RADIO PRODUCTION WORKTEXT
Fourth Edition

RADIO PRODUCTION WORKTEXT

Studio and Equipment

Fourth Edition

DAVID E. REESE
LYNNE S. GROSS

Focal Press

An Imprint of Elsevier

Boston   Oxford   Auckland   Johannesburg   Melbourne   New Delhi

Focal Press is an imprint of Elsevier.

 This book is printed on acid-free paper.

Library of Congress Cataloging-in-Publication Data
Reese, David E.
    Radio production worktext: studio and equipment/David E. Reese,
    Lynn S. Gross.-4ᵗʰ ed.
        p.   cm.
        Includes index.
        ISBN 0-240-80439-2 (pbk.:alk paper)
            1.   Radio stations-Equipment and supplies. 2. Radio-Production
and direction. 3. Sound-Recording and reproducing-Equipment and supplies.
I. Gross, Lynne S. II. Title.
TK6557.5.R44 2001
621.389's-dc21

                                        2001023632
British Library Cataloguing-in-Publication Data
A catalogue record for this book is available from the British Library.

The publisher offers special discounts on bulk orders of this book.
For information, please contact:
Manager of Special Sales
Elsevier Science
200 Wheeler Road
Burlington, MA 01803
Tel: 781-313-4700
Fax: 781-313-4802

For information on all Focal Press publications available, contact our World
Wide Web homepage at http://www.focalpress.com

10 9 8 7 6 5 4
Printed in the United States of America

*For anyone with a desire to get into the business of radio
production, we hope the following pages expand your interest in
the technologies and techniques involved.*

D.E.R.
L.S.G.

Contents

5 DIGITAL AUDIO PLAYERS/RECORDERS

6 ANALOG AUDIO PLAYERS/RECORDERS

7   AUDIO EDITING

8 MONITOR SPEAKERS, CABLES, CONNECTORS, AND STUDIO ACCESSORIES

9 SIGNAL PROCESSING EQUIPMENT

12 INTERNET RADIO AND OTHER DISTRIBUTION TECHNIQUES

Preface

This edition of *Radio Production Worktext* has been written to reflect the changes that digital technology has brought to the radio production studio and the techniques of audio production. The text follows the concept of the previous editions by offering a solid background in the mechanics of modern radio production, and it will be valuable for those who wish to become engaged in radio production or those who are already producing for radio but wish to know more about equipment and production techniques. Some production texts seem to offer burdensome amounts of information and explanations that don't have practical applications in the day-to-day world of radio, and other texts wander into aspects of radio broadcasting that have only vague implications for radio production. This text sticks to the subject at hand, and although radio production can seem complex to the beginner, *Radio Production Worktext* simplifies the understanding of the radio production process.

Radio is a very competitive field, and those with both a firm understanding of the basics of audio production and a basic knowledge of digital audio production will stand the best chance of succeeding in the future. Reading this text will get you started. However, as the title implies, this isn't a book just to read, but rather a text that will become an integral part of your study and practice of radio production. The worktext approach is an admission that this subject is really only taught by a combination of theory and discussion *and* practical, hands-on use of broadcast equipment. Each chapter of the text is divided into a section of **Information**, a section of **Self-Study Questions** and **Answers**, and a section of **Projects**.

The Information sections are further divided into modularized units so that all the primary concepts can be easily learned. These concepts are illustrated with drawings, photographs, and images that help the student grasp the specific ideas being presented.

The Self-Study Questions include multiple choice and true/false questions covering the material presented in the chapter. Answers, as well as suggested procedures for those who don't answer correctly, guide the student through this section. These questions are not really test questions, but rather are intended to be instructional so that by the time the student has read the Information section and answered the questions correctly, he or she will feel confident about knowing the information.

The Projects sections of the chapters contain practical projects that should give readers a degree of expertise in equipment manipulation and, we hope, lead them on to further, creative radio production work. It is assumed that the reader has completed both the Information section and Self-Study Questions before beginning the various projects. The importance of practical production experience should not be overlooked, and these projects should be viewed as a starting point for the developing radio production person. Additional hands-on work in the production studio is never wasted time and is highly recommended.

The book is organized primarily by equipment, but it doesn't deal strictly with a nuts-and-bolts approach. Techniques as well as mechanics are included within each chapter. In fact, the book isn't intended to be that technical. It's written in an easy-to-read style that should enable people without technical training to understand the nature and makeup of the radio process.

The fourth edition of this book continues to refine its organization and content. As a result, we have expanded the sections on digital equipment and procedures throughout the book. For example, while we still look at "cut and splice" editing in Chapter 7, "Audio Editing," the focus of the chapter is now on digital audio editing.

At the suggestion of some of our readers, we've added a chapter, Chapter 12, "Internet Radio and Other Distribution Techniques." The Internet has changed the nature of the radio industry in some ways. As an outlet for creative audio production, it has been of particular benefit to college radio stations.

This edition of *Radio Production Worktext* includes a CD-ROM that illustrates many of the important concepts discussed in the text. For example, when the terms "crossfade" and "segue" are explained in Chapter 3, "The Audio Console," not only is there a definition of the terms and a diagram showing the concept, but there's also an audio clip that lets you readily hear the difference between these two sound transitions. Those sections of the text that include an "audio clip" are noted throughout the text with a small "compact disc" icon.

In addition to various audio clips, the CD-ROM provides our readers with access to a demo version of *Cool Edit Pro*, one of the leading digital audio editing software programs for the PC. We've used this program to illustrate many digital production concepts in the text, and now you can easily use the program to duplicate our demonstrations or create your own audio production projects.

There are also files on the CD-ROM that provide material you can use to create audio production projects. Some of these files are for particular production projects in the text, but most of them are music and sound effects that can be used with a variety of projects. These files are noted next to the appropriate projects by means of a "file folder" icon.

Throughout the book we have freshened and updated both the copy and artwork to reflect the modern production studio. As with earlier editions, Chapter 1, "The Production Studio Environment," introduces the reader to the layout and design of the radio production studio—the environment in which you'll accomplish your production work—and describes briefly the equipment that's detailed in succeeding chapters. The initial chapter also discusses some basic concepts regarding "sound" that will help the production person to understand the "raw material" being worked with.

The reader is quickly immersed in digital audio production in Chapter 2, "Digital Audio Production." After a brief look at how audio is converted from analog to digital, this chapter introduces some of the digital equipment that can almost replace an entire studio. For example, once audio is recorded into equipment with audio editing capability, you can often edit the audio, add signal processing to the audio, and work in a multitrack format with the audio, among other things.

Chapter 3, "The Audio Console," introduces the heart of all production work. New material on digital consoles and "virtual" consoles brings this chapter into the digital age. A firm understanding of this chapter is important, because most other broadcast equipment operates through the audio console. Having mastered the audio board, students should be ready to work with the sound sources that can serve as inputs or outputs for the console. One of these is covered in Chapter 4, "Microphones." Chapter 5, "Digital Audio Players/Recorders," deals with the players and recorders beyond those covered in Chapter 2, "Digital Audio Production." Compact discs, MiniDiscs, DATs (Digital Audio Tapes), and hard disc players and recorders are all considered here.

Chapter 6, "Analog Audio Players/Recorders," looks at the turntable and audio tape recorders still found in many facilities and is an admission that the production studio hasn't completely forgone all analog technology. Chapter 7, "Audio Editing," deals with both analog and digital editing.

Equipment that is often overlooked is included in Chapter 8, "Monitor Speakers, Cables, Connectors, and Studio Accessories." Monitor speakers and headphones are first discussed, and then the connectors, cables, and accessories that complement the major pieces of equipment in the production studio are surveyed. Chapter 9, "Signal Processing Equipment," provides an introduction to the most popular signal processing equipment employed in radio production work. Once again you will learn that digital equipment can often replicate most of the signal processing effects—usually faster and more easily.

Chapter 10, "Multitrack Production Techniques," looks at the basics of multitrack production. Some analog-based production studios have multitrack capability, and almost all digital-based studios do, so it's important for the production person to learn the basic techniques of multitrack recording and the creative possibilities that they open up.

Chapter 11, "Production Situations," considers some production situations beyond basic spot production. Many of the techniques and skills used for regular commercial production are also employed for radio announcing, newscasting, interviewing, and sport play-by-play, to name a few. The last chapter, Chapter 12, "Internet Radio and Other Distribution Techniques," explains how to develop an Internet radio station and briefly looks at some of the other distribution methods for getting radio production work to the listener.

In each chapter you'll also find **Production Tip** boxes that provide interesting notes relevant to various production topics. Throughout the book, key terms are listed in **boldface** when first introduced. These terms are explained in the text, and/or definitions are also included in the Glossary. A selected list of additional Suggested Readings is provided for students who wish to continue their study in this area.

We are indebted to many people for their help and encouragement while we put together this newest edition of *Radio Production Worktext*. Our colleagues within the Communications Departments at John Carroll University and California State University, Fullerton offered generous support for this project's realization. Many changes to the fourth edition of this text are a result of the helpful comments that came from instructors using previous editions. A special "thanks" goes to our reviewer for this edition— Samuel J. Sauls, Ph.D., University of North Texas. Their comments and suggestions were very helpful throughout our revision process. The CD-ROM that comes with the text is the result of the skill and effort of Brian Gross (*www.b12x12.com*), who developed and produced it using some of the materials recorded for the last edition's CD by David Conrad of Sound Concepts (Manhattan Beach, CA). We are also appreciative of Chris Sterling, Associate Dean at George Washington University, who served as one of the voices on the original CD. And once again, *Radio Production Worktext* is as good as it is because of the expert help and backing of the staff at Focal Press, especially Marie L. Lee, Senior Editor, and Diane Wurzel, Assistant Editor.

CHAPTER ONE

The Production Studio Environment

Information

1.1 INTRODUCTION

The room that houses the equipment necessary for radio production work and in which a broadcaster's finished product is assembled is known as the **production studio**. What may initially appear to be merely a roomful of electronic equipment will become a comfortable environment, once you've become familiar with the space and components that make up the production facility. If your facility has several studios, they may be labeled "Production 1" or "Prod. B" or simply identified with a common abbreviation for the production studio, "PDX."

Most radio facilities have at least two studios; however, one is usually delegated as the **on-air studio** and is used for the live, day-to-day broadcasting. The other studio or studios are production studios, used for putting together programming material that is recorded for playback at a later time. This includes such items as commercials, public-service announcements (PSAs), and station promotional announcements (promos). Some stations also have a studio that is considered a **performance studio** or **announce booth**. It houses nothing more than microphones, a table, and chairs. The output is usually sent to a production studio to be recorded, although sometimes it's sent directly to the on-air studio for live broadcast. A performance studio can be used for taping interviews, for discussions involving several guests, or for putting a small musical group on the air.

Today most radio work is done **combo**; that is, the announcer is also the equipment operator. Because of this, the equipment and operator are in a single studio, be it a production room or an on-air room. In earlier radio days, the announcer was often located in a separate room or announce booth adjacent to the studio that housed the actual broadcast equipment. Visual contact and communication were maintained via a window between the two rooms. An engineer was required to manipulate the equipment, and all the announcer did was provide the voice. Many larger-market radio stations still use a similar announcer/engineer arrangement, popularly known as "engineer assist."

Two of the biggest concerns for studio design looked at in this chapter are acoustics and ergonomics. Acoustics refers to how sound "behaves" within an enclosed space, and ergonomics refers to design considerations that help reduce operator fatigue and discomfort. While you will probably never build or remodel a broadcast studio, an understanding of the characteristics of the production room can help you assess your facility and suggest ways you can improve the surroundings you'll be working in.

1.2 THE AUDIO CHAIN

Figure 1.1 shows a map of the typical radio production studio. Starting with various sound sources, such as an announcer's voice, a CD, or an audio recorder, it shows the routes that sound takes to ultimately be broadcast or recorded. This is often called an **audio chain** because the various pieces of equipment are linked together. The trip can be complicated since the sound can go through several changes along the way. For example, it can be dubbed, or copied, from CD to MiniDisc, or it can be **equalized,** which is a form of signal processing. The solid lines show sound being sent to the audio console, through **signal processing** equipment, and then to the transmitting system; this would be normal for an on-air studio. The broken line shows the sound being sent back to the audio recorder after signal processing; this would be common for a production studio. In both cases the sound can be heard in the studio through monitor speakers or headphones. You'll learn more about all of this as you work your way through this text, but for now the diagram in Figure 1.1 provides a look at where you are headed.

The equipment shown is also representative of that found in the typical radio production studio. The **microphone** transforms the announcer's voice into an audio signal. It is not uncommon for a production facility to have

1

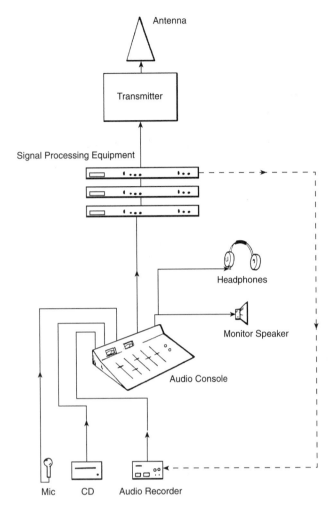

FIGURE 1.1 The audio chain shows how sound moves through the production studio.

FIGURE 1.2 Many radio studios use modular furniture components arranged in a U-shaped design that allows the operator to see and easily reach the equipment. (Image courtesy of Arrakis Systems, Inc.—*www.Arrakis-Systems.com*.)

usually put into the audio chain between the audio console and the transmitting equipment or recording equipment. Monitoring the sound during production work is accomplished with studio **speakers** or **headphones**. Compare Figure 1.1 with Figures 1.3 and 1.10 to see how the audio chain translates into the actual production studio.

1.3 STUDIO LAYOUT

Almost all radio production studios use a U-shaped layout (see Figure 1.2) or some variation of it because this allows the operator to reach all the equipment control surfaces, and puts the operator immediately in front of the audio console. With the use of remote start/stop switches for equipment that's out of arm's reach of the operator, all equipment manipulation can occur at the audio console once everything has been set up and cued.

1.4 STUDIO CABINETS AND COUNTERS

Studio equipment is often installed on and in custom-built cabinets and counters. A less expensive but equally functional approach is to lay out the studio using modular stock components (see Figure 1.2 again). Audio cabinets have been designed expressly for recorders, audio consoles, and other pieces of studio equipment. Today's studio furniture systems also include space and cabinet modules for computer monitors and other computer equipment that's being integrated with traditional broadcast equipment in the radio studio, as shown in Figures 1.3 and 1.10. The computer monitor should be about 2 feet away from the announcer and the top-most screen line should fall slightly below eye level. Monitors that are placed too high, perhaps on top of a studio module, can cause neck strain.

one or more auxiliary mics for production work that requires two or more voices. Most production rooms also have two **CD players,** enabling different CDs to be played back-to-back or simultaneously. Many production studios still house a turntable so the occasional vinyl record can be played, but some have eliminated this piece of equipment. Audio recorder/player sources can include **reel-to-reel**, **cassette**, and **cartridge** machines, although these analog devices, like the turntable, are becoming obsolete. Modern studios utilize **digital** gear, such as the **MiniDisc** recorder, personal audio editor, **CD-R** (compact disc recorder), or computer-controlled **digital audio workstation**. The number of recorder/players found in the production room depends on the complexity of the studio and the budget of the station.

All of this equipment feeds into the **audio console**, which allows the operator to manipulate the sound sources in various ways. Signal processing equipment, such as an **equalizer**, **noise-reduction** system, or **reverb** unit, is

FIGURE 1.3 Computer equipment must be integrated with traditional broadcast equipment in the modern production studio. (Image courtesy of Applied Construction Technology—KEZR-FM Production studio.)

The computer keyboard should be placed in-line with the monitor rather than off-to-the-side. Sometimes the keyboard can be placed on an under-counter drawer to accomplish this, but you have to watch the announcer's knee space in this situation. If possible, avoid putting a keyboard near hard counter edges that can cause wrist problems and make sure the computer mouse can be reached without stretching.

Studios can be designed to fit the equipment a station has, and studios can even be expanded as new equipment is added. Both custom-built and modular cabinets and counters are also designed to provide easy access to the myriad cables necessary to wire all the studio equipment together yet maintain an attractive image for the look of the studio. Digital equipment will offer the advantage of better cable management as linking equipment via digital inputs/outputs will actually require less cable. Other cabinets or storage modules are also available for CDs, records, tapes, and other material that's kept in the production studio.

Does stylish furniture make a studio sound better? Although that notion would be hard to quantify, a positive studio image does imply a commitment to high-quality professional production, and this often translates into more creativity, more productivity, and a better "sound" produced from that production studio.

1.5 SOUND SIGNAL VERSUS AUDIO SIGNAL

Much of the design of a production studio has to do with manipulating sound. It will be worthwhile to take a brief look at sound since this will help you understand many aspects of the production process, whether it involves a sound signal or an audio signal. When sound is naturally produced (for example, an announcer speaking into a microphone), we think of that sound as a **sound signal.** In radio production, when that sound signal is then manipulated electronically (such as recorded on audio tape), it's called an **audio signal.** Obviously most radio production must start at some point with a sound signal, but during the actual production process, we are often manipulating an audio signal. To further complicate things, these terms are sometimes interchanged when people talk about various radio production processes.

1.6 SOUND DEFINED

When something vibrates, sound is generated. For example, plucking a single guitar string causes a mechanical vibration to occur, which we can easily see by looking at the string. Of course, we can also hear it. The vibrating string sets adjacent air molecules in motion, which in turn sets neighboring air molecules in motion, and on and on. Sound develops waves (like a stone dropped into water), which vibrate up and down and set the air molecules in a push **(compression)** and pull **(rarefaction)** motion.

In addition to the vibration noted above, we need a medium for the sound to travel through. Of course, the medium we're usually concerned with is the atmosphere, or air. Sound can also travel through other materials, such as water or wood, but will often be distorted by the medium. Sound vibrations can't travel in a vacuum.

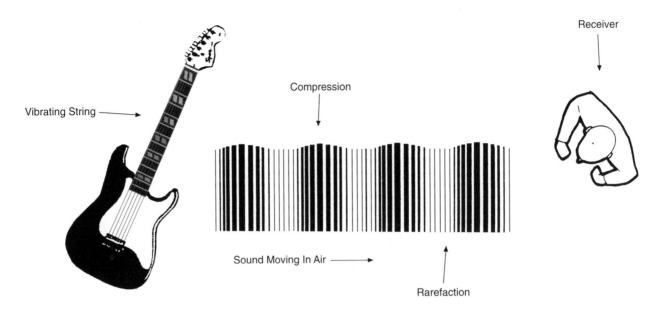

Vibrating String

Compression

Receiver

Sound Moving In Air ⟶

Rarefaction

FIGURE 1.4 The production of sound requires vibrations, which are transmitted through a medium, and a receiver.

Finally, for sound to exist technically, we need a receiver. Someone (a person) or something (a microphone) must receive it and perceive it as sound. Figure 1.4 shows a representation of sound being produced. We can't actually see sound waves, but they act very much like water waves as we've noted. The sine wave (shown in Figure 1.5C) is used to represent sound because it can readily show the wave compression (the portion of the wave above the center line) and the wave rarefaction (the portion of the wave below the center line).

1.7 CHARACTERISTICS OF SOUND WAVES

There are four key characteristics of sound that determine why one sound is different from another sound: amplitude, frequency, timbre, and the sound envelope. A sound wave's **amplitude** relates to its strength, which we hear as **volume,** or loudness. The loudness of a sound can be thought of as the height of the sound wave. The louder the sound, the higher the amplitude (see Figure 1.5A). As a sound gets louder, greater compression and rarefaction of air molecules takes place, and the crest of the wave will be higher while the trough of the wave will be deeper. A sound wave's actual amplitude is readily measured; however, loudness is a subjective concept. What is loud to one person isn't necessarily loud to another person. Sound amplitude is measured in **decibels** (dB). Decibels represent the ratio of different audio levels on a logarithmic scale and measure the relative intensity of sound. Sounds in the range of 0 dB (the threshold of hearing) to 120 dB (the threshold of pain) are detected by the human ear, but those sounds near and exceeding the high end can be painful and can damage your hearing.

Frequency relates to the number of times per second that a sound wave vibrates (goes in an up and down cycle), which we hear as **pitch** (see Figure 1.5B). The faster something vibrates, or the more cycles per second, the higher the pitch of the sound. Like amplitude, frequency can be objectively measured, but like volume, pitch is subjective. In radio jargon, cycles per second are know as **hertz** (Hz). A sound wave that vibrates at two thousand cycles per second is said to have a frequency of 2,000 hertz. When the cycles per second gets higher, for example 20,000 hertz, the term **kilohertz** (kHz) is often used. It denotes 1,000 cycles per second, so 20,000 hertz could also be called 20 kilohertz. Humans hear frequencies that fall in the approximate range of 20 Hz to 20 kHz, but most of us do not hear sounds near the extremes of this range. A sound's **wavelength** is the distance between two compressions (crests) or two rarefactions (troughs). Sound wavelength can vary from around three-quarters of an inch for a treble sound near 16 kHz to around 36 feet for a bass sound near 30 Hz. There is an inverse relationship between wavelength and pitch, so higher pitched sounds have the shorter wavelength.

A sound's **timbre** (which is pronounced "TAMbur"), or **tone,** relates to the **waveform** of the sound. It's the characteristic of sound that distinguishes one announcer's voice from another, even though both may be saying the same thing at the same volume and pitch. A graphic representation of a pure tone is shown as the shape of a sine wave, as in Figure 1.5C. Each sound has one basic tone that is its **fundamental;** most sound, however, is a combination of many tones with different strengths at different frequencies, so the waveform is much more complex, as shown in Figure 1.5D. These other pitches are either exact frequency multiples of the fundamental (known as **harmonics**) or pitches that are not exact multiples of the fundamental (known as **over-**

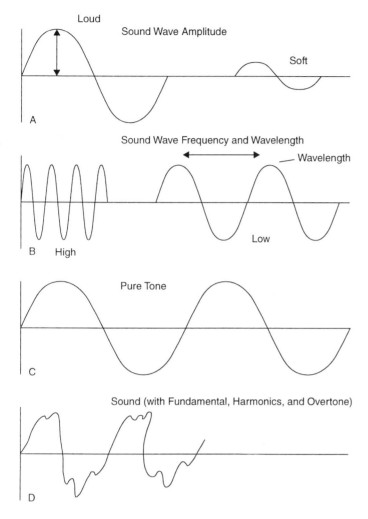

Loud
Sound Wave Amplitude
Soft

A

Sound Wave Frequency and Wavelength
Wavelength

B High Low

Pure Tone

C

Sound (with Fundamental, Harmonics, and Overtone)

D

FIGURE 1.5 Characteristics of sound waves include volume, pitch, and tone, here visualized as sine waves.

tones). For example, striking an A note (above middle C) on a piano would produce a fundamental tone of 440 Hz. In other words, the piano string is vibrating 440 times per second. The harmonics of this note will occur at exact (or whole number) multiples of the fundamental tone, such as 880 Hz (twice the fundamental) or 2,200 Hz (five times the fundamental). The interaction of the fundamental, harmonics, and overtones creates the timbre of any particular sound.

A sound's wave **envelope** relates to its **duration**, or the change in volume of a sound over a period of time, as shown in Figure 1.6. Normally a sound's wave envelope develops through four specific stages: **attack**, the time it takes an initial sound to build to maximum volume; **decay**, the time it takes the sound to go from peak volume to a sustained level; **sustain**, the time the sound holds its sustain volume; and **release**, the time it takes a sound to diminish from sustain volume to silence. In essence, decay, sustain,

and release refer to the time it takes a sound to die out. Some sounds, like a percussive drum beat, have a very fast attack; other sounds, like a piano chord, have a long decay-sustain-release. Audio equipment must be able to accurately reproduce any sound wave envelope.

1.8 STUDIO SOUND CONSIDERATIONS

The radio production studio is a unique space in that the physical room that comprises the studio will impact the sound produced in it. Because of this, several additional characteristics of sound need to be considered in designing the studio, including sound isolation, noise and vibration control, and room acoustics.

When sound strikes a surface (such as a studio wall), some of that sound is reflected back, some is absorbed within the material of the surface, and some is transmitted

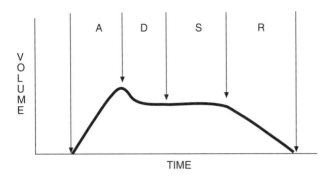

FIGURE 1.6 The sound wave envelope depicts the change in volume of a sound over a period of time.

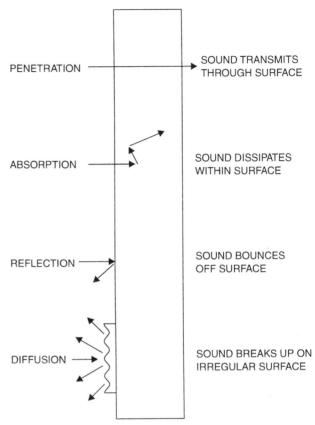

FIGURE 1.7 Sound striking a studio wall will reflect, penetrate, be diffused, or be absorbed by that surface.

through the surface. Most of the sound that hits a hard, flat surface will be reflected back. However, if the surface is irregular, it will break up the sound wave and disperse the reflections—a phenomenon known as diffusion. Sound that's absorbed into the surface is dissipated within it, but **penetration** occurs when sound goes through a surface and is transmitted into the space on the other side of the surface. Figure 1.7 illustrates that penetration, absorption, reflection, and diffusion are all characteristics that help determine the sound that is both produced and reproduced in the studio.

When a sound (such as an announcer's voice) is produced, the **direct sound** is the main sound that you hear. In a production situation, it is sound that goes from the announcer (the sound source) straight to the microphone. On the other hand, **indirect** or **reflected sound** reaches the microphone fractions of a second after the direct sound does because it has traveled a roundabout route. Reflected sound consists of **echo** and **reverberation**. This indirect sound has bounced off or been reflected from one surface (echo) or two or more surfaces (reverb) before reaching the microphone (see Figure 1.8). Since it's an early reflection, echo provides a distinct repetition of the sound, such as "hello—hello—hello." On the other hand, reverb's repeated later reflections provide a continuous decay of the sound, such as "hello—oo—oo." The components of direct and indirect sound make up what is commonly called the sound's "life cycle."

In designing the radio studio, the goal is to manipulate these sound characteristics to create a proper sound environment for production work. When considering reflected sound, we think in terms of reverb ring and reverb route, with the same concepts being true for echo but to a lesser extent. **Reverb ring** or **reverb time** is the time that it takes for a sound to die out or go from full volume to silence—in other words, the decay-sustain-release portion of a wave envelope. **Reverb route** is the path that sound takes from its source to a reflective surface and back to the original source (or a microphone, if recording).

Excessive reflected sound tends to accent high and midrange frequencies, which produces a "harsh" sound; to

blur the stereo image, which produces a "muddy" sound; or to cause standing waves (see section 1.10), which produces an "uneven" sound. Reflected sound can also be **reinforced** by causing objects or surfaces within the studio to vibrate at the same frequencies as the original sound in a sympathetic fashion.

Both **absorption** and diffusion are utilized to control reflected sound. Part of the reflected sound can be absorbed within the carpeting, curtains, and walls of the studio. Absorption soaks up sound and shortens reverb time to prevent excessive reflection. Absorption provides a **dead studio**, which has a very short reverb ring and a long reverb route that produces a softer sound. Excessive absorption produces a totally dead studio, which provides a "dry" sound that is unlike any normal acoustic space and isn't really desirable. In contrast, a **live studio** has a longer reverb ring and a short reverb route that produces a harder, or more brilliant, sound.

Diffusion uses irregular room surfaces to break up sound reflections. This decreases the intensity of the reflections, making them less noticeable, but doesn't deaden the sound as much because the sound reflects are redirected rather than soaked up. Most studio designs control reflec-

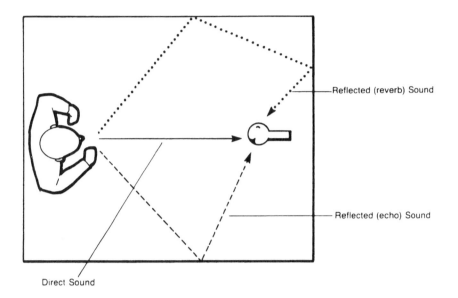

Reflected (reverb) Sound

Reflected (echo) Sound

Direct Sound

FIGURE 1.8 Direct sound goes directly from the announcer to the microphone, but reflected sound is also produced in the studio.

tions by a combination of absorption and diffusion techniques.

One common studio design is a **live end/dead end** (**LEDE**) approach. The front of the studio (where the announcer and equipment are located) is designed to absorb and diffuse sounds. This dead end quiets some of the equipment operation noise, picks up the direct sound of the announcer's voice, and absorbs the excess reflections that pass by the microphone from the live end. The live end, or back, of the studio adds a desirable sharpness to the sound by providing some reflected sound. This LEDE studio design was first devised by Synergetic Audio Concepts, a leading audio education company, and has since been employed in many production studio situations.

1.9 STUDIO CONSTRUCTION MATERIALS

Part of these design considerations involve the actual construction materials used for the studio. Ideally, you want to keep penetration to a minimum by keeping outside (unwanted) sound from entering the studio and inside sound from escaping from the studio, except via the audio console. Radio studios utilize **soundproofing** to accomplish this sound isolation. Doors are heavy-duty and tightly sealed; windows are often double glass with the interior pane slanted downward to minimize reflected sounds; and walls, ceiling, and flooring use special sound-treatment materials. For example, studio walls may be covered with acoustically treated and designed panels that both absorb and trap reflected sounds (see Figure 1.9). Some stations use carpeting on the studio walls, but this type of soundproofing doesn't absorb low frequencies very well. Some pro-

duction studios have actually used egg cartons on the walls as a sound treatment. If you compare the design of an egg carton bottom with the design of the acoustic panel shown in Figure 1.9, you'll see why some stations have gone the inexpensive egg carton route.

All materials absorb sound to some degree, but each material will have a different **absorption coefficient,** which is the proportion of sound that it can absorb. A coefficient of 1.00 means that all sound is absorbed in the material. On the other hand, a coefficient of 0.00 means no absorption and that all the sound is reflected back. Hard, smooth surfaces like plaster or panel walls and hardwood floors have low absorption coefficients. Heavy, plush carpets,

FIGURE 1.9 Acoustic panels help control reflected sound through both absorption (foam material) and diffusion (irregular surface). (Image courtesy of Illbruck, Inc.—Sonex Acoustical Products.)

drape-covered windows, and specially designed acoustic tiles will have higher coefficients. For example, using a 1,000 Hz tone as the sound source, the absorption coefficient of a sheetrock wall would be .04 while a 2-inch Sonex foam tile would be .81; a glass window would be .12 while a window curtain would be .75; and a painted concrete block wall would be .07 while a carpeted concrete wall would be .37. The purpose of any soundproofing material is to help give the studio a dead sound. Soundproofing absorbs and controls excess reverb and echo and helps produce a softer sound.

1.10 STUDIO SIZE AND SHAPE

The size and shape of a production studio can also determine how reflective the studio is. As noted, the radio production studio doesn't want to be overly reflective because sound produced or recorded in the studio can become too bright and even harsh. Unfortunately, normal room construction often goes counter to good broadcast studio design. For example, studios with parallel walls (the normal box-shaped room) produce more reflected sound than irregularly shaped studios. Sound waves that are reflected back and forth within a limited area, such as between studio walls that are parallel, can produce standing waves. In basic terms, a **standing wave** is a combination of a sound wave going in one direction and its reflected wave going in the opposite direction. If the distance between the walls is the same as the wave length (or a multiple of it), the waves interact and produce an undesirable combined sound that tends to be uneven, as previously mentioned. To help prevent standing waves, adjacent studio walls can be splayed (joined at more than a 90-degree angle) to help break up reflected sound and control excessive reverb and echo.

The actual size of the production facility is partially determined by the equipment that must be housed in it. However, in constructing the radio production room, consideration should be given to the fact that when rooms are built with height, width, and length dimensions that are equal or exact multiples of each other, certain sound frequencies tend to be boosted, and certain sound frequencies tend to be canceled. Since this "peaks and valleys" sound is not desirable in the radio production room, cubic construction should be avoided when possible.

1.11 STUDIO AESTHETICS

There are some studio design considerations that can be categorized as the "aesthetics" of the production room. In general, the radio studio should be pleasant to work in; after all, the operator is confined to a rather small room for long stretches of time. For example, fluorescent lighting should be avoided when possible. Not only does it tend to introduce hum into the audio chain, but it's harsher and

more glaring than incandescent light. If possible, the studio lights should be on dimmers so that an appropriate level of light can be set for each individual operator. If the lighting causes glare on a computer monitor, use a screen filter to diminish this problem or use track lighting that can be directed away from the screen.

Stools or chairs used in the radio studio should be comfortable and functional. User-friendly adjustments should allow the announcer to set the seat height so that the entire sole of the foot rests on either the floor or a footrest. Chairs must move easily because even though most of the equipment is situated close to the operator, he or she must move around to cue CDs, thread tapes, or select production music. The production stool must also be well constructed so that it doesn't constantly squeak if the operator moves slightly while the microphone is open. This may not be a factor for production studios designed for a stand-up operation, wherein there is no stool, and the counters are at a height appropriate for the operator to be standing while announcing. This allows the operator to be more animated in his or her vocal delivery and actually provides a better posture for speaking than a sitting position.

Many radio production rooms are decorated with music posters or radio station bumper stickers and paraphernalia. Not only does this keep the studio from being a cold, stark room, but it also gives the studio a radio atmosphere. Figure 1.10 shows the interior of a typical radio production studio.

Production Tip #1— "Static Electricity"

Static electricity can be a problem in radio production studios because of the heavy use of carpeting. Most radio people don't enjoy getting shocked every time they touch the metal control surface of an audio console. Also, some modern audio equipment and computer systems have electronic circuits that can be disrupted by static discharges. There have been instances where tape recorders have switched into "play" mode when an announcer just "sparked" the faceplate of the machine. If design factors can't keep the studio static free, commercial sprays can be put on the carpeting or spray fabric softener can be used to provide an antistatic treatment at a modest cost. Dilute the fabric softener a bit or you'll build up a dangerous, slippery gloss on your carpets. A static touch pad could also be provided in the studio which the operator merely placed a finger on to harmlessly discharge static buildup. Some studios have even been built with conductive laminate countertops connected to the studio's ground system to help keep static problems to a minimum.

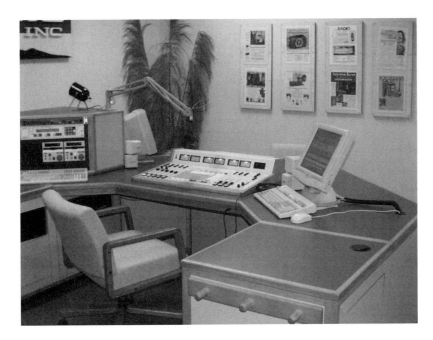

FIGURE 1.10 The production studio should be a comfortable and functional environment for the announcer. (Image courtesy of Arrakis Systems, Inc.—www.Arrakis-Systems.com.)

FIGURE 1.11 When lit, the on-air or recording light indicates that a microphone is "live" in that studio.

1.12 ON-AIR/RECORDING LIGHTS

On-air lights (see Figure 1.11) are usually located outside the radio production room or studio. Normally they are wired so that whenever the microphone in that studio is turned on, the on-air light comes on. A light outside a production studio will often read "recording" instead of "on-air." In either case, a lit light indicates a live microphone. Good production practice dictates that when an on-air light is on, you *never* enter that studio, and if you're in the vicinity of the studio, you are quiet. *Inside* the studio, another alert light may come on when the mic is turned on and announcers often say "stand by" just before turning on the mic to alert others in the studio that he or she is preparing to turn on the mic.

1.13 RADIO HAND SIGNALS

Radio **hand signals** don't play a major role in modern radio production; however, there are situations when vocal communication isn't possible and hand signals are necessary. For example, if an announcer and engineer are working an on-air show from separate rooms, they must be able to communicate with each other. There are also times when two announcers must communicate, but an open or live microphone in the studio prevents them from doing so verbally. Because of situations like these, hand signals have evolved over the years to communicate some basic production information. Figure 1.12 shows some of the basic radio hand signals.

Often hand signals concern getting a program started or stopped. A **standby** signal is given just prior to going on-air by holding one hand above the head with the palm forward. The standby signal is immediately followed by the **cue talent** signal. Meaning, "You're on," this signal is given by pointing your index finger (using the same hand that gave the standby signal) at the person who's supposed to go on-air. The common hand signal for stopping a program is the **cut** signal, which is given by drawing the index finger across the throat in a "slitting" motion. This signal terminates whatever is happening at the moment and usually "kills" all live microphones and stops all recorders.

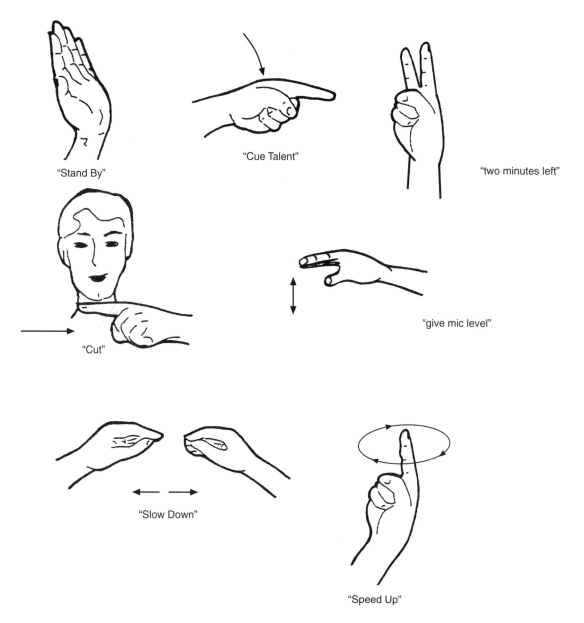

"Stand By"

"Cue Talent"

"two minutes left"

"Cut"

"give mic level"

"Slow Down"

"Speed Up"

FIGURE 1.12 Hand signals allow announcers to convey information when a live microphone prevents verbal communication.

Some hand signals are used to give directions to the announcer regarding the microphone. To get an announcer to **give mic level**, for example, hold one hand in front of you with the palm down and thumb under the second and third fingers. Open and close the thumb and fingers in a "chattering" motion to indicate that the announcer should talk into the mic so that levels can be checked.

Other hand signals are often used during a production to let the talent know how things are going or to convey some necessary information. Timing cues are given with the fingers. To indicate that 2 minutes are left in the program, you would hold up the index and second finger of one hand in front of you. Using both index fingers to form a cross in front of you means there are 30 seconds left. Timing cues always tell the announcer how much time remains in the program because there is nothing you can do about the time that has already gone by. When everything is going fine, the radio hand signal is the traditional "thumbs up" given with clenched fist and extended thumb.

There is no universal set of hand signals, so you may find that your facility uses some that are different, uses some not presented here, or doesn't use any at all. In any case, an understanding of radio hand signals should prove helpful in some production situations.

1.14 NOISE AND DISTORTION

The next few chapters will deal with the equipment that's housed in the production studio. Inherent in any of this electronic equipment is noise. Any unwanted sound element that is introduced in the production process that was not present in the original sound signal is thought of as **noise**. For example, a microphone that employs an extremely long cable might add noise to the audio signal. Turntables and recorders can introduce noise from mechanical gears or just through the electronic circuits used in amplifying or recording the signal.

In broadcast production, the noise level should be kept as low as possible. Most radio production equipment is designed to produce a **signal-to-noise ratio (S/N)** of at least sixty-to-one. S/N is an audio measurement, usually in decibels, which notes the amount by which a signal at a standard test level exceeds the level of noise produced by an electronic component. The higher the signal-to-noise level the better. For most analog equipment, a S/N around 60 dB is considered good quality; modern digital equipment, such as a CD player, can show a signal-to-noise ratio of 98 dB. The signal-to-noise ratio gives an indication of the equipment's ability to reproduce sound cleanly.

Distortion is an unwanted change in the audio signal due to inaccurate reproduction of the sound. One type of distortion is loudness distortion, which can occur when a signal is recorded at a level too loud for the equipment to handle. An overdriven signal sounds "muddy," and the reproduced signal does not have the same clarity or sharpness that the original signal did.

You should be aware of noise and distortion when working with audio equipment, especially analog equipment. Digital equipment, in many instances, reduces the chance of introducing noise or distortion into your production work, but most of your production work will be accomplished with a combination of analog and digital equipment.

1.15 PRODUCTION STUDIO SETUP

Before beginning any production work, set up the production studio. This means cleaning up any mess left behind from previous work in the studio. Theoretically, there shouldn't be anything to clean up since good production practice dictates that each person cleans up the production facility after each work session; but theory doesn't always translate into practice, so, if necessary, put away background music CDs, take old tapes off the recorders, zero counters, and clear some working space for yourself.

Set all audio console controls to a neutral position. In other words, turn on only those pieces of equipment that

you're going to use. Not only is it easier to keep track of and manipulate the volumes for just the equipment you need, but it also prevents any additional audio noise from being introduced into your production work from a piece of equipment that you're not even using.

If possible, use a **tone generator** to set reference levels to the audio recorders; some audio consoles have a built-in tone generator for this purpose. At the very least, read some copy into the mic and set a good level on the audio board, and then balance that level with the input levels of the recorders. Do the same for the CD player and other sound sources you'll be using.

If you're working with audio tape, clean all tape-recorder heads. When cut 'n' splice editing has been done in the studio, some residual grease pencil may have been left on the heads, and even normal use leaves some oxide material on or near the heads. If you need to dispose of a "dull" razor blade, be sure to put a piece of masking or cellophane tape over the sharp edge of the blade before you toss it into the waste basket. (Putting the tape just a bit beyond the blade edge will keep people who are emptying the trash from possibly cutting themselves.)

Bulk erase the tapes that you plan to use with a **degausser**. In general, you don't need to worry about erasing anything that may already be on these tapes because the custom in most studios is that any tape left in the production studio is up for grabs. If you want to save something that you've recorded, take the tape out of the production studio. Take a look at the audio tape, too. If it's excessively worn or damaged in any way, throw it out. If you're using reel-to-reel tape, spool off a few feet from the front of the reel, and throw it away. That part of the tape gets the wear and tear of threading and handling and will wear out before the rest of the tape. If you're producing something that's very important or something that you know will be aired over and over, start with fresh tape.

It's also good practice to keep notes while you're doing any production work. For example, if you're using any signal processing equipment, note the settings for the effect you're producing so that you'll be able to recreate it easily at another time. Also, write down the production music you use for music beds. That way you'll avoid using the same piece of music over and over. Make note of any sound effects or special recording techniques, so you can duplicate what you've produced at some future time, if need be. Use a **track sheet** to keep notes regarding multitrack productions.

The few minutes that you take now to set up the studio will make the production go more smoothly later. It will also save you time in the overall production process.

1.16 CONCLUSIONS

Unless you're building a radio facility from the ground up, it's probable that you will have little control over the construction of the studio; sound treatment is an important consideration, however, and some aspects of improving the sound environment can be put into practice in almost any situation. Completion of this chapter should have you in the radio production studio and ready to learn the procedures and techniques for operating all the equipment you see in front of you.

Self-Study

■ QUESTIONS

1. To work *combo* in radio means that the announcer _____.
   a) has an engineer to operate the studio equipment for him or her
   b) operates the studio equipment and also announces
   c) works at two different radio stations
   d) is announcing in both the on-air and the production studio

2. Which type of studio is least likely to contain an audio console?
   a) on-air studio
   b) production studio
   c) PDX studio
   d) performance studio

3. Sound produced in the radio studio that causes objects or surfaces within the studio to vibrate sympathetically is said to be _____.
   a) absorbed
   b) reflected
   c) reinforced
   d) diffused

4. In the radio production studio, sound that has bounced off one surface before reaching the microphone is_____.
   a) echo
   b) reverberation
   c) direct sound
   d) indirect sound

5. Reverb ring in the production studio refers to _____.
   a) the circular route reflected sound takes before it reaches the mic
   b) the time it takes reflected sound to go from full volume to silence
   c) just another common name for echo
   d) a sound that has bounced off two or more surfaces

6. The use of carpeting on the walls of some radio production facilities is an example of _____.
   a) an inexpensive way of decorating the studio
   b) producing reverb in the studio
   c) producing a live sound in the studio
   d) soundproofing the studio

7. Studios with parallel walls produce less reflected sound than irregularly shaped studios.
   a) true
   b) false

8. Most production studios use a U-shaped layout because _____.
   a) this design places equipment within easy reach of the operator
   b) this design must use incandescent lights rather than fluorescent lights

    c) this design necessitates custom-built cabinets
    d) this design uses the least amount of wire to connect the equipment

9. Static electricity is not a problem in the modern production studio because state-of-the-art audio equipment is impervious to static.
    a) true
    b) false

10. Which hand signal almost always follows immediately after the standby hand signal?
    a) 2 minutes to go
    b) thumbs up
    c) cue talent
    d) give mic level

11. If you hold up the index, second, and third fingers of one hand in front of you, the announcer knows _____.
    a) there are 3 minutes left in the program
    b) there are 30 seconds left in the program
    c) he or she should move three steps closer to the microphone
    d) 3 minutes have gone by since the beginning of the program

12. The linking of a CD player to an audio console, the console to an equalizer, and the equalizer to an audio recorder would be called an _____.
    a) audio road map
    b) audio linking
    c) audio processor
    d) audio chain

13. When sound waves are reflected between parallel walls in such a manner that a wave reflected in one direction is combined with an identical wave going in the opposite direction, it produces an uneven sound known as a _____.
    a) diffused wave
    b) standing wave
    c) absorbed wave
    d) sympathetic wave

14. When a "recording" light is on outside a production studio, it means a microphone is "live" in that studio.
    a) true
    b) false

15. In the audio production studio, a tone generator is used to _____.
    a) set audio console controls in a neutral position
    b) bulk erase audio tapes
    c) set volume levels
    d) keep track of music played

16. When sound produced in the production studio strikes a hard, flat surface, which of the following does *not* happen?
    a) reflection
    b) absorption
    c) penetration
    d) diffusion

17. A production studio wall that has an absorption coefficient of .50 will absorb half the sound striking it and reflect back half the sound.
    a) true
    b) false

18. Posters and other radio station paraphernalia should not be put up in a production studio as it will distract the announcer from doing good production work.
    a) true
    b) false

19. Some of the acoustic tiles used in production studios use irregular surfaces to break up sound reflections. This is called _____.
    a) absorption
    b) reflection
    c) penetration
    d) diffusion

20. The production studio should be cleaned up by _____.
    a) the first person to use the studio in the morning
    b) each production person when he or she finishes a session
    c) the last person to use the studio at night
    d) the station receptionist

21. Which statement about "sound" is *not* true?
    a) sound is generated when something vibrates
    b) sound, to technically exist, must be heard
    c) sound vibrations develop waves by setting adjacent air molecules in motion
    d) sound vibrations travel faster in a vacuum than in air

22. An unwanted change in the audio signal due to inaccurate reproduction of the sound is _____.
    a) reverb
    b) noise
    c) distortion
    d) diffusion

23. Which of the following is *not* part of a sound wave's envelope?
    a) attack
    b) decay
    c) sustain
    d) rarefaction

24. The number of times a sound wave vibrates (goes in an up and down cycle) per second determines its _____.
    a) frequency
    b) amplitude
    c) wavelength
    d) wave envelope

25. The standard unit of measure to gauge the relative intensity of sound is the _____.
    a) signal-to-noise ratio
    b) hertz
    c) absorption coefficient
    d) decibel

■ ANSWERS

If You Answered A:
1a. No. This is not working combo. (Reread 1.1.)
2a. No. An on-air studio needs one for sending the mixed signal out. (Reread 1.1 and 1.2.)

3a. No. If anything, absorbed sound would be diminished. (Reread 1.8.)
4a. Yes. Echo is sound that has reflected off a single surface.
5a. No. This is close to (but not exactly) describing reverb route. (Reread 1.8.)
6a. No. Painted walls would be less expensive, so this can't be correct. (Reread 1.9 and 1.11.)
7a. No. Just the opposite is true. (Reread 1.10.)
8a. Right. The operator can reach around the "horseshoe."
9a. No. Just the opposite is true. (Reread Production Tip #1.)
10a. Wrong. The two minute signal would not come until the end of a program. It won't be right after a standby signal. (Reread 1.13.)
11a. Yes. This is the correct hand signal.
12a. No. Although you could map out this audio signal route, this is not the best answer. (Reread 1.2.)
13a. No. Diffused waves would be sound reflections that have been broken up. (Reread 1.8 and 1.10.)
14a. Right. On-air and recording lights usually come on automatically when a microphone is on in that studio.
15a. No. It does set something, but it has nothing to do with a neutral position. (Reread 1.15.)
16a. No. Most of the sound that strikes a hard, flat surface will be reflected. (Reread 1.8.)
17a. Yes. This would be a true statement.
18a. Wrong. Posters and other studio decorations aren't likely to cause poor production work, and they do add "atmosphere" to the studio. (Reread 1.11.)
19a. No. This would be a "soaking up" of sound reflections. (Reread 1.8 and 1.9.)
20a. Wrong. No one would want to be first. (Reread 1.15.)
21a. No. This is a true statement. (Reread 1.6.)
22a. No. Reverb is a form of reflected sound. (Reread 1.8 and 1.14.)
23a. Wrong. Attack is the time it takes an initial sound to build up to full volume. (Reread 1.7.)
24a. This is the correct answer.
25a. No. While S/N is expressed in decibels, it measures the nominal output of audio equipment in relation to the equipment's noise level. (Reread 1.7 and 1.14.)

If You Answered B:
1b. Correct. The announcer is also the equipment operator when working combo.
2b. No. A production studio needs one for mixing. (Reread 1.1 and 1.2.)
3b. Wrong. Reflected sound is sound that has bounced off a surface. (Reread 1.8.)
4b. No. Reverb is sound that has reflected off two or more surfaces. (Reread 1.8.)
5b. Yes. This is what we call reverb ring.
6b. Wrong. Carpeting absorbs sound and reduces reverb. (Reread 1.8 and 1.9.)
7b. Yes. This is the correct response.
8b. No. Lights have no relevance, so this can't be correct. (Reread 1.3 and 1.11.)
9b. Yes. Modern electronics, especially logic circuits, can be disrupted by static discharges.
10b. Wrong. You wouldn't know the production was going well if it hadn't started yet. (Reread 1.13.)
11b. No. Crossed index fingers indicate 30 seconds. (Reread 1.13.)
12b. No. This is not correct. (Reread 1.2.)
13b. Correct. This is the right answer.
14b. Wrong. This is exactly what it means. (Reread 1.12.)
15b. Wrong. It has nothing to do with erasing tapes—a degausser does. (Reread 1.15.)
16b. This isn't a bad choice, but some sound will be absorbed and dissipated even with hard surfaces. (Reread 1.8.)
17b. No. A coefficient of 1.00 would mean total absorption and a coefficient of 0.00 would mean no absorption. (Reread 1.9.)
18b. This is the correct answer.
19b. No. This would be sound that has bounced off a surface. (Reread 1.8.)
20b. Yes. All production people are responsible for their own cleanup.
21b. No. This is a true statement. (Reread 1.6.)
22b. No. You're close because noise is an unwanted element introduced into the audio signal that was not present in the original sound, but there's a better response. (Reread 1.14.)
23b. Wrong. Decay is the time it takes sound to go from peak volume to a sustain level. (Reread 1.7.)
24b. Wrong. Amplitude relates to volume and the height of a sound wave. (Reread 1.7.)
25b. No. Hertz is another term for cycles per second and is a measure of frequency. (Reread 1.7.)

If You Answered C:

1c. No. This is not working combo. (Reread 1.1.)

2c. No. This is just another term for production studio. (Reread 1.1 and 1.2.)

3c. Right. This is the correct response.

4c. No. Direct sound doesn't bounce off any surface before reaching the mic. (Reread 1.8.)

5c. No. Echo and reverb are both reflected sound but distinctly different. (Reread 1.8.)

6c. No. Just the opposite would happen. Soundproofing with carpeting would help produce a dead sound in the studio. (Reread 1.8 and 1.9.)

8c. No. In a cost-minded facility, this could be a negative. (Reread 1.3 and 1.4.)

10c. Correct. Standby and cue talent hand signals are always given one after the other.

11c. No. There is another hand signal to move the announcer closer to the mic, and exact steps are never indicated. (Reread 1.13.)

12c. No. You are way off base with this answer. (Reread 1.2.)

13c. No. Absorbed waves would be sound reflections that have been soaked up. (Reread 1.8–1.10.)

15c. Correct. A tone generator is used to help set volume levels.

16c. Wrong. Some sound will penetrate a hard surface and be transmitted to the adjoining space. (Reread 1.8.)

19c. No. This would be sound that has been transmitted through a surface. (Reread 1.8.)

20c. No. This wouldn't be fair to whoever was last. (Reread 1.15.)

21c. No. This is a true statement. (Reread 1.6.)

22c. Yes. You're correct.

23c. Wrong. Sustain is the time a sound holds its volume. (Reread 1.7.)

24c. Wrong. Wavelength refers to the distance between two wave compressions or rarefactions. (Reread 1.7.)

25c. No. Absorption coefficient measures the degree to which materials can absorb sound. (Reread 1.7 and 1.9.)

If You Answered D:

1d. No. This seems improbable and is not working combo. (Reread 1.1.)

2d. Correct. It usually only has mics that are fed to an audio console in either a production studio or an on-air studio.

3d. Wrong. (Reread 1.8.)

4d. You're partly right, but echo and reverb are both indirect sound, and one is a better response to this question. (Reread 1.8.)

5d. No. While this describes reverb, there is a better response. (Reread 1.8.)

6d. Correct. Carpeting walls helps to soundproof, as would use of acoustic tiles designed for the production studio.

8d. While this may be true, it really is not the best reason. (Reread 1.3.)

10d. No. The give-mic-level signal, if used, would have been given before a standby signal. (Reread 1.13.)

11d. Wrong. Time signals are usually given only to show how much time remains in a program. (Reread 1.13.)

12d. Correct. The term "audio chain" describes how broadcast equipment is connected together.

13d. No. Sympathetic waves would be sound reflections that have been reinforced. (Reread 1.8 and 1.10.)

15d. No. This would be a track sheet. (Reread 1.15.)

16d. Right. Sound is diffused when it strikes an irregular surface.

19d. Correct. This is diffusion.

20d. Naturally not. (Reread 1.15.)

21d. Yes. Sound vibrations can't travel in a vacuum.

22d. No. Diffusion is sound that has been "broken up" by an irregular surface. (Reread 1.8 and 1.14.)

23d. Correct. Rarefaction is not part of a sound's wave envelope.

24d. Wrong. Wave envelope refers to a sound's duration. (Reread 1.7.)

25d. You're right, the decibel is the standard unit or ratio used to measure a sound's volume.

Projects

■ PROJECT 1

Tour a radio station and write a report describing its production facilities.

Purpose

To enable you to see a commercial radio production facility firsthand.

Advice, Cautions, and Background

1. Don't push a station that seems reluctant to have you come. Some stations (especially smaller ones) are happy to have you. Others are pestered to death with would-be visitors or aren't equipped to handle them.
2. Make sure that before you go you have some ideas about what you want to find out so that you can make the most of your tour.
3. Keep your appointment. Once you make it, don't change it, for this will breed ill will for you and your school.

How to Do the Project

1. Select a station that you would like to tour. (If the instructor has arranged a station tour for the whole class, skip to step 4.)
2. Call the station, tell them you would like to see that station so that you can write a report for a radio production class, and ask if you may come.
3. If they're agreeable, set a date; if they're not, call a different station.
4. Think of some things you want to find out for your report. For example:
   a. How many production studios do they have?
   b. What types of equipment (CD player, audio recorder, etc.) do they have?
   c. What manufacturers (brand names) have they bought equipment from?
   d. How is the production studio soundproofed?
   e. How is the on-air studio different from the production studio(s)?
   f. Do the announcers ever use hand signals during a production?
   g. Are their studios designed for stand-up operation?
   h. What is the physical layout of the studios and the station?
5. Go to the station. Tour to the extent that they'll let you, and ask as many questions as you can.
6. Immediately after leaving the station, jot down notes so you'll remember main points.
7. Write your report in an organized fashion, including a complete description of the production studio and the other points you consider most pertinent. It should be two or three typed pages. Write your name and RADIO FACILITY TOUR on a title page.
8. Give the report to your instructor to receive credit for this project.

■ PROJECT 2

Redesign your production studio.

Purpose

To suggest improvements to your production facility, utilizing some of the techniques mentioned in this chapter.

Advice, Cautions, and Background

1. While you may initially feel your production studio is "perfect" just the way it is, almost every studio can be configured better.

2. You won't be judged on artistic ability, but make your drawings as clear as possible.
3. You may find it useful to complete Project 1 before attempting this project.

How to Do the Project

1. Draw a rough sketch of your production studio, showing approximate dimensions, door and window location, equipment placement, etc.
2. Draw another sketch of the studio, suggesting changes or improvements to it. For example, if there currently is a CD player on the left side of the audio console and another on the right side, you may suggest moving them both to one side. If you notice a paneled or painted sheet rock wall in the studio, you may suggest putting acoustic tile on that area. You may want to employ an idea for your studio that you noticed when you did Project 1, but be creative, and try to design the best possible production studio.
3. On a separate sheet of paper, provide a reason for each change you suggest.
4. Write your name and STUDIO DESIGN on a title page, and put your two sketches and reasons together.
5. Turn in this packet to the instructor to receive credit for this project.

■ PROJECT 3

Draw an audio chain flowchart for your production studio.

Purpose

To help you understand that the audio chain maps the route an electronic audio signal takes as it goes from one place to another in the production studio.

Advice, Cautions, and Background

1. It may be helpful to review Figure 1.1 before beginning this project.
2. Use simple shapes to represent equipment and arrowed lines to represent the sound signal.
3. You won't be judged on artistic ability, but make your drawings as clear as possible.

How to Do the Project

1. Pick a single sound source in your production studio, such as a CD player.
2. Draw a figure to represent the CD player toward the left side of a sheet of paper, and label it appropriately.
3. Determine where the sound goes as it leaves the output of the CD player. (Most likely, to the audio console.)
4. Draw a figure to the right of the CD player to represent the audio console, and label it.
5. Draw an arrowed line going from the CD player to the audio console to represent the signal flow.
6. Now determine where the sound goes next. (It could go to a signal processor or maybe directly to an audio recorder.)
7. Continue in this manner until you've drawn all the possible signal paths that the CD player sound could take. (Don't forget to include the signal to the studio monitors!)
8. Pick another sound source, such as the studio microphone, and repeat the above steps. Do the same for all the other sound sources in your studio—audio recorders, turntables, etc.
9. Write your name and AUDIO CHAIN on your sketch, and turn it in to the instructor to receive credit for this project.

Digital Audio Production

Information

2.1 INTRODUCTION

Digital technology has revolutionized how the radio production person can record, edit, and otherwise manipulate an audio sound signal. The days of pushing buttons to start a tape recorder are quickly being replaced with manipulating a mouse or keyboard and viewing a computer monitor screen to accomplish the tasks of audio production.

From the advent in the early 1980s of the compact disc player, to the total digital production studio of the early 2000s, radio has eagerly embraced digital technology. This chapter introduces you to some basic information about digital audio. It looks at some of the digital audio equipment used in the modern studio that has had this revolutionary impact on radio production.

2.2 THE DIGITAL AUDIO PROCESS

In the radio production domain, digital technology is replacing analog technology. By digital technology we mean the process of converting audio information into an electrical signal composed of a series of on and off pulses. In other words, the digital process is a conversion into **binary** numbers. All computers handle information in this manner by associating a binary number with each letter of the alphabet and each number, then manipulating this binary data.

Before digital technology was developed, audio recording relied on an **analog** process. An analog signal (for example, the audio signal produced by a microphone) is a continuously variable electrical signal whose shape is defined by the shape of the sound wave produced (see Figure 2.1A). In the analog recording process, a duplicate, or electromagnetic representation, of the sound wave of the original sound source is stored on magnetic tape.

Each time the analog signal is recorded or processed in some fashion, it is subject to degradation because the signal changes shape slightly. Analog encoding is similar to creating a line graph to show a statistical analysis. All measure-ments are on a continuous line that curves up and down with no discrete points. The recording process is like trying to retrace a curve on a graph; the reproduction is always slightly different than the original.

In addition to this generation loss, because analog recording relies on magnetic pulses stored on tape, any defect or decrease of the magnetic properties of the tape means a loss of signal quality. Typical problems for analog recording have included noise and distortion, print-through and crosstalk, flutter and hiss, and limited dynamic range. You'll learn more about the limitations of analog recording in Chapter 6, "Analog Audio Players/Recorders."

On the other hand, digital encoding is accomplished in a discrete fashion, in a manner similar to looking at individual numbers in a statistical analysis and writing them down in a set order. The audio signal (from a microphone) starts out as analog, but it can be converted to digital by going through four stages: filtering, sampling, quantizing, and coding. First, the original sound signal is sent through a low-pass **filter** that "strips" off frequencies that are above the range of human hearing. Although originally inaudible, these frequencies can be shifted, or **aliased**, into an audible range during recording and playback, so this process is known as **anti-aliasing**.

The filtered analog signal is next divided many times a second in a process known as **sampling** (see Figure 2.1B). Each sample represents the amplitude of the audio signal at the moment the sample is taken. By taking enough samples and converting the samples to binary data, an exact reproduction of the original sound signal can be recorded onto tape or some other medium. Most digital equipment utilizes **sampling rates** of 32, 44.1, and 48,000 times per second. The sampling rate must be at least twice the highest frequency in the audio signal to enable accurate encoding and decoding. Since we can't hear sounds above 20 kHz, the sampling rate should be slightly greater than twice 20 kHz, which is one of the reasons why the most common digital sampling rate is 44.1 kHz. Lower sampling rates can be utilized for lower quality recordings.

Quantizing and coding are the stages that assign a numerical value to each individual sample. **Quantizing**

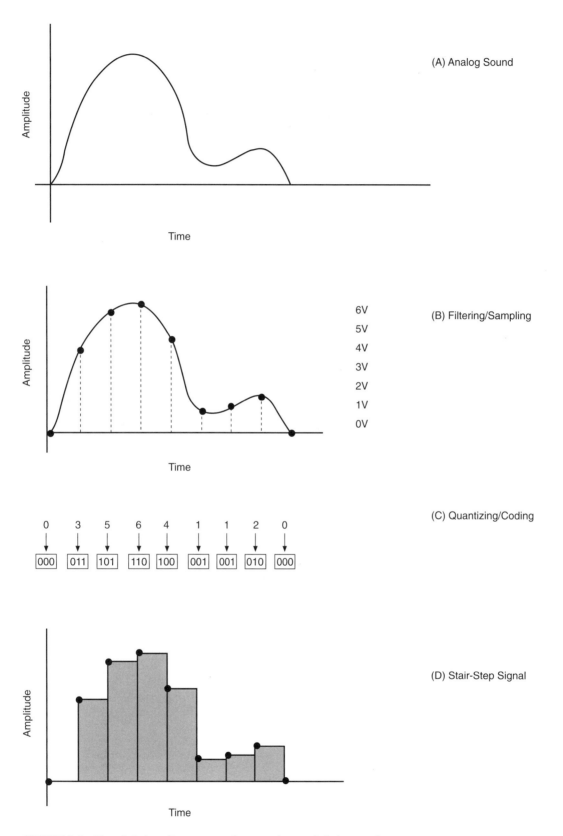

FIGURE 2.1   The digital audio process—from analog to digital to analog.

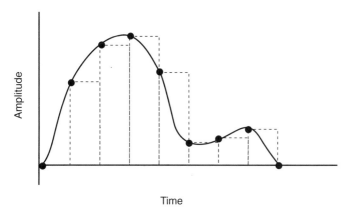

(E) Recreated Analog Signal

FIGURE 2.1 Continued.

determines how many levels or values the sample will be broken down into or how many "places" the binary number will have. The term "bit," short for binary digit, references the quantizing levels; the more levels, the more information you would have about the signal. For example, a 1-bit system would signify just two quantizing levels—either there's a voltage or there isn't—and not much information about the sound. Each additional bit doubles the number of levels. The standard bit rate for most digital recording is 16 · bits, with some compact disc recording now being done with 20-bit technology. Sixteen bits can represent 65,536 values.

Coding is putting "0s" and "1s" in a precise order corresponding to the values measured during the quantizing process. This binary, or digital, "word" (see Figure 2.1C) represents each individual sample's voltage level at that particular moment. The analog-to-digital (A/D) converter is the electronic circuit that accomplishes this task.

Remember, it's the binary data that is actually recorded, not an analog representation of the signal. With digital technology, we can copy from tape to tape with no measurable loss of quality. Along with the improved frequency response, wide dynamic range, and unmeasurable noise and distortion, this ability to rerecord with no decrease in quality has been a big part of the acceptance of digital in radio production.

To transform the digital signal back to analog, the recorded "numbers" are sent to a digital-to-analog (D/A) converter where each sample is read and decoded. A signal of the corresponding analog amplitude is produced and "held" for the individual samples producing a stair-step signal (see Figure 2.1D) that represents the analog signal. Finally, a filter employs an exact mathematical attribute for each sample to recreate a correct reproduction of the original analog signal, as shown in Figure 2.1E.

2.3 DESKTOP RADIO—THE DIGITAL AUDIO EDITOR

The simplest way to get into digital radio production is to put together an inexpensive digital audio editor that utilizes a standard off-the-shelf computer system, plus some specialized equipment, to make up an audio editing system. Often referred to as "desktop radio," this type of production system has the potential of replacing almost an entire production studio. Although some systems may run on a more basic computer setup, most will require at least Windows 95, a Pentium 133 or higher speed CPU, 32 MB of RAM (random access memory), a mouse or similar pointing device, a high-resolution VGA monitor, and a fast EIDE or ultrawide SCSI hard drive with about 10 megabytes of memory for each stereo minute of audio. There are also Mac-based systems that would require a similarly configured computer. In addition to the computer, the necessary specialized equipment includes a **DSP** (digital signal processing) **audio card**, and normally a PCI-bus design, as shown in Figure 2.2. A standard computer audio card could be used, but professional audio hardware usually offers higher sampling rate capability, greater bit resolution, and broadcast-style connectors. The audio card functions as both the analog-to-digital and digital-to-analog converter, and the interface or I/O (input/output) device that moves the audio signal from its source in the production studio into the editing system, then back into the production studio. The final component of a desktop radio system is a computer software program to perform the actual editing of the audio.

There are several software programs (see Figure 2.3) that can turn a PC into a powerful digital audio editor—IQS's *SAW* series, Sonic Foundry's *Sound Forge*, and Syntrillium's *Cool Edit Pro*, to name a few. Bare-bone audio editing soft-

FIGURE 2.2 The DSP audio card is an important component of the computer-based desktop audio editor. (Image courtesy of Lynx Studio Technology, Inc.)

FIGURE 2.3 Audio editing software can transform an off-the-shelf computer into a desktop audio editor. (Image courtesy Syntrillium Software Corporation.)

ware can be found for less than $100, but most professional programs used in the broadcast studio will fall in the $300 to $900 range—still a relatively inexpensive investment. With a budget of a couple thousand dollars, any radio station should be able to build a desktop system and begin doing digital audio production work.

With the most basic editing program, you can merely define segments of audio and then assemble the segments into a list to be played back. For example, the background to a "concert spot" might include several songs by the featured group. Segments of each song are recorded on the editor's hard disk as a **soundfile**. The exact portion of each segment that is to be used in the spot can then be selected, using the mouse to define an **event** or **region** in a fashion similar to standard editing: that is, selecting a range (start point and end point) for each "edit." In this case, the edit marks are made on the computer screen, which shows a "picture" of the audio (usually the actual waveform) that can be easily moved, or "trimmed," to the exact position desired. As shown in Figure 2.4, the portion of audio that is to be edited out is usually highlighted on the screen. The final step is to assemble the events into a **playlist** or sequential order. The various edits can be played back one event at a time or in a seamless montage. Chapter 7, "Audio Editing" and Chapter 10, "Multitrack Production Techniques" will further examine the techniques of manipulating audio with digital equipment or software programs.

One of the biggest advantages of this type of system is the *nondestructive* nature of the editing. The original audio isn't actually altered; edit information (where to start and stop playing the audio) is recorded in an "edit decision list." Some systems execute editing that's *destructive* because portions of the audio are actually deleted or cut out; however, even these systems usually allow you to preview the edit before it's performed and undo it if it isn't marked properly.

More sophisticated editing programs allow the recording of several "tracks" (just like a multitrack recorder) that can then be manipulated individually and ultimately mixed together to provide a completely produced spot.

2.4 RECORDING WITH THE DIGITAL EDITOR

Regardless of the software program employed, the first step in beginning an audio production project is to record a soundfile, and although each program will utilize different techniques, you should find that they are similar in procedure. To illustrate various digital production techniques, this text is using Syntrillium Software Corporation's *Cool Edit Pro* program. A demo version of this software is included on the CD-ROM that comes with this text. *Cool Edit Pro* is really two programs combined into one. The "edit view" screen (shown in Figure 2.5) puts the user in a single-waveform editor that is used to record and edit mono and stereo audio segments. The *Waveform Display* shows the audio soundfile and is utilized to edit or otherwise process the sound. The *Transport* buttons control recording and playback functions of the audio. A *Timeline Display* shows timing information, and *Horizontal* and *Vertical Zooms* allow you to scale the audio display to various sizes. Other options are available

FIGURE 2.4   A soundfile is pictured on the computer screen as the waveform of the audio, with the vertical axis indicating amplitude and the horizontal axis showing time. (Image courtesy of Syntrillium Software Corporation.)

FIGURE 2.5   The main screen of an audio production software program shows various navigation and functional controls for manipulating the audio being worked on. (Image courtesy of Syntrillium Software Corporation.)

through either *Menu Options* or *Toolbar* buttons. Switching to the "multitrack view" screen moves the operator to a multitrack hard disk recorder—capable of mixing and processing up to 64 tracks of audio—which shows the production being assembled, fine tuned, and ultimately finished. Other software programs will have similar screens and functions.

Before you can record, you'll need to have an audio signal coming to the "line inputs" on the audio card. In a radio studio, the output of the audio board is usually sent

FIGURE 2.6   Prior to recording with *Cool Edit Pro*, you need to select sample rate, bit resolution, and whether you want to record in stereo or mono. (Image courtesy of Syntrillium Software Corporation.)

FIGURE 2.7   The Personal Audio Editor is becoming a digital replacement for the two-track reel-to-reel recorder. (Image courtesy of 360 Systems.)

to your audio editor so that *any* audio source in the studio can be plugged into the system. To start recording, mouse click on the FILE option menu and select NEW. This will pop up a window (shown in Figure 2.6) that allows you to make settings that control the recording process. Key recording parameters include sample rate and bit resolution. As noted earlier, the higher the rate and resolution, the higher the quality of the recording. Most digital audio recording is done at 44.1 kHz (sample rate) and 16-bit (resolution), which is CD-quality audio. You'll also need to select either mono or stereo recording. Click the OK button to set your recording parameters. To begin recording, click on the RECORD button on the *Transport*; click on the STOP button to discontinue recording. You can check recording levels by watching the RECORD LEVEL METERS at the bottom of the "edit view" screen. Double-clicking activates the meters if they aren't already monitoring the audio amplitude. It's also probable that you can manipulate the source audio volume through an external control, such as the audio console noted previously. Once you've ended the recording session, you can immediately begin working on (editing) the audio. You'll find many additional recording features in the *Cool Edit Pro* software, but this should give you some familiarity with the basic recording techniques of a typical digital audio editor.

2.5 THE PERSONAL AUDIO EDITOR

Another type of digital audio editor that *doesn't* need a computer, mouse, monitor, or special plug-in card is beginning to see a lot of popularity in the production studio. 360 Systems Short/cut™ personal audio editor is configured in a compact, portable case, as shown in Figure 2.7, and

records audio directly to its internal hard disk. Beneath a two-track waveform display are three distinct sections of controls. To the right are the basic transport controls (like play, pause, record, etc.); in the center are editing controls (like edit in, cut, erase, and a large scrub wheel); and to the left are the system controls (like hot keys, menu directory, and a QWERTY keyboard for labeling functions).

Editing with the Short/cut™ is as easy as recording or loading in a file, scrubbing to the edit-in point, and then scrubbing to the edit-out point. The marked section of audio will become highlighted and can then be removed, copied, or erased, or new material can be inserted. As in most digital equipment, if you make a mistake an undo function will allow you to correct it. The Short/cut™ has a selectable 44.1 kHz or 48 kHz sample rate, and 360 Systems currently offers a 4-hour recording time model. Less complex than some of the PC-based audio editors, this type of digital audio editor is being touted as a digital replacement for the reel-to-reel recorder and is becoming very commonplace in the digital production studio.

2.6 DIGITAL AUDIO WORKSTATIONS

A further extension of digital editing technology in the radio production studio has been the development of the **DAW**, or **digital audio workstation**. These hard-disk-based systems incorporate proprietary computer technology to convert the original sound signal to digital form, which can then be stored, manipulated, and recalled using the workstation. While some digital audio workstations are quite similar to the earlier mentioned desktop radio systems (see Figure 2.8), some do not physically look like computers (see Figure 2.9). In either case, because the workstation has been developed as a dedicated audio recorder and editor, they often have built-in specialized functions and features.

The basic components of the DAW are similar to the elements that make up the simple digital audio editor mentioned earlier; however, DAWs are often "packaged" as a

FIGURE 2.8 Some digital audio workstations resemble desktop radio systems but utilize specialized cards, customized boxes, and proprietary software. (Image courtesy of SADiE.)

FIGURE 2.9 The swing to digital includes the increasing use of the dedicated digital audio workstation. (Image courtesy of Orban.)

single unit similar to the one shown in Figure 2.9. A **frame** houses the computer chassis, power supply, and motherboard. An internal **hard disc drive** stores and manipulates the digital audio data. Remember, each stereo minute of audio will "eat up" about 10 megabytes; however, data compression techniques can greatly reduce the capacity requirements, and low-cost, high-capacity hard drives have made this less and less of an issue. A **user interface**, such as a keyboard, touchscreen, or mouse, is necessary to actually operate the workstation. However, many workstations have tried to be more user-friendly to radio production people by making the interface include typical radio production elements, such as faders, cue wheels, and tape-transport buttons like "rewind" or "play." Sometimes these interfaces are shown in graphics form on a computer screen, but some systems actually attach to a mini-audio board (refer to Figure 2.9). A built-in audio card provides the connection between the workstation and the other audio equipment by converting analog audio into digital data and vice versa. Through the use of serial and parallel ports, many workstations have the ability to network with other workstations or interface with printers, modems, and other components.

2.7 AUDIO SYNCHRONIZATION

With analog audio, the audio signals are constant streams with no specific demarcation points; however, digital audio

has changed the audio environment. Digital audio signals are streams of digits broken up into digital words, as we noted earlier in this chapter. If two digital signals are "out of sync," then one may just be beginning a new digital word when the other is in the middle of a word. Switching from one to the other would result in an audible tick or pop. Synchronized audio signals would both start new digital words at precisely the same time. Some digital production equipment is self-synchronizing, but digital audio consoles that accept many different types of digital inputs will need to synchronize audio to a common clock.

Most digital audio workstations and many other pieces of digital broadcast equipment also have the ability to incorporate MIDI and SMPTE synchronization. **MIDI (musical instrument digital interface)** is an interface system that allows electronic equipment—mainly musical instruments like synthesizers, drum-machines, and samplers—to "talk" to each other through an "electronic" language.

SMPTE (Society for Motion Picture and Television Engineers) **time code** is an electronic language developed for videotape editing that identifies each video "frame" with an individual address. The time-code numbers consist of hour, minute, second, and frame. The frame digits correspond to the thirty video frames in each second.

Both MIDI and SMPTE signals can be used to reference various individual pieces of equipment and accurately start, combine, or stop them. Someone working in the production studio is more likely to make use of MIDI or SMPTE than someone in the on-air broadcast studio. MIDI, in particular, is often used to interface various musical sounds for an audio production.

2.8 ADVANTAGES OF THE DIGITAL PRODUCTION STUDIO

One of the main advantages of digital equipment like the CD player or DAW is improved audio signal quality. The digital format offers superior technical specifications in the area of frequency response, dynamic range, signal-to-noise ratio, wow, flutter, and other forms of audio distortion. Not only does this provide an improved initial audio signal, but the digital process doesn't build up any added noise during recording, dubbing, or transmitting.

Production people quickly realized that another advantage of digital editors like the DAW was the ability to utilize nondestructive editing. Not only does editing without using razor blades to physically cut the audio tape provide a safer work environment in the production studio, it also allows you to preview the editing before it's finalized. Most DAWs have some type of "undo" button to put the sound back into its original form if you don't like the way the edit came out. Another operational advantage of the DAW is fast random access (the ability to immediately cue up at any point) to all the material stored in the system. Faster and easier operation of digital equipment should lead to less time spent on basic production functions and more time spent on the creative aspect of the production process.

It is also easier to undertake many editing operations with digital editing than with traditional razor blade editing. For example, if you must remove a very short segment, such as someone momentarily stuttering on a word, it's easy to do because you can both hear the problem and see the waveform of the audio. If necessary, you can zoom in to make the audio segment larger, and then remove the stuttering section accurately. If you record something, but then need to make it slightly shorter or longer, you can do so easily with digital equipment. For instance, if you record what is to be a 15-second commercial and it turns out to be 17 seconds long, you can remove short bits of silence throughout the commercial to get it to 15 seconds. In fact, many digital audio software programs or DAWs can do this time-compression/expansion for you. You indicate how long you want something to be, and the program adjusts the material accordingly.

Digital equipment (see Chapter 5, "Digital Audio Players/Recorders"), such as the CD, MiniDisc, and digital audio cart recorders, offers a labeling function that's more convenient and comprehensive than paper labels. IDs and other types of label information can be encoded within the digital media. A "table of contents" can provide names, times, and other data through a front-panel window on the equipment or through the video monitor screen of a DAW.

Another technical advantage of digital is that there are fewer maintenance problems, such as dirty tape heads or alignment problems. Most digital equipment promises a longer interval between breakdowns than comparable analog equipment, and when there's a technical problem, digital equipment usually takes less time to repair. Since there are fewer internal operating parts in digital equipment, in many cases repair is a simple replacement of one circuit board or component for another.

In many cases, digital equipment is smaller than the analog equipment it is designed to replace, offering a space savings that can be important in the smaller radio studio. For example, some MiniDisc recorders take up just a single rack space (a height of about $1\frac{3}{4}$"), and the 360 Systems Short/cut™ is smaller and more portable than the analog reel-to-reel recorder it was designed to replace.

Production Tip #2— "Maintaining Digital Equipment"

There are fewer mechanical elements in digital broadcast equipment than older analog equipment, so maintaining that equipment is different, as noted in this chapter. In addition to typical broadcast maintenance, computer knowledge is becoming more and more important. To keep your studio computers running in their most efficient manner, you will need to reboot every week to ten days. Most computer programs, such as editing software, will cause the computer RAM to become fragmented as the program runs. You may not notice any problems with typical business programs (like a word processor) on computers that run during the normal workday and then are shut down until the next day. However, studio computers are often running 24 hours a day, every day of the week. RAM can become so fragmented that the computer will lock up, and that's a condition that you don't want to happen for a production or on-air computer. Set up a regular maintenance reboot during some station quiet time and you'll have fewer computer problems. In addition, memory management should become a regular part of your computer maintenance. As production work is accomplished, soundfile fragments and completed productions can be left on the hard drive. In a short period of time, hours of hard disc storage will dwindle down to minutes unless old files are deleted from the system or archived onto a removable storage medium for later use.

Originally the high cost of digital equipment was a definite drawback; however, the cost factor has decreased with continued development of digital technology, and today the majority of digital equipment is either less expensive or about the same price as the analog equipment it is replacing. Only the full-blown DAW systems or high-end digital multitrack recorders, at several thousands of dollars, would be considered expensive for some stations. The alternative, PC-based systems with consumer-grade equipment, offers the possibility of an "entry-level" approach to getting started with digital production, and many smaller market stations are successfully heading in this inexpensive direction.

2.9 DISADVANTAGES OF THE DIGITAL PRODUCTION STUDIO

The advantages of the digital studio far outweigh the disadvantages, but like any technology, there are a few minuses to go with all the pluses. One disadvantage of digital equipment is the learning curve tied to understand-

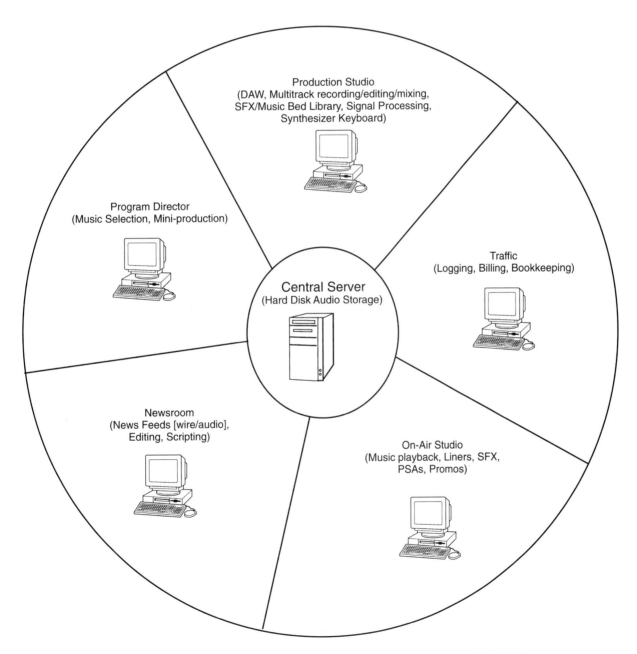

FIGURE 2.10 The all-digital station will integrate audio production with other aspects of the facility's operation.

ing the operation of various components. Although learning the basic editing functions of a MiniDisc recorder might be fairly straightforward, learning to operate a DAW in an expert manner can take several months, a factor that makes them somewhat user-unfriendly. Regardless of what manufacturers might claim, most digital equipment takes some time to learn, and production people must be willing to give the time and effort necessary to pick up new radio production techniques.

Most of the sound problems associated with analog recording are nonexistent with the digital process, but digital recording does have a unique, subjective problem of its own. The superior sonic quality of a digital signal is so clear and noise-free that some find that it sounds "harsh" or "mechanical" in comparison to the old "warmth" of analog distortion! It would be hard to argue against the superior sound quality that digital equipment provides, because it can be readily measured and compared to analog sound. Nonetheless, a criticism of digital sound still exists because, for some, the clear, brilliant sound has been likened to a "cold" or "mechanical" sound. It's not what we're hearing, but rather what we *don't* hear that our ears are used to hearing with old analog equipment. The tremendous frequency response, dynamic range, and lack of noise and other forms of distortion, for some people, is too "harsh." Of course, this judgment of sound quality is highly subjective, and for many if not most people, digital sound is just fine and highly superior to analog sound.

But there is a "noise" disadvantage of digital equipment—not audio noise, but noise from fans in computers or disk drives. If these have to be housed in a studio with live mics, there could be a problem. Some production facilities solve this potential problem by putting the computer CPUs in a separate equipment room; leaving only the keyboard/mouse and monitor in the actual studio. However, another potential noise problem is "buzz" from the video monitor interfering with the speaker monitors. Shielding or creative placement might be necessary to make the digital studio workable in the normal studio environment.

Only one advantage of the digital studio can, to a lesser extent, also show up as a disadvantage. Some production facilities will have to look carefully at the space requirements of new digital equipment. As we've noted, most digital equipment is smaller than the analog equipment it's replacing, but additional counter space for a video monitor and mouse will be necessary, as will additional rack space for hard-disk drives and perhaps other digital equipment. For a time, digital hardware will have to coexist with the traditional broadcast equipment in most production studios. Of course, this will become less of a problem as older analog equipment is totally removed from the production studio.

2.10 THE ALL-DIGITAL RADIO FACILITY

The future of digital technology, for those who embrace the concept, looks like more than just a very high-tech produc-

FIGURE 2.11 Digital distribution networks deliver CD-quality content, such as commercials, music singles, and news actualities to radio stations. (Image courtesy of DG Systems.)

tion studio. For example, most proponents of the DAW see it as a part of an all-digital radio station (see Figure 2.10). Not only can the DAW-based system produce a radio commercial, but it can store the commercial or several variations of it (while maintaining digital quality), play the commercial on-air by sending the signal to a digitized transmitter, and even send logging and bookkeeping information about the airing of the commercial to the appropriate station personnel. These types of systems are being used by more and more radio stations.

2.11 DIGITAL DISTRIBUTION NETWORKS

Another way digital technology has impacted radio and radio production is the ability to deliver CD-quality audio to radio stations using **digital distribution networks**. Two companies, DG Systems and Digital Courier International (DCI), provide such a service by linking radio stations with ad agencies, production houses, and record companies.

Under traditional analog techniques, radio spots were recorded onto audio tape masters, then dubbed to tape copies, and finally delivered by mail or courier to individual stations. The digital distribution networks feature PC-based servers in the ad agency, production house, or record company onto which audio files are loaded. This audio is sent via phone line to the network headquarters, and then, with appropriate instructions, sent to receivers at client stations (see Figure 2.11).

Since they employ digital lines (such as **ISDN** [Integrated Services Digital Network]), these networks offer fast, instantaneous delivery of digital quality audio to stations around the country. They have been used to send commercials, newly released singles, and other production materials. Digital distribution networks have also been used to facilitate simultaneous recording from two different locations.

2.12 CONCLUSIONS

There seems to be little doubt that radio production has and will continue to change because of various developments in digital audio production. The whole industry is gravitating toward digital, and those who aren't embracing the technology will find they are left behind. A basic understanding of digital technology and the operation of digital-based equipment has become a prerequisite for success for the radio production person.

Self-Study

■ QUESTIONS

1. In which area is digital technology superior to analog technology?
   a) signal-to-noise ratio
   b) frequency response
   c) dynamic range
   d) all of the above

2. A standard off-the-shelf computer can be converted into a basic digital audio editor by adding appropriate software and _____.
   a) an ESP audio card
   b) an ESPN audio card
   c) a DSP audio card
   d) an ASP audio card

3. In the digital recording process, an electromagnetic representation of the sound wave of the original sound source is stored on magnetic tape.
   a) true
   b) false

4. In general, a digital audio workstation's hard-disk drive will require _____ megabytes of memory for each stereo minute of audio the system is capable of handling.
   a) 5
   b) 10
   c) 15
   d) 20

5. Musical instruments (such as synthesizers or samplers) can interface to digital audio equipment through an electronic communications language known as _____.
   a) Short/cut
   b) SAW
   c) MINI
   d) MIDI

6. Which stage of the digital recording process breaks down the analog signal into discrete values or levels?
   a) filtering
   b) sampling
   c) quantizing
   d) coding

7. One of the main advantages of the digital audio workstation in radio production is _____.
   a) it's an inexpensive system to put together and maintain
   b) it's easy to operate
   c) it's capable of nondestructive editing
   d) it offers better recording quality than a personal audio editor

8. Digital audio workstations have the potential to introduce noise into the production process through two ways: cooling fan noise picked up by a mic and _____.
   a) video monitor interference picked up by a studio monitor speaker
   b) hiss picked up during the recording process
   c) clicks picked up at edit points during editing
   d) none of the above

9. The digital audio workstation has very little practical use outside the radio production studio.
   a) true
   b) false

10. Nondestructive editing is a feature of all desktop radio systems.
    a) true
    b) false

11. Digital recordings can be copied over and over with no measurable loss of sound quality because _____.
    a) the sound signal is a continuously variable electrical signal, the shape of which is defined by the shape of the sound wave produced
    b) the original sound source is sampled over 44,000 times per second
    c) it is binary data that is recorded, and this can be accurately copied
    d) the laser beam is focused directly on the data track

12. Most digital equipment promises a longer interval between breakdowns than comparable analog equipment; however, when there is a technical problem, repair time for the digital equipment will probably also be longer.
    a) true
    b) false

13. Which disadvantage of the digital production studio would be easiest to argue against?
    a) It can be difficult to learn digital equipment operation.
    b) The cost of digital equipment.
    c) The need for additional studio space for digital equipment.
    d) The sound of digital equipment.

14. Which digital sampling rate is used most frequently?
    a) 32 kHz
    b) 44.1 kHz
    c) 48 kHz
    d) 88.2 kHz

15. A _____ delivers CD-quality radio content, such as commercials, to radio stations around the country.
    a) digital audio workstation
    b) digital distribution network
    c) digital audio card
    d) digital audio editor

ANSWERS

If You Answered A:
1a. You're partially correct, but this is not the best response. (Reread 2.1 and 2.8.)
2a. No. You didn't "sense" the correct answer. (Reread 2.3.)

3a. Wrong. This statement describes analog recording, not digital recording. (Reread 2.2.)
4a. No. Hint: this would work for a mono signal. (Reread 2.6.)
5a. Wrong. 360 Systems' Short/cut™ is a personal audio editor, not a communications language. (Reread 2.7.)
6a. No. Filtering cuts off unwanted high frequencies before sampling begins. (Reread 2.2.)
7a. No. DAWs are relatively expensive. (Reread 2.8.)
8a. Correct. This could be a problem with incorrectly positioned monitors.
9a. No. (Reread 2.10.)
10a. No. Some desktop radio systems have a destructive edit mode and actually delete the audio that has been edited, but usually only after a preview of the edit. (Reread 2.3.)
11a. Wrong. This refers to an analog signal. (Reread 2.2.)
12a. No. Only half of this statement is true. Although digital equipment will probably break down less than analog equipment, repair for digital equipment also promises to be shorter in many cases. (Reread 2.8.)
13a. No. Some digital equipment isn't very user-friendly and has a considerable learning curve. (Reread 2.9.)
14a. No. This is another sampling rate that some digital equipment is capable of utilizing. (Reread 2.2.)
15a. No. A DAW could be utilized to produce a commercial, but it's not used to send spots around the country. (Reread 2.6 and 2.11.)

If You Answered B:

1b. You're partially correct, but this is not the best response. (Reread 2.1 and 2.8.)
2b. No. You might have just taken a "sporting" guess to get this answer. (Reread 2.3.)
3b. Right. This is not digital recording, but rather analog recording.
4b. Yes. This is the correct answer.
5b. Wrong. SAW is an audio editing software program, but not a communication language. (Reread 2.7.)
6b. No. Sampling is when the signal is "sliced" into thousands of individual samples (voltages). (Reread 2.2.)
7b. No. DAWs are complicated and require some time to learn to operate proficiently. (Reread 2.8.)
8b. Wrong. Digital recording will add virtually no hiss. (Reread 2.9.)
9b. Yes. DAWs could well become the heart of a completely digital radio station.
10b. Yes. There are desktop radio systems that have both destructive and nondestructive edit modes.
11b. Wrong. But you're heading in the right direction. Sampling rate is important for exact reproduction of the original sound, but it isn't really the reason why digital recordings can be copied over and over. (Reread 2.2.)
12b. Yes. Only part of this statement is true. Digital equipment repair time should be shorter than analog.
13b. No. While some digital equipment is costly, as more and more digital equipment hits the market, this is less and less of a disadvantage. However, there is a better answer. (Reread 2.9.)
14b. Correct. This is the most common digital sampling rate.
15b. Yes. This is the correct response.

If You Answered C:

1c. You're partially correct, but this is not the best response. (Reread 2.1 and 2.8.)
2c. Correct. A DSP audio card is a standard audio interface for the PC platform.
4c. No. (Reread 2.6.)
5c. Wrong. You're probably confusing this with the MiniDisc. (Reread 2.7.)
6c. Yes. This is correct.
7c. Yes. DAWs offer nondestructive editing capability.
8c. Wrong. DAW electronic editing is noiseless. (Reread 2.9.)
11c. Correct. Binary data can be accurately recorded over and over, making digital copies sound exactly like the original.
13c. No. It's true some digital equipment is smaller than comparable analog equipment, but usually additional studio space is required for keyboards, computer monitors, etc. (Reread 2.9.)
14c. No. This is another sampling rate that some digital equipment is capable of utilizing. (Reread 2.2.)
15c. No. A digital audio card is part of a desktop radio system. (Reread 2.3 and 2.11.)

If You Answered D:

1d. Correct. Digital technology offers all these technical improvements over analog.
2d. No. You got "bitten" on this answer. (Reread 2.3.)
4d. No. (Reread 2.6.)
5d. Right. MIDI (musical instrument digital interface) is the correct response.
6d. No. Coding is when a series of binary digits are assigned to each individual sample. (Reread 2.2.)

7d. No. Both DATs and DAWs record with the same digital quality. (Reread 2.8.)

8d. Wrong. There is a correct response, but this isn't it. (Reread 2.9.)

11d. Wrong. While the use of a laser is an important part of CD technology, it is not the reason. (Reread 2.2.)

13d. Yes. This is the weakest disadvantage of digital equipment because in most ways digital audio is obviously superior in quality to analog and in other ways it's a highly subjective judgment.

14d. Wrong. This is not a common sampling rate. (Reread 2.2.)

15d. No. A digital audio editor could be used to produce a commercial, but it's not used to send spots around the country. (Reread 2.3, 2.4, and 2.11.)

Project

■ PROJECT 1

Write a report that compares various recording/editing software programs.

Purpose

To allow you to further investigate some of the computer software that is available for digital production systems.

Advice, Cautions, and Background

1. Prepare a list of questions that you want answered before you begin your research.
2. This project requires obtaining material through the Internet from various manufacturers.
3. The manufacturers shown below are not the only ones who produce audio editing software. You could also complete the project by looking at other programs.

How to Do the Project

1. Develop some questions that you want answered about audio editing software. For example:
   a. What are the computer system requirements for each software program?
   b. What exactly can each do in the area of radio production?
   c. How much do they cost?
   d. Are there any problems associated with these programs?
   e. What sample rate does each program use?
2. Gather information by going to the Web site of the manufacturers. (Some addresses are provided below.)
3. If your facility has this software or you know of a station in your area that does, try to talk with someone who uses it on a regular basis to further research the programs.
4. Organize your material into an informative report that compares the various software programs. It should be several pages long. Write your name and Editing Software Programs Comparison on a title page.
5. Turn in the report to your instructor for credit for this project.

Syntrillium Software Company (Cool Edit Pro)
P.O. Box 62255
Phoenix, Arizona 85082
www.syntrillium.com

Innovative Quality Software (SAW32)
4680 S. Eastern Avenue, Suite H
Las Vegas, Nevada 89119
www.iqsoft.com

Sonic Foundry Inc. (Sound Forge)
754 Williamson Street
Madison, Wisconsin 53703
www.sonicfoundry.com

Cakewalk Music Software (Cakewalk)
5 Cambridge Center, 10th Floor
Cambridge, Massachusetts 02142
www.cakewalk.com

Digidesign, a division of Avid Technology (Pro Tools)
3401-A Hillview Avenue
Palo Alto, California 94304
www.digidesign.com

Minnetonka Audio Software (Fast EdDit)
17113 Minnetonka Blvd., Suite 300
Minnetonka, Minnesota 55345
www.minnetonkaaudio.com

■ PROJECT 2

Using a digital audio editor or digital workstation, build a short music bed.

Purpose

To give you experience with digitally based recording and editing.

Advice, Cautions, and Background

1. Obviously, you can't do this assignment unless you have the hardware and software to complete it available to you.
2. CD music that you can use is provided on the CD-ROM that accompanies this text, but if you prefer, you can use your own music from some other source—a DAT, an analog tape, a record. Keep in mind that a CD or music on a DAT tape will already be in digital form, whereas music from a record or analog tape will be in analog form.
3. You'll be laying the same 10 seconds of music down three times, so select some music that will lend itself to this. Find 10 seconds at the beginning or in the middle of a piece of music that won't sound like it has been cut off abruptly.
4. The project is written to be 30 seconds long, but feel free to make a music bed 60 seconds long, if you prefer.

How to Do the Project

1. Select music from the CD-ROM provided or from some other source and record a soundfile of about 20 seconds onto your computer.
2. Activate your computer editing program.
3. Select a 10-second region of music from the 20 seconds, and lay it down on one track made available through your computer editing program.
4. Lay the same 10 seconds of material down again right next to the first region, and then lay it down one more time right after the second 10-second segment.
5. Listen to it and improve upon it so that it could be used as a 30-second music bed under someone talking about a commercial product. You may want to change volume or fade it in or out or tighten it a bit. What you can do and exactly how you do it will depend on the computer program that you're using.
6. Record from the computer to an audio tape (DAT or analog). Label this tape with your name and DIGITAL EDITED MUSIC BED. Give the tape to your instructor to receive credit for this project.

■ PROJECT 3

Record a basic "voice and music bed" commercial.

Purpose

To develop your skill in creating one of the most common types of radio spots.

Advice, Cautions, and Background

1. This project assumes you have enough familiarity with your studio equipment to accomplish basic recording and production techniques.

2. The production incorporates a single announcer voice and a music bed.
3. You will need to write a simple script that can be read in about 23 seconds. Write the copy about a desktop item, such as a ballpoint pen, stapler, or paperclip holder.
4. There are many ways to accomplish this project, so don't feel you must follow the production directions exactly.

How to Do the Project

1. Record the script (voice only) onto a recorder, such as a reel-to-reel or digital recorder. Rerecord it to correct any vocal mistakes, to get the timing correct, or just to get it to sound the way you want.
2. Select a music bed that is appropriate for the style of the spot. You might use the bed you produced in Project 2, or you might find something on a production music CD, or on the CD-ROM with this text.
3. You can play back the music bed directly from a CD, or you may have to record it on another recorder.
4. Set correct playback levels for both the vocal track and the music bed. Both will start at full volume. Then cue both to the beginning sound.
5. Record your completed spot onto an audio cassette, so set your cassette recorder to record mode.
6. Begin recording. Start the music bed at full volume. Start the vocal track and simultaneously fade the music bed slightly so the vocal track is dominant.
7. As the vocal ends, bring the music bed back to full volume and then quickly fade it out as you approach 30 seconds.
8. It may take you several attempts to get the spot to come out correctly. If you need to "do it over," just recue everything and try again.
9. Listen to the finished commercial. Make sure you've gotten a good balance between the music and the voice.
10. On the tape write your name and BASIC RADIO SPOT, and turn it in to your instructor to receive credit for this project.

CHAPTER THREE

The Audio Console

Information

3.1 INTRODUCTION

The audio console, or **control board**, is the primary piece of equipment in any production facility. It can be more difficult to understand than other equipment in the radio production studio, but most other pieces of equipment operate in conjunction with the audio console. Therefore, unless you can operate the audio console, you can't really utilize other studio equipment, such as a compact disc player or audio recorder. The broadcast, or on-air, consoles used in most radio stations are fairly straightforward in their construction and operation; however, some control boards used in audio production and music recording become much more complex with additional controls and features. Regardless of their complexity, all control boards have basic similarities. Even though you'll run across many different brands of audio consoles in your radio production work, a thorough knowledge of any one control board will enable you to use any control board after a brief orientation.

Look at the audio console shown in Figure 3.1. Most boards, from the simplest to the more complex, include some method for input selection (mic/line switch, A/B/C source selectors) and input volume control (faders and pots), as well as some method for output selection (program/audition/auxiliary switch, output selectors) and volume control (master gain control). They should also have some method of indicating to the operator the strength of the signal (VU meter), and a way of allowing the operator to hear the mix of sources (monitor speakers, cue speakers, headphones). Boards also have amplifiers at various stages so that the signal is loud enough when it eventually goes to the transmitter or an audio recorder. These amplifiers are buried inside the board and are not something the board operator can control. In addition, audio consoles can have many other special features to help the board operator work more efficiently and creatively. The board may look intimidating because of all the buttons, knobs, and levers, but most of them are repeats of each other since the board has many different inputs and outputs. These will be explained in detail as we begin to explore the operation of the audio console.

3.2 THE DIGITAL AUDIO CONSOLE

Like most other audio production equipment, the audio console is facing transformation from analog to digital. The first generation of digital boards were quite a bit more expensive than the analog consoles they were designed to replace, which kept many stations from making the transition. Current digital audio consoles are just slightly more expensive than their analog counterparts and often offer additional features that justify the small extra expense. Some production facilities haven't felt the need for a digital board because many of their audio sources were still analog and a digital board wouldn't offer any particular advantage. However, as more and more studios become fully digital, moving the console from analog to digital becomes the last step in building a totally digital audio chain. During this transitional stage, most digital boards have the capability to handle both analog and digital inputs with modular designs that include plug-in channels that can be easily updated from an analog to a digital format as the studio adds additional digital equipment.

There are several options for digital audio console design. Some boards emulate traditional audio consoles and are self-contained units as shown in Figure 3.2. The various audio sources are fed directly into the standalone console following the most common wiring practice and allowing console replacement to be a simple matter of "pick up the old, drop down the new." Other digital consoles are designed so that the "board" is merely an interface or control unit for an audio "engine" that can be installed in a rack in the studio or in an equipment room down the hall (see Figure 3.3). In this instance, the audio console works in a fashion like the keyboard for your computer. The audio engine is essentially an audio router that accepts both analog and digital inputs with a capacity that greatly exceeds even the largest analog board. Generally, analog inputs are converted to digital signals and digital signals with different sample rates are synchronized at the audio engine.

Rather than having a physical audio board containing individual input and output modules with multiple controls, the operator may also simply manipulate a "virtual

FIGURE 3.1 The audio console is the heart of the production studio because other equipment is manipulated through it. (Image courtesy of Arrakis Systems, Inc.—*www.ArrakisSystems.com.*)

a

b

c

FIGURE 3.2 Some digital audio consoles feature a self-contained, modular architecture much like older analog boards. (Image courtesy of Studer Professional Audio Equipment.)

FIGURE 3.3 Some digital audio consoles feature the board as an interface and a separate audio engine that allows the electronics to be centralized in a rack or equipment room. (Image courtesy of Wheatstone Corporation.)

console," or a representation of an audio console, on a computer screen, as shown in Figure 3.4. This is already common practice on some digital audio workstations that include mixing functions and other audio software programs.

Another feature of the new digital audio console is the inclusion of a touchscreen interface (review Figure 3.2) or similar type of LCD (liquid crystal display) window. Because digital boards can be so readily customized to individual users, assigning different sources to different channels, a visual display helps with programming the board setup and operating the console.

3.3 AUDIO CONSOLE FUNCTIONS

Any control board has three primary functions: to mix audio, to amplify audio, and to route audio. First, the audio console enables the operator to select any one or a combination of various inputs. In other words, it must first be determined where the signal is coming from: a microphone, a CD player, or an audio recorder, for example. Audio consoles are sometimes referred to as mixing boards because of their ability to select and have several inputs operational at the same time. Much of the production work you do will

FIGURE 3.4 "Virtual" audio console controls emulate the functions of the traditional audio board. (Image courtesy of Arrakis Systems, Inc.—*www.Arrakis-Systems.com*)

be a mix of voice, music, and sound effects through the audio console.

The second function of the control board is to **amplify** the incoming audio signal to an appropriate level. Although all sound sources are amplified to a degree, some sound sources (especially microphones or turntables) produce such a small electrical current they must be amplified to be used. What is also meant by "amplify" is that the volume of an audio signal going through the console can be raised or lowered and you'll learn more about level adjustment later in this chapter. The third function of the audio console is to enable the operator to route these inputs to a number of outputs, such as monitor speakers, the transmitter, or an audio recorder. This allows us to determine where the signal is going and to provide a means for listening to the signal.

3.4 BASIC AUDIO CONSOLE PARTS

All control boards, whether digital or analog, operate in basically the same way. For the purpose of simplicity, let's consider a small audio console with just two channels; Figure 3.5 shows such a board. Each channel has two inputs (labeled A and B) so that, for example, a microphone could be assigned to channel 1 (position A) while channel 2 has a CD player assigned to input A and an audio recorder assigned to input B. In general terms, a channel refers to the path an audio signal follows. On an audio console, a **channel** refers to a group of switches, faders, and knobs that are usually associated with one or two sound sources. On this board, note the individual input selectors, output selectors, volume controls, and on/off switches associated with both channel 1 and channel 2. The cue, headphone,

and studio monitor gain controls are associated with both channels, as are the VU meters.

3.5 INPUT SELECTORS

The **input selectors** on this particular model of audio console are pushbuttons that can be put in either an A or B position. This allows two different sound sources to be associated with each channel. Although channel 1 and channel 2 look identical, there is a major difference between them. Channel 1 has been designed to accept only mic level inputs. Microphones generally do not have amplifiers built into them, whereas CD players and audio recorders have already put their signals through a small amount of amplification. When a sound source comes into channel 1, it sends the signal coming into it through a stage of preamplification that is not present for signals coming into channel 2. In other words, a mic level input allows a signal to catch up to a signal coming into the line position in terms of amplification. Then they both often go through additional amplification.

The way the input selector switches in Figure 3.5 are arranged, a microphone comes into the first channel (A input), a CD player comes into the second channel (A input), and an audio recorder comes into the second channel (B input). Nothing is assigned to the B input of channel 1. Wiring the equipment to the board involves running a cable from the mic, CD player, and audio recorder to the back (or bottom) of the audio console. Such wiring is usually done in a semipermanent way by the engineer.

Not all audio boards have input selector switches. Some radio production boards have only one input per channel that must be either at the mic level, or other inputs that can only accommodate equipment that has been preamplified and is ready for a line level. On boards of this type, usually only microphones can be patched into the first two inputs, and only CD players, audio recorders, and other line-level equipment can be patched into the remaining inputs.

On the other hand, some boards have input selector switches that have three or more positions for one input. For these boards, it's possible to patch a CD player at position A, a turntable at position B, and an audio recorder at position C all into the same input. The use that the facility is going to make of the various equipment has to be carefully studied because, of course, no two pieces of equipment could be used at the same time on a single channel. Regardless of the configuration of an audio board, the first two channels (from the left) are almost always utilized as mic level channels. Channel 1 is normally the main studio mic, and channel 2 is often an auxiliary microphone.

Digital audio consoles are changing the concept of input selection somewhat. Most digital boards allow the user to assign *any* audio source to *any* channel using a type of audio router, as shown in Figure 3.6. In other words, the console configuration can be personalized to each individual user,

FIGURE 3.5 A simple two-channel audio console.

so that channel 3 can be associated with a CD player for one person and then a DAT recorder for the next person. Once the source is selected for any of the console's channels, the source name is usually displayed on an alpha display for that channel module.

3.6 INPUT GAIN CONTROL

The input **gain controls** shown in Figure 3.5 are called **sliders**, or **faders**. They are merely **variable resistors**. Although they are called **volume controls**, or gain controls, they don't really vary the amount of amplification of the signal. The amplifier is always on at a constant volume. Raising the fader (moving it from a "south" to a "north" position) decreases the amount of resistance to this signal. When the fader is raised and the resistance is low, a great deal of the signal gets through. The dynamic is like that of a water faucet. The water volume reaching the faucet is

always the same, even when the faucet is closed. When you open the faucet (decrease the resistance), you allow the water to flow, and you can vary that flow from a trickle to a steady stream.

Some older boards have rotary knobs called **potentiometers**, or **pots**, instead of faders. These provide the same function. As the knob is turned to the right (clockwise), the resistance is decreased and the volume is increased. Some production people feel the fader is easier to work with. For one thing, the fader gives a quick visual indication of which channels are on and at what level. This is much harder to see with a rotary knob.

The numbers on both rotary knobs and faders may be in reverse order on some audio consoles to show their relationship to resistance. For example, if a knob is completely counterclockwise, or off, it may read 40; at a twelve o'clock position it may read 25; and completely clockwise, it may read 0. These figures represent decreasing amounts of resistance and thus higher volume as the knob is turned clock-

FIGURE 3.6 On most digital audio consoles, any available audio source can be assigned to any of the console's input channels. (Image courtesy of Wheatstone Corporation.)

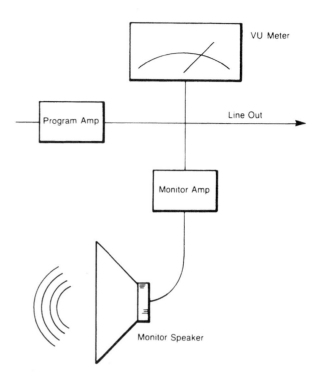

FIGURE 3.7 The monitor amplifier section of an audio console.

wise. Modern boards with fader volume controls often use a range of numbers from –55 to 0 to +10 or +15. While the same relationship to resistance is true (the more the fader is raised, the less resistance), these numbers actually relate to decibels and the VU meter. If the board has been set up properly, a 0 setting of the fader will produce a 0 reading on the VU meter. Some boards avoid using any numbers at all and merely use equally spaced indicator lines to provide some kind of reference for various knob and fader settings.

Of course, most boards have more than the two channels of our example board. In most radio production studios, boards have 10 to 12 channels. Each channel has its own gain control and with two inputs per channel, twenty or so individual pieces of audio equipment can be manipulated through the console. In professional audio production facilities, 16 to 20 channels are not uncommon.

In addition to the gain controls just mentioned, some boards have a **gain trim**, or **trim control**, that fine-tunes the volume of each input. For example, if the sound signal coming from a CD player has the left channel louder (stronger) than the right channel, a stereo trim control can decrease the left level or increase the right level until the sound signal is equal for both channels. Each input channel on an audio console usually has a gain trim feature, and often there is a similar trim adjustment for the program and audition output of the audio board. While these trim controls may be on the face of the audio board, they are sometimes an internal adjustment that is taken care of by the engineer when the control board is initially set up.

3.7 MONITORING—SPEAKERS AND HEADPHONES

Once the signal is through the input gain controls, it's amplified in a program amplifier and then sent several

places (see Figure 3.7). One of these is a **monitor amplifier**. This amplifies the signal so that it can be sent into a **monitor speaker** to enable the operator to hear the signal that is going out. Boards usually contain a simple potentiometer to control the gain of the monitor speaker. For example, our simple board has a pot labeled *STUDIO* which controls the volume of the monitor speakers. This control in no way affects the volume of the sound being sent out to an audio recorder (or transmitter, etc.). It only controls the volume for the person listening to it in the control room. A common mistake of beginning broadcasters is to run the studio monitors quite loud and think all is well, while in reality they have the signal going through the audio board (and therefore to a recorder or on-the-air) at a very low level. It's important for the operator to be aware of the level of sound going out the line.

Most audio consoles also have provision for listening to the output of the board through **headphones**. Since live microphones are often used in production work, the monitor speakers are muted when the mic is on so that **feedback** doesn't occur. To be able to hear an additional sound source, such as a CD, headphones are necessary. Audio consoles often allow you to monitor any of the outputs with headphones by selecting an appropriate switch. There is usually a volume control to adjust the signal level going to the headphones. On our simple board, this control is labeled *HDPN*.

3.8 CUE

Another function found on most boards is called **cue**, which allows you to preview an input sound source. Both rotary pots and fader controls go into a cue position, which is below the off position for that control. If you turn the rotary pot all the way counterclockwise to off, it will reach a detent, or stop. Keep turning the knob (with a little extra pressure) until it clicks into the cue position. Faders are brought down, or "south," until they click into cue (see Figure 3.5 again). Some faders can be put into cue with a separate pushbutton (see Figure 3.8) that, when depressed, puts that channel into cue regardless of where the fader control is set. Cue position is usually marked on the face of the audio console.

In the cue position, the audio signal is routed to a cue amplifier and then to a small speaker built into the control board. Since the quality of this small internal speaker is usually marginal at best, the cue signal is often sent to a small, but better quality, external speaker located near the audio console. Some audio consoles send the cue signal to the main studio monitor speakers. The program signal is automatically turned down, or "dimmed," when a channel is put into cue and the cue signal is heard "on top of the program signal." On our simple audio console, the cue volume level is controlled with the pot labeled *CUE*.

As the name implies, this position is designed to allow the operator to cue up a sound source. For example, an audio recording can be cued to the exact beginning so that the sound will start immediately when the recorder is turned on. If an input is in cue, the signal doesn't go to any other output such as the transmitter or an audio recorder. Its only purpose is to allow off-air cueing.

Many beginning announcers and production people forget to move the volume control out of the cue position after cueing up the sound source. If something is left in cue, it won't go out on the air or be routed to an audio recorder. It will only play through the cue speaker.

3.9 VU METERS

Another place the signal is sent after program amplification is the volume unit indicator, or VU meter (see Figure 3.9). This is a metering device that enables the operator to determine what level of sound is going out the line.

One common type of VU meter has a moving needle on a graduated scale. Usually the top position of the scale is calibrated in **decibels (dB)**, and the lower portion of the scale is calibrated in percentage. In audio engineering, a reading of 0 dB is 100 percent volume, or the loudest you want the signal to go. The VU meter is important for consistent audio production work. As noted in Chapter 1, "The Production Studio Environment," how loud something sounds is very subjective. What is loud to one announcer may not be deemed loud by another, especially if they set

FIGURE 3.8 Whether digital or analog, a single channel of an audio console consists of a group of switches, pushbuttons, and a fader that can be used to manipulate a sound source assigned to that channel. (Image courtesy of Wheatstone Corporation.)

FIGURE 3.9 The standard VU meter has both a percent and decibel scale.

the monitor speaker volume differently. The meter gives an electronic reading of volume that is not subjective.

The accuracy of VU meters is sometimes questioned in two areas. First, VU meters have trouble indicating transients, or sudden sharp, short increases in volume of the sound signal. Most VU meters are designed to indicate an average volume level and ignore these occasional sound bursts. Secondly, VU meters tend to overreact to the bass portion of the sound. In other words, if a sound signal is heavy in the bass frequencies, it will probably indicate a higher VU reading than the total sound signal is actually providing. In spite of these concerns, the VU meter remains the best indicator of volume levels in broadcast production.

Generally, an operator should control the signal so that it stays approximately between 80 percent and 100 percent. When the needle swings above 100 percent, we say the signal is **peaking in the red** because that portion of the VU meter scale is usually indicated with a red line. This is a warning to the operator to lower the gain of the fader or pot. Occasional dips into the red portion of the scale are likely, but having the needle consistently above 0 dB should be avoided. Sound signals above 100 percent are over-modulated and can cause a distorted sound.

Users of digital production equipment will quickly find that, unlike analog equipment, digital equipment is very unforgiving in regards to recording "in the red." Most digital equipment will not tolerate recording at any level above 100 percent and will distort or add "pops" to any recorded signal that exceeds it. Good production practice would be to record everything around −10 db when recording on digital equipment.

Often at the end of the needle's movement is a metal peg to prevent the needle from going off the dial. Allowing the gain to become so high that the needle reaches the upper peg is called **pegging the meter**, or **pinning the needle**, and should be avoided to prevent damage to the meter as well as distortion of the signal.

When the signal falls below 20 percent consistently, we say the signal is **undermodulated** or **in the mud**, and the operator should increase the volume. If it's necessary to adjust the level during the program, we say that the operator is **riding the gain** or **riding levels**. Gain is an audio engineer's term for loudness or volume. This is why a radio operator is often called a disc jockey. He plays record discs and *rides* the gain.

Our simple audio board (review Figure 3.5) has a set of VU meters that indicates the left and right volume of the program sound going out and another set of meters that show the audition output. Most boards have multiple VU meters. For example, they might have separate meters for each individual channel. Boards that have multiple outputs also have multiple meters. For example, a board that is stereo, like our example board, will have one meter for the right channel and one for the left.

On some boards the VU meter isn't an electromagnetic meter as has been described so far, but a succession of digital lights (LEDs, or light-emitting diodes) that indicate

FIGURE 3.10 VU meters with fluorescent or liquid crystal displays can indicate volume changes more quickly and accurately than electromechanical meters. (Image courtesy of Dorrough Electronics.)

how high the volume is. Other electronic meters replace the LEDs with liquid crystal or fluorescent displays, and the advantage of these meters over mechanical meters is that they can indicate volume changes more quickly and accurately (see Figure 3.10).

3.10 OUTPUT SELECTORS

The most common arrangement for the **output selectors** on a radio production board is a bank of three buttons for **program**, **audition**, and **auxiliary** outputs. The simple board in Figure 3.5 has this type of configuration except the auxiliary output is labeled *UTL* for utility. When no button is pushed in, the output is stopped at this point. When the program button is pushed, the signal normally goes to the transmitter if the board is in an on-air studio or to an audio recorder if the console is in a production room. The program position would be the normal operating position when using an audio console.

If the audition button is depressed, the signal is sent to an audition amplifier and then can be sent out to the monitor speakers, an audio recorder, another studio, and so on. The audition signal will *not* normally be sent to the transmitter. The purpose of the audition switch is to allow off-air recording and previewing of the sound quality and volume levels of a particular signal. For example, you could be playing a CD on one CD player through channel 3 of the audio console (in the program position) and at the same time be previewing another CD on a different CD player through channel 4 in the audition position. Each channel of the audio console can be used either in the program or audition position.

The auxiliary (**aux**) or utility position is just like either the program or audition position and is another output for the audio board. For instance, some studios are set up so that the aux position of one control board feeds another studio and becomes an input on the audio console in the other studio. Unlike most input selectors, which allow only one input to be selected at a time, output selectors usually allow more than one output to be active at a time. If all output buttons were depressed, you could send the same audio signal to three different locations at the same time.

The configuration of output selector buttons varies from board to board. If there are a large number of outputs—six, for example—then there may be six output buttons for each input. The input signal will be sent to whichever buttons are down, or selected. For instance, the microphone could be sent to the transmitter; the turntable, to a DAT recorder; and the CD, to a MiniDisc recorder. Sometimes there are no output selectors; every input either goes out or it doesn't, depending on the master volume control. Other boards have buttons labeled "send" that determine where the signal goes. Some boards just use a single toggle switch in place of push buttons. The functions are exactly the same, depending on which way the toggle is switched; if the toggle is in the middle, or neutral, position, the signal stops at that point (just like having no button pushed in a three-button bank).

Audio boards are often referred to by their number of inputs and outputs. A sixteen-in/four-out board has sixteen inputs and four outputs.

3.11 OUTPUT GAIN CONTROL

There is no output gain control on our simple board in Figure 3.5 that can be adjusted by the operator. Some audio consoles include a **master fader** that controls the volume of the signal leaving the board. Even if an input sound source is selected, program output is selected, and fader volume is up, if the master fader is all the way down, no signal will go from the console. Many boards have more than one output gain control. Again, a stereo board requires two masters, one for the right channel and one for the left. If there are multiple volume controls, then there's usually a master gain control that overrides all the other output volume controls. In other words, if the master is down, the signal won't go anywhere, even though one or more of the output volume controls are up.

3.12 REMOTE STARTS, CLOCKS, AND TIMERS

Other "bells and whistles" that frequently appear on audio boards include **remote start switches** (see Figures 3.5 and 3.8). These are usually located below each individual channel fader, and if the equipment wired into that channel (such as a CD player or audio recorder) has the right interface, it can be turned on, or started, by depressing the remote start. This makes it easier for the announcer to start another sound source while talking into the microphone without having to reach off to the side and possibly be pulled off mic. For most consoles, these switches also turn that channel on and off. In other words, even if you have the fader for that channel turned up, no sound signal will

---

> **Production Tip #3— "Audio Board Echo"**
>
> You can add an echo effect to your voice using your audio console if you still have a reel-to-reel recorder in your studio. Digital recorders, such as a MiniDisc, will give you an entirely different effect—that you don't want! Set up the reel-to-reel to record; if it has a *tape/input* switch, make sure this is in the *tape* position. On the audio console, make sure the recorder is selected as the input for a channel and make sure the program output selector is "on." (This assumes that the program output of the board "feeds" the recorder.) Have the reel-to-reel channel fader on just *slightly*. Set your microphone levels. Now start the tape recorder in "record" mode and begin talking into the microphone. You should be wearing headphones and you should hear an echo effect on your voice. The more you turn up the reel-to-reel volume control on the audio console the greater the echo will be; however, if you turn it up too far, you'll find it's too much effect and it won't be usable. Most announcer voices sound better with just a little echo; in other words, it should be hardly noticeable. Of course, you can create a similar effect a lot easier with digital editing software such as *CoolEdit Pro* or signal processing equipment, but this isn't a bad way to still make some use of that old reel machine sitting in the corner of your studio.

---

go through the channel until it has been turned on. However, some consoles are set up so that they will automatically turn the channel on when the fader is moved upward.

Many control boards include built-in clocks and timers. Digital clocks conveniently show the announcer the current time (hours, minutes, and seconds), and timers (see Figure 3.5) can be reset at the start of a CD or tape to count up the elapsed time or count down the remaining time. Many timers will begin automatically when an "on" or remote start button is pressed.

3.13 FREQUENCY RESPONSE

In radio production, we often mention the frequency response of equipment or, for that matter, the frequency response range of human hearing. In very general terms, we can think of the human ear as able to hear frequencies within the range of 20 to 20,000 cycles per second. For most of us, it's not quite so low nor quite so high. In any case, radio production equipment, such as an audio console, should be able to reproduce an audio signal in that range, and most modern equipment is measured by how well it does so. For example, a monitor speaker may have a frequency response of 40 hertz to 18 kilohertz, meaning that that speaker can accurately reproduce all frequencies within that range. An inexpensive broadcast microphone may have a frequency response of only 80 hertz to 13 kilohertz. It would not be able to pick up any of the higher frequencies, or those above 13,000 hertz. This would not be a problem if the mic were used primarily to record speech because the human voice usually falls in a frequency range of 200 to 3,000 hertz. Obviously, if you wanted to record a musical group (which often produces sounds in the full range of frequencies), you would want to use a microphone with a wider frequency response. Frequency response is often shown with a frequency response curve because some equipment may not pick up or reproduce some frequencies as well as others. Since most broadcast equipment is designed to pick up all frequencies equally well, its response is considered to be **flat**, although few components have a truly flat frequency response curve.

Although there are no standard figures, the audio frequency spectrum is often divided into three regions: bass, midrange, and treble. The low frequencies (bass) are those between 20 and 250 hertz and provide the "power," or "bottom," to sound. Too little bass gives a "thin" sound, and too much bass gives a "boomy" sound. The midrange frequencies fall between 250 and 4,500 hertz. These frequencies provide a lot of sound's substance and intelligibility. Too little midrange gives a lack of "presence," but too much midrange gives a "harsh" sound. High frequencies (treble) are those from 4,500 hertz to 20,000 hertz. The treble frequencies provide the brilliance and sharpness to sound. Too little treble gives a "dull" sound, and too much treble gives an excess "sparkle" to the sound as well as increasing the likelihood of hearing noise or hiss in the sound.

As frequencies change, we think in terms of the musical interval of the **octave**, or a change in pitch caused by doubling or halving the original frequency. For example, a sound going from bass to midrange to treble frequencies by octave intervals would go from 110 hertz to 220 hertz to 440 hertz to 880 hertz to 1,760 hertz to 3,520 hertz to 7,040 hertz and so on. As humans, we are subject to an awkwardly named **equal loudness principle**, by which we hear midrange frequencies better than either high or low frequencies. In radio production (and other forms of sound manipulation), we often compensate for this by equalization of the signal.

3.14 EQUALIZERS AND PAN POTS

Many boards have simple equalizers (EQ). These increase or attenuate certain frequencies, thus altering the sound of the voice or music by changing the tonal quality of the sound. In some instances they eliminate unwanted sound. For example, scratches in records are heard mainly on high frequencies. By filtering out these frequencies, the record could sound scratch-free. Likewise, a low rumble can be removed by eliminating or turning down low frequencies. Equalizers can also be used for special effects, such as making a voice sound like it is coming over a telephone line. It's important to note that when you equalize a sound, you affect both the unwanted and wanted sound; equalization is usually a compromise between eliminating a problem and keeping a high-quality, usable audio signal.

Usually the equalizers are knobs or switches that increase or attenuate a certain range of frequencies. They are placed somewhere above each input volume control. As shown in Figure 3.8, the input signal of this channel is split into three frequency ranges: high, midrange, and low. Turning the control clockwise increases the volume of that range of frequencies; counterclockwise rotation of the control will decrease its level. The "EQ in" button on this channel is actually a bypass switch that allows the operator to hear and compare the signal with or without equalization. Equalizers and other signal processing equipment will be discussed in further detail in Chapter 9, "Signal Processing Equipment."

Audio console channel inputs that are **monaural** (such as a microphone channel) often have a **pan pot**, or **pan knob**. By turning (panning) this knob to the left or right, you can control how much of the sound from that input goes to the right channel and how much goes to the left channel output. In other words, if the pan pot of a mic channel is turned toward the L position, upon monitoring the vocal would sound stronger, or louder, from the left speaker. Normally, the pan pot would be in the center position and the input sound would be directed equally to the left and right outputs of that channel. **Stereo** input channels may have a **balance control**, which serves a similar purpose.

3.15 OTHER FEATURES

Some boards have a built-in **tone generator**. This reference tone is usually placed on a recording before the actual program material. The tone generator sends out a tone through the board that can be set at 100 percent, using the board VU meter. The VU meter on the source to which the signal is being sent (e.g., an audio recorder) is simultaneously set at 100 percent. After the two are set, any other volume sent through the board will be the exact same volume when it reaches the recorder. Having a tone generator allows for this consistency. Otherwise, sounds that register at 100 percent coming through the board might peak in the red and be distorted on the recorder.

The tone on the recording is also used during play back. The audio engineer or board operator listens to the tone and sets that recorder VU meter to 100 percent. That way the recording will play back exactly as it was recorded.

Some audio consoles have a **solo switch** above each input. When this switch is on, only the sound of that particular input will be heard over the monitor. Other boards have a **mute switch** for each channel, which prevents

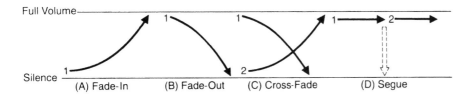

FIGURE 3.11   Sound transitions are used frequently in radio production work.

the signal from going through that channel when it's depressed. A mute switch acts just like an on/off switch.

A few boards have a **talk-back switch**, which is a simple intercom system consisting of a built-in microphone and a pushbutton control that turns the mic on or off. The normal position of this switch is off so that the button must be pushed in to activate the mic. The signal from the talk-back mic is sent to a speaker in another studio—for example a performance studio—which would allow the operator at the audio console to communicate with the announcer in a studio at a separate location.

3.16 SOUND TRANSITIONS AND ENDINGS

As mentioned early in this chapter, one of the functions of the audio console is to mix two or more sound sources together. Often this mix is really a sound transition, or the merging of one sound into another. In radio production, the basic transition is the **fade** (gradually increasing or decreasing volume), where you mix one sound with silence. For example, to **fade-in** a CD means to slowly increase the volume from silence to the desired level (see Figure 3.11A). A **fade-out** accomplishes just the opposite as the CD goes from normal, full volume to silence (see Figure 3.11B). Most compact discs are recorded so that they fade out at the end naturally, but in production work it's sometimes necessary to end a song early, and the production person can do so with a manual fade-out. The other common transitions are the cross-fade and the segue. As the name implies, a **cross-fade** occurs when one sound is faded down as another sound is faded up (see Figure 3.11C). There is a point as the two sounds cross when both sounds are heard. Because of this, care should be taken in choosing music to cross-fade. Some combinations of songs can sound extremely awkward. The speed of a cross-fade is determined by the

board operator and depends on the type of effect desired; however, most cross-fades are at a medium speed to give a natural, brief blending of the two sounds. A **segue** is quite different; it is the transition from one sound to the next with no overlap or gap (see Figure 3.11D). A segue can best be accomplished when the first song ends cold. Music with a **cold ending** doesn't fade out, but rather it has a natural, full-volume end. Unlike fades of any kind, the segue is accomplished with both sounds at full volume. Most disc jockey work is a mixture of cross-fades and segues, but all the sound transitions are used frequently in radio production work.

In addition to the fade-out and cold ending, one other music ending that should be noted is the **sustain ending**. Songs with a sustain ending will hold the final chord or notes for a short period of time and then very gradually fade out. This is distinctly different from either a normal fade-out or a cold ending. Music that is specifically designed for radio use will often have an indication of the ending—F (fade-out), C (cold ending), or S (sustain ending)—as part of the timing information about the song.

3.17 CONCLUSIONS

If you have followed the descriptions and explanations offered in this chapter, the audio console should be a less frightening assemblage of switches, knobs, and meters than it was when you began. You should begin to have a good idea of how to operate each board and feel comfortable working with the controls of the board in your own studio. You should also be aware that the audio console is becoming a digital board, one that you may manipulate very similarly to older analog boards, or that you may maneuver the controls of a virtual audio console with a few mouse clicks.

Self-Study

■ QUESTIONS

1. It's possible to have music from an audio recorder go into a control board and then come out and be recorded on another recorder.
   a) true
   b) false

2. In Figure 3.8, according to the pan pot position, what is the relationship between the sound signal going to the left channel and the signal going to the right channel?
   a) left would be less than right
   b) left would be the same as right
   c) left would be greater than right
   d) there would be no signal going to the right

3. In Figure 3.8, if the fader were at 15 and you changed it to 40, you would have _____.
   a) amplified the signal
   b) put the channel in cue
   c) decreased the resistance
   d) decreased the volume

4. In Figure 3.5, sound would not get to program out on channel 2 unless _____.
   a) the fader is at 0
   b) the PGM output selector switch is on
   c) the HDPN volume control is at 3
   d) the A input selector switch is set to CD

5. In Figure 3.7, audible sound comes from the _____.
   a) VU meter
   b) monitor amplifier
   c) program amplifier
   d) monitor speaker

6. In Figure 3.9, 50 percent on the scale is roughly equivalent to _____.
   a) −6 dB
   b) −4 dB
   c) 50 dB
   d) −10 dB

7. If the position of the needle of the VU meter in Figure 3.9 were at 20 percent; this would be an example of _____.
   a) peaking in the red
   b) turning up the pot
   c) being in the mud
   d) riding the gain

8. If the position of the needle of the VU meter in Figure 3.9 were at +3 dB; this would be an example of _____.
   a) riding the gain
   b) broadcasting in stereo
   c) peaking in the red
   d) pegging the meter

9. A line-level channel of an audio console would have what type of equipment assigned to it?
   a) CD player and audio recorder
   b) microphone and CD player
   c) microphone and audio recorder
   d) only microphones

10. The monitor/speaker is an example of _____.
    a) an input
    b) a mix
    c) an output
    d) an equalizer

11. Look at Figure 3.5. If the PGM/AUD/UTL output selector switch of channel 1 is in the audition position, _____.
    a) sound will not reach the input A switch
    b) sound can be going to an audio recorder
    c) sound can be going to the transmitter
    d) sound will go to the cue speaker

12. A master volume control on an audio board _____.
    a) must be up for sound to leave the board
    b) is required only if the board is stereo
    c) controls only the volume of the line inputs
    d) controls only the volume of the mic inputs

13. Which control might be used to help eliminate scratches on records?
    a) the pan knob
    b) the gain trim
    c) the solo button
    d) the equalizer

14. The cue position on a fader _____.
    a) allows sound to go to the transmitter
    b) sometimes substitutes for the trim control
    c) sends sound to a small speaker in the audio board
    d) allows sound to fade from the left to right channel

15. Which of the following can help assure that the level that's being recorded on an audio recorder is the same as that coming from the audio board?
    a) tone generator
    b) remote switch
    c) digital timer
    d) pan pot

16. Which of the following statements about digital audio consoles is *not* true.
    a) digital consoles are more expensive than analog consoles
    b) digital consoles include some type of display screen
    c) digital consoles do not accept analog inputs
    d) digital consoles offer several design architectures

17. When a disc jockey fades down one CD at the same time as another CD is faded up, this is known as a _____.
    a) fade-in
    b) fade-out
    c) segue
    d) cross-fade

18. On an audio console, the term _____ refers to a group of switches, faders, and knobs that are usually associated with one sound source, such as a CD player.
   a) input selector
   b) remote start switch
   c) channel
   d) output selector

19. A segue is the basic sound transition in which one sound is "mixed" with silence.
   a) true   *Its fade ↗*
   b) false

20. Most audio consoles used in radio broadcasting are identical to the consoles used in music recording.
   a) true
   b) false

21. Which feature of an audio console would allow the operator to alter the tonal quality of a sound going through the board?
   a) mute switch
   b) gain trim control
   c) equalizer control
   d) talk-back switch

22. The channel of the digital audio console shown in Figure 3.8 can be put into cue by _____.
   a) moving the fader up to "0"
   b) moving the fader down to "50"
   c) depressing the "on" button
   d) depressing the "cue" button

23. Which feature of an audio console is a simple intercom system?
   a) talk-back switch
   b) tone generator
   c) pan knob
   d) output selector

24. Because of the complexity of the numerous buttons, switches, and knobs associated with the audio console, this is one piece of production equipment that is *not* likely to be moving from an analog to a digital configuration.
   a) true
   b) false

25. If you were attempting to segue from one song to another, how should the first song end?
   a) fade-out
   b) cold ending
   c) fade-in
   d) sustain ending

■ ANSWERS

If You Answered A:
1a. Right. A tape recorder can be both input and output.
2a. No. Check the setting of the pan pot. (Reread 3.14.)
3a. No. The fader never actually amplifies the signal. This is done with preamp or amplifer circuits. (Reread 3.6.)
4a. Wrong. When a fader or pot is at 0, it is usually on. (Reread 3.6 and 3.10.)
5a. No. This indicates level, but you hear nothing from it. (Reread 3.7 and 3.9.)

6a. Right. You read the scale correctly.

7a. No. The needle would be at the other end of the scale for this. (Reread 3.9.)

8a. No. Riding gain means to keep the volume at proper levels, and this is not being done. (Reread 3.9.)

9a. You're correct. Both a CD player and an audio recorder are line-level inputs.

10a. No. You're at the wrong end. (Reread 3.3.)

11a. No. The input selector switch is before the output selector switch and really has nothing to do with it. (Reread 3.5 and 3.10.)

12a. Right. The purpose of the master volume is to allow all appropriate sounds to leave the audio console.

13a. No. This controls how much sound is going to the left and right channel. (Reread 3.14.)

14a. No. When a channel is in cue, sound will not go to the transmitter. (Reread 3.8.)

15a. Right. If the board VU meter and the tape recorder VU meter are both set at 100 percent tone, the levels should be the same.

16a. No. While the difference between the price of an analog board and a digital console is becoming less and less, digital boards are still more expensive than their analog counterparts. (Reread 3.2.)

17a. No. This is a different sound transistion. (Reread 3.16.)

18a. No. This is one of the switches involved, but this is not the correct term. (Reread 3.4 and 3.5.)

19a. No. You've confused this with the fade. (Reread 3.16.)

20a. No. While there are similarities between all audio consoles, those most often found in radio are more basic than those used in the music recording studio. (Reread 3.1.)

21a. Wrong. This control turns off a console channel. (Reread 3.14 and 3.15.)

22a. No. This will turn the volume of the channel up. (Reread 3.6 and 3.8.)

23a. Correct. The talk-back feature allows a board operator to talk with an announcer in another studio via a simple intercom system.

24a. No. You're wrong. Digital consoles are already a part of production room equipment. (Reread 3.1 and 3.2.)

25a. Wrong. A segue should happen with both songs at full volume with no overlap or silence between songs; if the first song fades out this won't happen. (Reread 3.16.)

If You Answered B:

1b. Wrong. A tape recorder can be fed in and another tape recorder can be placed at the output. (Reread 2.2 carefully.)

2b. No. Check the setting of the pan pot. (Reread 2.14.)

3b. No. Cue most likely would be even below the −55 mark. (Reread 2.5 and 2.7.)

4b. Right. When the PGM output selector switch is in the on position, normally sound would be sent to the transmitter or an audio recorder.

5b. No. This amplifies so that the sound can come out, but you don't hear the sound from it. (Reread 3.7.)

6b. No. You went the wrong direction. (Reread 3.9.)

7b. No. If anything, the pot is being turned down. (Reread 3.9.)

8b. No. This is not correct. (Reread 3.9.)

9b. No. A microphone should come into a mic input because it needs to be amplified to reach the line level of amplification. A CD player would be plugged into the line position. (Reread 3.5.)

10b. No. This is way off. (Reread 3.3.)

11b. Yes. The purpose of the audition position is to send the sound somewhere other than the transmitter. Sound would not necessarily need to go to an audio recorder, though it could.

12b. No. A master volume control functions the same for both mono and stereo. Stereo boards, however, usually have two master volume controls, one for each channel. (Reread 3.11.)

13b. Wrong. This allows fine-tuning of input or output levels on an audio board. (Reread 3.6 and 3.14.)

14b. No. The two have nothing to do with each other. (Reread 3.6 and 3.8.)

15b. No. This will turn on the recorder remotely but will do nothing about levels. (Reread 3.12 and 3.15.)

16b. No. Whether it's a simple alpha-display on the channel module or a full LCD screen, because they can be readily reconfigured, digital boards have some type of display screen. (Reread 3.2.)

17b. No. This is a different sound transition. (Reread 3.16.)

18b. No. This is one of the switches involved, but this is not the correct term. (Reread 3.4 and 3.12.)

19b. Correct. The basic sound transition that mixes one sound with silence is the fade, not the segue.

20b. Yes. Radio consoles are usually not as complex as the boards used in music recording.

21b. Wrong. This control varies the input level of a sound source of a console channel. (Reread 3.6 and 3.14.)

22b. No. While some consoles are put into cue by moving the fader down, it would have to go all the way down and usually "click" into a cue position. (Reread 3.6 and 3.8.)

23b. Wrong. The tone generator provides a reference level for setting correct recording levels. (Reread 3.15.)

24b. Yes. This is a correct response because digital audio consoles are readily available now.

25b. Yes. The first song should have a cold ending if you're going to segue into the next song.

If You Answered C:

2c. Right. The pan pot is set so that more of the sound from the input goes to the left channel.

3c. You're warm but not right. Changing the level from −5 to −25 would increase resistance. (Reread 2.5.)

4c. Wrong. The HDPN volume control only controls the volume of the headphone's audio. (Reread 3.7 and 3.10.)

5c. No. This amplifies sound, but you don't hear sound from it. (Reread 3.7.)

6c. There is no such thing on a VU meter. (Reread 3.9 and review Figure 3.9.)

7c. Right. "In the mud" is the term for a low reading.

8c. No. It is worse than that because the needle is all the way to the end of the scale. (Reread 3.9.)

9c. No. A microphone should come in a mic input because it needs to be amplified to reach a useable level. An audio recorder would be plugged into the line position. (Reread 3.5.)

10c. Right. Sound comes out to the monitor/speaker.

11c. No. The audition position is not normally used to send the sound to the transmitter. (Reread 3.10.)

12c. No. It controls all the sound that is set to leave the board. Line and mic positions have no bearing on it. (Reread 3.5 and 3.11.)

13c. No. This allows you to hear one input channel by itself. (Reread 3.14 and 3.15.)

14c. Right. Cueing is just for the person operating the board.

15c. No. This is simply a type of clock. It has nothing to do with levels. (Reread 3.12 and 3.15.)

16c. Yes. Digital boards have modules that accept analog signals and convert them to digital.

17c. No. This is a different sound transition. (Reread 3.16.)

18c. Yes. This is the correct term.

21c. Right. EQ controls increase or decrease certain frequencies of the sound, thus changing the tone.

22c. No. If the fader was up, this would let us hear audio, but not in cue. (Reread 3.8 and 3.12.)

23c. Wrong. Pan pots control the amount of sound that goes to the left or right output of a channel. (Reread 3.14 and 3.15.)

25c. No. You're confused here; a fade-in isn't a way a song ends. (Reread 3.16.)

If You Answered D:

2d. No. That would not be correct. (Reread 2.14.)

3d. Right. This is an increase in resistance to the signal; not as much of the signal gets through, and it's softer.

4d. Wrong. It wouldn't matter if the A input was assigned to a CD, audio recorder, or some other piece of equipment. (Reread 3.5 and 3.10.)

5d. Right. You hear sound from the monitor speaker.

6d. You might be thinking of half of the dB scale, but that isn't correct. (Reread 3.9.)

7d. No. If anything, the operator is not properly riding the gain. (Reread 3.9.)

8d. Right. Pegging the meter is correct. We could also have used the term "pinning the needle."

9d. Wrong. Microphone signals must be amplified to reach line level and should only come into a mic input. (Reread 3.5.)

10d. No. An equalizer affects frequencies. (Reread 3.3 and 3.14.)

11d. Wrong. The cue speaker will be activated when a channel is put into cue, regardless of where the PGM/AUD/UTL switch is. (Reread 3.8 and 3.10.)

12d. No. It controls all the sound that is set to leave the board. Mic and line positions have no bearing on it. (Reread 3.5 and 3.11.)

13d. Right. This can help eliminate high frequencies where scratches reside.

14d. No. You're confusing this with a pan pot. (Reread 3.8 and 3.14.)

15d. No. This allows sound to fade from the left to right channel. (Reread 3.14 and 3.15.)

16d. Wrong. Digital boards have more than one design approach, for example, the mainframe and control-surface system. (Reread 3.2.)

17d. This is the correct response.

18d. No. This is one of the switches involved, but this is not the correct term. (Reread 3.4 and 3.10.)

21d. Wrong. This control is a form of studio intercom. (Reread 3.14 and 3.15.)

22d. Yes. On this console, any channel can be put into cue merely by pressing the cue button associated with that channel, regardless of where other switches or buttons are set.

23d. Wrong. Output selectors determine where sound goes when it leaves the audio console. (Reread 3.10 and 3.15.)

25d. No. A segue should have no overlap or silence between songs; if the first song has a sustain ending this won't happen. (Reread 3.16.)

Projects

■ PROJECT 1

Learn to operate an audio console.

Purpose

To acquaint you with the operation of an audio console, to make you somewhat proficient at some of its functions, and to practice basic sound transitions.

Advice, Cautions, and Background

1. Audio boards are generally the most complicated pieces of equipment in a radio station. It may take you a while to master a board, but don't despair. Take it slowly, and don't be afraid to ask for help.
2. Audio boards all have the same general purpose. Sounds come into the board, are mixed together, and are sent out to somewhere else.
3. The actual exercise should be done as quickly as possible. You won't be judged on aesthetics. In other words, when you're fading from one source to another, do it quickly. Don't wait for the proper musical beat, phrase, or pause.

How to Do the Project

1. Familiarize yourself with the operation of the audio console in your production studio. Learn the inputs, the outputs, the method for changing volume, and other special features of the board.
2. As soon as you feel you understand the board, do the following exercise as rapidly as possible while recording it on an audio recorder. Practice as much as you like first.
   a. Cue up a CD, play part of it, and fade it out.
   b. Using the studio mic, announce your name and the time.
   c. Begin a second CD.
   d. Cross-fade to another CD, and then fade it out.
   e. Bring in an auxiliary microphone, and ad-lib with another announcer.
   f. Fade in either a record or a CD, segue to another CD, and fade it under.
   g. Announce something clever on the studio mic.
3. Listen to your recording to make sure it recorded properly.
4. Label your tape AUDIO CONSOLE OPERATION, and hand it in to your instructor for credit for the project.

■ PROJECT 2

Diagram and label the audio console in your production room.

Purpose

To familiarize you with the positioning of the various switches and controls so that you can access them quickly.

Advice, Cautions, and Background

1. Some boards are very complicated and have more functions than are discussed in this chapter. Usually this is because they're intended to be used for sound recording of music. If you have such a board, you only need to label the parts that you will be using frequently.
2. If you can't find controls for all of the functions given in this chapter, ask for help. Because there are so many different brands and types of boards, sometimes functions are combined or located in places where you cannot identify them easily.
3. You don't need to label each switch and knob. If your board has ten inputs, it will obviously have ten channel volume controls. You can circle them all and label them together, or make one label that says INPUT VOLUME CONTROLS and draw arrows to all ten.
4. You will be judged on the completeness and accuracy of your drawing. You won't be graded on artistic ability, but be as clear as possible.

How to Do the Project

1. Sketch the audio console in your production studio.
2. Label all the basic parts: input selectors, channel gain controls, VU meters, output selectors, and master gain controls (if your board has them).
3. Also label any other parts of the board that you will be using frequently, such as equalizers, cue positions, and headphone connections.
4. Label your sketch AUDIO CONSOLE, and give your completed drawing to the instructor for credit for this project.

■ PROJECT 3

Record a "two-voice" commercial.

Purpose

To develop your skill in creating a radio spot while working with another announcer.

Advice, Cautions, and Background

1. This project assumes that you have enough familiarity with your studio equipment to accomplish basic recording and production techniques.
2. The production incorporates two announcer voices and a music bed.
3. You will need to write a dialogue script that can be read in about 23 seconds. Write the copy about a fast food restaurant, such as Burger King, Arby's, or Kentucky Fried Chicken.
4. There are many ways to accomplish this project, so don't feel you must follow the production directions exactly.

How to Do the Project

1. Record the script (voices only) onto a recorder, such as a reel-to-reel or digital recorder. Make sure both voices are close to the same volume level. Rerecord to correct mistakes or just to get it to sound the way you want.
2. Select a music bed that is appropriate for the style of the spot. You might find something on the CD-ROM that accompanies this text.
3. You can play back the music bed directly from a CD, or you may have to record it on another recorder.
4. Set correct playback levels for both the vocal track and the music bed. Both will start at full volume. Then cue both to the beginning sound.
5. Record your completed spot onto an audio cassette, so set your cassette recorder to record mode.
6. Begin recording. Start the music bed at full volume. Start the vocal track and simultaneously fade the music bed slightly so the vocal track is dominant.
7. As the vocal ends, bring the music bed back to full volume and then quickly fade it out as you approach 30 seconds.

8. It may take you several attempts to get the spot to come out correctly. If you need to "do it over," just recue everything and try again.

9. Listen to the finished commercial. Make sure you've gotten a good balance between the music and the voice and all recording levels were proper.

10. On the tape write your name and Two-Voice Radio Spot, and turn it in to your instructor to receive credit for this project.

CHAPTER FOUR

Microphones

Information

4.1 INTRODUCTION

In the radio production room, the microphone takes on an important role because it's the first element in the audio chain. It's the piece of equipment that changes the announcer's voice into an electrical signal that can then be mixed with other sound sources and sent to a recorder or broadcast over the air. Because the purpose of the microphone is to change sound energy into electrical energy, it's called a **transducer**, which is a device that converts one form of energy into another.

Unlike much of the other studio equipment, microphones are generally analog based, although some very expensive digital mics are now coming on the market. Putting an A/D converter in an external mic preamplifier or immediately after the mic in the audio chain could quickly transform *any* mic's electrical output to a digital signal. One manufacturer, beyerdynamic, has a digital mic with the preamp and analog-to-digital converter built into the mic housing. In both instances, the sound signal is changed to an analog signal by the microphone, and then that signal is changed into a digital signal. Currently, there is no microphone that converts the mic sound signal *directly* into a digital data stream; however, it's highly likely we'll see one in the not too distant future.

4.2 CLASSIFYING MICROPHONES

There is no one correct mic to use in radio production work, but specific types of microphones will work better than others in certain situations. For example, a microphone that is perfect for voiceover work in the studio, may not work well for recording a sound effect. Microphone types are usually determined by two key factors—the internal, sound-generating element and the pickup pattern of the mic. Categorized by their sound-generating element, there are two types of microphones commonly used in radio: the dynamic mic and the condenser mic.

4.3 DYNAMIC MICROPHONES

The **dynamic mic** is sometimes known as the **moving-coil microphone** or occasionally as the **pressure mic**. This microphone's sound-generating element is constructed of a diaphragm, a magnet assembly, and a voice coil, as shown in Figure 4.1. The flexible diaphragm, which responds to the pressure of the sound, is positioned so the attached small wire coil is within the field of the permanent magnet. Movements of the diaphragm caused by sound waves result in a disturbance of the magnetic field, and this induces a small electric current into the coil of wire. In Chapter 8, "Monitor Speakers, Cables, Connectors, and Studio Accessories," you'll see that the basic loudspeaker consists of similar elements and works much like a dynamic microphone in reverse when changing electrical energy into sound energy.

The dynamic mic is very commonly used in radio and has many advantages that make it so popular. Because of its relatively simple construction, it is a modestly priced mic that produces very low self-noise and has excellent **frequency response** so that both highs and lows reproduce accurately. The main reason it has seen such acceptance by broadcasters is its sturdy design. The dynamic mic can withstand a moderate amount of abuse, which often occurs in the broadcast setting. Dynamic mics can handle extremely high sound levels, making it almost impossible to overload this style of microphone. It's also fairly insensitive to wind, and this, along with its ruggedness, makes it an excellent remote mic. The dynamic mic can be used in most broadcast situations—as a stand mic, a handheld mic, or a lavalier (a small mic hung around the neck or clipped to clothing below the neck).

The main disadvantage of the dynamic mic is that it does not satisfactorily reproduce the voices of certain individuals. With some announcers, the mic exaggerates plosives (popping on *p*) and sibilance (hissing on *s*).

Even though the dynamic mic is fairly rugged, all microphones are fragile to some extent and should be handled

Dynamic Microphone

FIGURE 4.1 The internal components of a dynamic microphone include a diaphragm, magnet, and voice coil. (Image courtesy of Shure Incorporated.)

Condenser Microphone

FIGURE 4.2 The internal components of a condenser microphone include two oppositely charged plates—a moveable diaphragm and a fixed backplate. (Image courtesy of Shure Incorporated.)

with care like any other piece of audio production equipment. Beginning announcers often misuse a mic by blowing into it to see if it's live or to set a level. This is the worst way to test a mic and can result in serious damage to the microphone. In fact, the higher the quality of the microphone, the more likely that it *will* be damaged in this manner.

4.4 CONDENSER MICROPHONES

The other common type of broadcast microphone is the **condenser mic**. Also known as a **capacitor mic**, it uses an electronic component—the capacitor—to respond to the sound. The sound-generating element consists of a charged conductive diaphragm and an oppositely charged metallic backplate separated by an insulating material that creates an air space between them and forms a sound-sensitive capacitor (see Figure 4.2). The thin metal, or metal-coated, plastic diaphragm responds to sound waves, changing the distance between the diaphragm and the backplate; this alteration changes the capacitance and generates a small electrical signal that is further amplified within the electronics of the microphone.

The condenser mic requires a power supply, such as a battery, to charge the backplate and diaphragm and related electronic components. Because batteries used to be large and cumbersome, early condenser mics were both inconvenient and expensive. Today's condenser mics utilize small internal power supplies or **phantom power** supplies. The latter usually comes from a recorder or an audio board through the mic cable to the microphone. Because all condenser mics are powered, the electronics of the mic can produce a little noise, and there is a limit to the sound level signal the mic can handle. Still, the condenser microphone is an excellent radio mic because it's fairly rugged and produces excellent sound quality and wide frequency response. Although the dynamic mic is the most-used radio

production mic, the condenser mic is also frequently found in the modern radio production studio. In addition, the built-in microphone on modern portable cassette recorders is usually a condenser mic that provides fairly good quality on both consumer and professional models.

Another form of condenser microphone is the **electret mic**. Its capacitor is permanently charged during manufacture, but it still needs a power supply (albeit much less power) for its electronic circuit. The lower power requirement offers some flexibility in usage, but the electret mic possesses less dynamic range than the regular condenser microphone, so you may not find an electret mic in many radio production studios.

4.5 OTHER MICROPHONES

There are other types of microphones, but they are less likely to be encountered in the broadcast studio. For many years the **ribbon mic** was common in radio. Another form of a dynamic microphone, the ribbon mic contains a sound-generating element that consists of a thin, corrugated metallic ribbon stretched in the field of a magnet. Sound waves vibrating the ribbon generate an electrical signal. The ribbon mic has an excellent warm, smooth sound, but it is bulky and fragile and has been largely replaced by the condenser mic, which has a similar high-quality sound.

A **regulated phase microphone** can be thought of as part dynamic mic and part ribbon mic. A wire coil is attached to or impressed into the surface of a circular diaphragm. The diaphragm is suspended between two circular magnets that are designed to be acoustically transparent. An electrical current is generated as sound waves vibrate the diaphragm. Because of its design, the regulated phase mic exhibits some of the qualities of a ribbon mic with some of the ruggedness of the dynamic mic. This mic is used more in the recording industry than in radio, but you may run across one in some production studios.

4.6 SPECIAL PURPOSE MICROPHONES

There are other microphone "types," but these are not based on internal sound-generating elements. In fact, these microphones usually employ one of the basic designs mentioned in the previous sections; however, they are often designed for a specific usage and are frequently considered another variety of mic. For example, the **lavalier mic** (see Figure 4.3) mentioned previously is a tiny microphone, usually less than 1 inch long, that can be unobtrusively clipped to an announcer's lapel or tie. There are both dynamic and condenser models, and although the lavalier mic is occasionally used in a radio remote situation, its small size makes it more appropriate for television than radio.

A **stereo microphone** like the one shown in Figure 4.4 incorporates small, multiple sound-generating elements within a single mic housing that can duplicate the various stereo miking techniques. You'll learn more about these stereo miking techniques later in this chapter.

FM microphones—also known as **RF** (radio frequency), **wireless**, and **radio mics**—are used occasionally in radio production situations when a microphone cable might hinder the recording or production. A wireless mic is really a system—a microphone, a radio transmitter, and a radio receiver (see Figure 4.5). The audio signal generated by the mic (employing either a dynamic or condenser element) is sent out from the mic by a low-power transmitter rather than a microphone cable. This transmitter is either in the mic housing or contained in a small pack designed to be worn by the announcer. The transmitted signal is picked up by a receiver located nearby and converted from a radio frequency signal back into an audio signal at that point. One problem associated with wireless mics is interference. Since they broadcast on specific FCC-assigned frequencies that are not exclusive to FM mics, they sometimes pick up interference from VHF TV, cordless telephones, and other radio frequency users.

The **pressure zone mic**, or the **PZM** (also known as a **boundary**, **plate**, or **surface-mount mic**), is a small microphone capsule mounted next to a sound-reflecting plate (or boundary), as shown in Figure 4.6. Designed to be used on a flat surface, such as a tabletop, the mic picks up sound from all directions above the table surface. Boundary mics offer exceptional microphone sensitivity because both direct sound and reflected sound reach the mic at the same time, since the mic is so close to the reflective surface. This boosts the incoming sound signal, which improves the clarity of the microphone.

Figure 4.7 shows that the **shotgun microphone** is appropriately named. A mic capsule is at one end of a tube, or barrel, that is "aimed" like a gun toward the sound source. The design of the mic rejects sound from the side and rear

FIGURE 4.3 Because of their unobtrusive design, lavalier microphones are more appropriate for television than radio. (Image courtesy of Audio-Technica U.S., Inc.)

FIGURE 4.4 Stereo microphones often employ multiple sound-generating elements within a single mic housing. (Image courtesy of AKG Acoustics, Inc.)

HAND-HELD MICROPHONE
W/BUILT-IN TRANSMITTER

LAV MIC
W/BODY-PAK TRANSMITTER

RECEIVER

FIGURE 4.5 Since it's wireless, the FM microphone can be used when the microphone cable would get in the way. (Image courtesy of beyerdynamic.)

but picks up a very narrow angle of sound from the front of the mic's barrel. The highly directional nature of the mic makes it good at picking up sound from a considerable distance from the sound source; however, sound quality is somewhat less than mics designed to pick up only nearby sounds.

There are other specialized microphones available, but in typical radio production work you aren't likely to run across them. In fact, even the mics mentioned in this section will only be useful on occasion, but an understanding of them may prove helpful from time to time.

4.7 MICROPHONE PICKUP PATTERNS

Another way of classifying microphones is by their pickup patterns. Microphones can be constructed so that they have different directional characteristics. In other words, they

pick up sound from varying directions, as shown in Figure 4.8. Sound picked up at the front of the microphone, or at 0 degrees, is said to be on-axis. Sound picked up from the mic's side is 90 degrees off-axis, and sound picked up from the rear of the microphone is 180 degrees off-axis. The microphone housing, by the use of small openings and ports, can be designed so that unwanted sound (often off-axis sound) is canceled out or attenuated as it enters the mic. The on-axis sound received directly from the front of the mic fully impacts the mic's diaphragm. An understanding of the microphone pickup patterns helps the user place the mic relative to the sound source to maximize picking up the desired sound and minimize picking up unwanted background noise.

Three basic sound patterns are omnidirectional, bidirectional, and cardioid. Although most microphones will have one fixed pickup pattern, **multidirectional mics** have switchable internal elements that allow the microphone to

FIGURE 4.6 The PZM microphone is designed to be used on a flat surface, such as a tabletop. (Image courtesy of Crown International, Inc.)

FIGURE 4.8 On-axis sound, picked up directly from the front of the microphone, fully impacts the mic's diaphragm.

FIGURE 4.7 A shotgun microphone has a long tube or barrel that is "aimed" at the sound source. (Image courtesy of Sennheiser Electronic Corporation.)

employ more than one pickup pattern—most commonly cardioid and omnidirectional.

4.8 THE OMNIDIRECTIONAL PICKUP PATTERN

The **omnidirectional** mic is also known as a **nondirectional** mic. These two terms may seem to contradict each other—*omni* (all) and *non* (no). Both terms are correct, however. The

mic picks up sound in all directions, but it also has no particular pickup pattern. Omnidirectional mics pick up sound equally well in just about any direction. Think of an orange with a microphone right in the middle. No matter where the sound comes from, the mic responds to it equally well. Figure 4.9 illustrates the pickup pattern for a typical omnidirectional microphone.

Omnidirectional mics are used whenever it is desirable to pick up sound evenly from all sides of the mic, including above and below it. Omnidirectional mics are com-

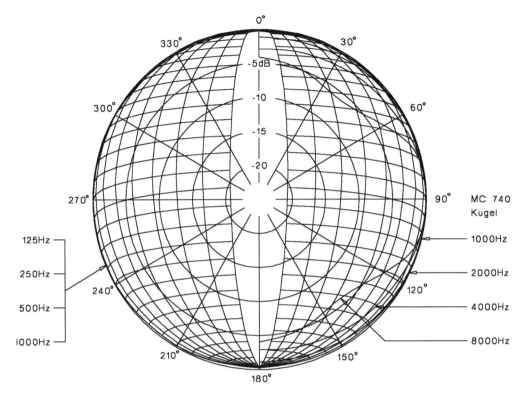

FIGURE 4.9 The omnidirectional pickup pattern shows that the microphone picks up sound equally well from all directions. (Image courtesy of beyerdynamic.)

monly used in broadcast situations outside the studio when the ambience of the location needs to be picked up along with the announcer's voice. Of course, the fact that they pick up sound equally well from all directions can also be a disadvantage. You may pick up unwanted background noise (such as traffic noise) in addition to the announcer when recording in a remote situation. Omnidirectional mics used in a highly reflective room may also produce a "hollow" sound, since they tend to pick up more reverb than other types of mics.

4.9 THE BIDIRECTIONAL PICKUP PATTERN

The **bidirectional** mic picks up sound mainly from two directions: the front and the rear of the mic, or on-axis and off-axis (see Figure 4.10). Its pickup pattern can be visualized as a figure 8, with the microphone located at the intersection of the two circles, or, to maintain the fruit analogy, as two grapes side-by-side. It was often used for radio dramas so that actors could face each other, but it is not a common pickup pattern for today's broadcast mics. Although you may not utilize it in many radio production situations, it's a good mic for the basic two-person interview and is sometimes used, in combination with other mic types, for stereo recording.

4.10 THE CARDIOID PICKUP PATTERN

The **cardioid** mic is sometimes referred to as **unidirectional** because it picks up sound coming mainly from only one direction—the front of the microphone. Its pattern is actually heart shaped, hence the name cardioid (refer to Figure 4.11). Another way to visualize its pickup pattern is to think of an upside-down apple, of which the stem represents the mic and the rest of the apple approximates the cardioid pickup pattern. Although the mic picks up sound from the front and sides, the level of pickup from the sides is only about half that of the front. The mic doesn't pick up sound well from the rear at all—less than one-tenth of the sound it can pick up from the front.

Variations on the basic cardioid design include the **super-cardioid**, **hyper-cardioid**, and **ultra-cardioid** microphones. They continue to offer great rejection of the sound from the sides, but each mic also picks up a narrower scope of on-axis sound. In other words, each of these mics becomes more and more directional in nature.

All cardioid mics are popular because they do reject unwanted sounds (excessive reverb, feedback, background noise), but the announcer must be careful to stay "on mic" and not move too far off-axis, especially when using super-, hyper-, or ultra-cardioid mics. Cardioid mics are

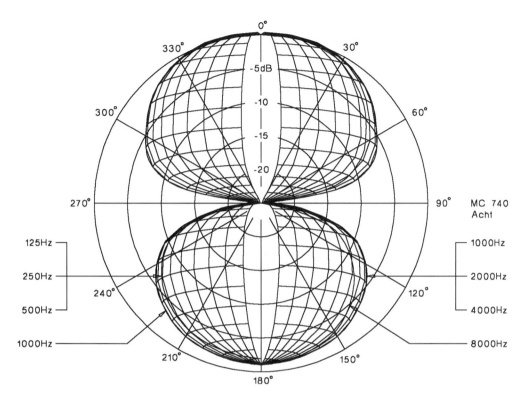

FIGURE 4.10   The bidirectional pickup pattern shows that the microphone picks up sound from the front and back of the mic. (Image courtesy of beyerdynamic.)

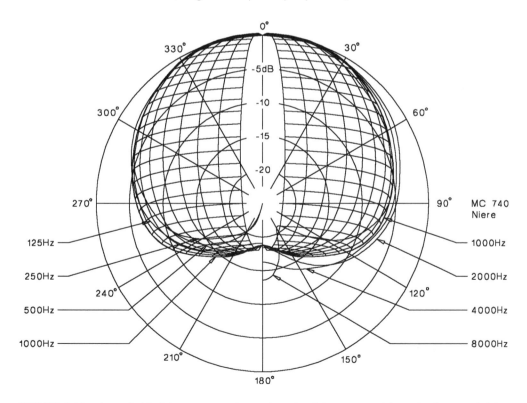

FIGURE 4.11   A cardioid pickup pattern shows the mic picks up sound from the front and sides, but not from the back. (Image courtesy of beyerdynamic.)

often employed in sports remote broadcasts; the sportscaster talks into the live side (front) of the mic, and the crowd and action sounds coming from the rear and sides are limited.

4.11 POLAR RESPONSE PATTERNS

The diagrams shown in Figures 4.9 to 4.11 indicate pickup patterns. One of the concepts that you need to understand is the difference between **pickup pattern** and **polar pattern**. We have already described a microphone's pickup pattern as the area around the microphone in which the mic best "hears" or picks up the sound. This is actually a three-dimensional shape (see Figure 4.12), as demonstrated by the orange, grape, and apple analogies. When a microphone's pickup pattern is shown by a two-dimensional drawing, we call that drawing the mic's polar pattern or polar response pattern, as shown in Figures 4.9 to 4.11. Compare the cardioid pickup pattern shown in Figure 4.12 with the cardioid polar response pattern shown in Figure 4.11.

A polar pattern is drawn around a full circle, or 360 degrees. As noted earlier, the line from 0 degrees to 180 degrees represents the mic's axis, and sound entering the mic from the front (0 degrees) is on-axis. The concentric circles show decreasing dB levels and allow us to see how the sound will be attenuated as it is picked up off-axis. For example, Figure 4.11 shows that sound picked up directly in front of the mic will experience no attenuation. On the other hand, sound picked up from either side (90 degrees off-axis) will be attenuated about 5 dB, and sound coming directly from the rear of the mic (180 degrees) will be attenuated almost 20 dB. The lines labeled at various frequencies show that microphone patterns usually vary somewhat by frequency. In most cases, lower frequencies are picked up in a less directional fashion.

FIGURE 4.12 A three-dimensional view of the cardioid microphone pickup pattern. (Image courtesy of Sennheiser Electronics Corporation.)

4.12 IMPEDANCE OF MICROPHONES

Another factor sometimes used to categorize microphones is **impedance**, a characteristic similar to resistance and common to audio equipment. Impedance is expressed in ohms, and mics can be either high-impedance (10,000 ohms or higher) or low-impedance (600 ohms or less). Most broadcast mics are low-impedance, since this type of mic provides the best frequency response, and most broadcast equipment is designed to accept this type of mic. High-impedance mics are also quite limited in the length of mic cable that can be used with them before hum and severe signal loss occurs. High-impedance mics should not be plugged into tape recorders or other equipment designed for low-impedance; similarly, low-impedance mics should not be used with high-impedance equipment, although the negative effects aren't as noticeable with this combination. If impedance is mismatched, sound will be distorted. There are impedance converters that can convert one type of impedance to the other.

4.13 SENSITIVITY OF MICROPHONES

Sensitivity refers to a microphone's efficiency or ability to create an output level. For the same sound source (say, one particular announcer's voice), a highly sensitive mic produces a better output signal than a less sensitive mic. To compensate for this, the gain control (volume) must be increased for the less sensitive mic; this increased gain produces more noise. Although different sensitivity-rating systems can be employed, generally condenser mics have high-sensitivity specifications, and dynamic mics have medium sensitivity. Obviously, if you're trying to pick up a loud or close-up sound, a microphone with a lower sensitivity rating would be desirable.

4.14 PROXIMITY EFFECT AND BASS ROLL-OFF

Announcer use of microphones sometimes produces a sound phenomenon known as the **proximity effect**. The proximity effect is an exaggerated bass boost that occurs as the sound source gets closer to the microphone. This should be noticeable as the announcer gets about 2 or 3 inches from the mic and is especially noticeable with mics that have a cardioid pickup pattern. Although it could help deepen a normally high voice, the proximity effect is usually defeated by a **bass roll-off switch** on the mic. This switch, when turned on, will electronically "roll off," or turn down, the bass frequencies that would be boosted by the proximity effect, thus leaving the desired flat response. Bass boost can also be controlled at the audio console, using the equalizer controls associated with the mic channel (review 2.14).

4.15 MICROPHONE FEEDBACK

Feedback is a "howling" signal generated when a sound picked up by a microphone is amplified, produced through a speaker, picked up again, amplified again, and so on—endlessly. Generally, reducing the volume or turning off the mic ends the feedback. Feedback is a common mic problem in public address situations but not usually in radio production, since the speaker is muted when the mic is switched on as was mentioned in Chapter 3, "The Audio Console." Occasionally, announcers can produce feedback in the production studio by operating their headphones at an excessive volume or accidentally picking up a stray speaker signal from an outside source, such as another studio speaker.

4.16 MULTIPLE MICROPHONE INTERFERENCE

Sometimes when two or more microphones receiving the same sound signal are fed into the same mixer, the combined signal becomes **out-of-phase**. What happens is that the sound reaches each mic at a slightly different time so that while the sound wave is up on one mic, it's down on the other. Under these circumstances, the resulting sound will have frequency peaks and cancellations causing very poor sound quality.

This situation is known as **multiple microphone interference** and can be avoided by remembering a three-to-one ratio. That is, if the mics are about 1 foot from the announcer (sound source), they should be at least 3 feet apart from each other. In this way the signals won't overlap (see Figure 4.13A). Another solution to this problem is to place microphones that must be close together head to head; then they will receive the signal at the same time (see Figure 4.13B). Although multiple microphone interference isn't usually a problem in the studio, it can occur in some radio remote situations.

4.17 STEREO

We hear sound in stereo because most sounds arrive at one ear before the other. In other words, the right ear hears a slightly different sound perspective from the left ear. This allows us to locate sound by turning our head until the sound is "centered." Most modern production work is done with stereo equipment. For example, the audio console has two master channels—a left and a right channel—and often we can pan the audio signal in such a fashion that more of it is assigned to the left or right channel. When we compare stereo sound to monophonic sound, we quickly realize that stereo adds both "depth" and "imaging" to the sound. *Imaging* is the apparent placement of the sound between the left and right plane and as noted provides location of the sound in space. *Depth* is the apparent placement of the

A

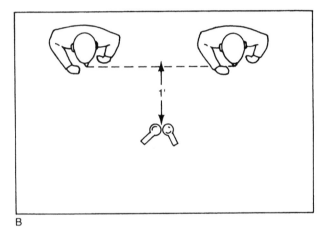

B

FIGURE 4.13 One method of avoiding multiple-microphone interference is to make sure the distance between the two mics is three times the microphone-to-source distance.

sound between the front and back plane and often provides the ambience of the space where the sound is produced. Good stereo sound allows us to record and reproduce sound as it is in real life.

4.18 STEREO MIKING TECHNIQUES

Much radio production work is done with a mono microphone. Even in "stereo" studios, usually the same mono mic signal is just sent to the left and right channels. However, there may be times when you will want to employ true stereo miking. Using traditional microphones, there are several common stereo miking techniques: **A-B** (or **spaced pair** or **split-pair**) **miking, X-Y** (or **cross-pair**) **miking, ORTF miking, stereosonic miking,** and **M-S** (or **mid-side**) **miking**.

All of these techniques, except spaced pair, is a form of **coincident miking** because they simultaneously employ two microphones whose pickup patterns overlap. Since the ultimate goal of stereo recording is to have separate sound signals come from the left and right speakers, one common way to accomplish this would be to split a pair of omnidirectional mics to the left and right of center about 18 to 36 inches apart. This A-B technique uses one mic to feed the left channel of the stereo signal and another one to feed the right channel. As long as phase problems are watched and the sound source is kept a somewhat equal distance from the mics, a true stereo signal will be obtained. However, when using this technique, the sound is often "spacious," with a great deal of separation. Room ambience may be overbearing, with individual sounds seeming to "wander" in the stereo image.

Another stereo miking technique requires placing two mics (usually cardioid) like crossed swords forming an X and Y axis, as shown in Figure 4.14. The angle formed between the heads of the mics is somewhere between 90 and 140 degrees, with the right microphone facing the left side of the announcer and the left mic facing the right side of the performance area. This X-Y miking allows the sound signal to reach both mics at the same time, that is, in phase. Although this solves some of the split-pair arrangement problems, it can cause a loss of "focus" on the image because the mics are off-axis to the center of the stereo image.

ORTF technique comes from a microphone placement developed by the French broadcasting organization Office de Radio-diffusion-Television Francaise. Similar to X-Y miking, two cardioid mics are crossed so that the heads are 17 centimeters apart (6.7 inches) and form an angle of 110 degrees. Unlike X-Y miking, the right mic provides the right channel output, and the left mic provides the left channel output. ORTF miking provides a very natural stereo sound with an "openness" that surpasses typical X-Y placement.

A lesser known stereo miking technique, stereosonic miking, involves placing two bidirectional mics one on top of the other. The front of each mic faces the announcer at about a 45-degree angle, and the rear of each mic faces the back of the performance area.

Mid-side miking, or M-S miking, offers superior imaging by using mics arranged in an "upside down "T" pattern. The mid mic (often a super-cardioid) is aimed at the sound source and the side mic (usually a bidirectional) is placed at 90 degrees to the mid mic to pick up the sound to the left and right. Both microphones must be fed into a mixer designed to *matrix*, or decode, the incoming signals into a stereo signal.

Variations of these techniques, using different types of microphones and mic placements, are also employed to achieve stereo miking. Furthermore, stereo microphones can duplicate X-Y or M-S techniques using a single micro-

FIGURE 4.14 Cardioid microphones arranged for stereo (X-Y) miking look like crossed swords. (Image courtesy of Shure Incorporated.)

phone with specially designed internal sound-generating structures (review Figure 4.4). In addition to the basic microphone, the radio production person will find one or more of the following accessories necessary for proper audio production work: windscreens, shock mounts, and stands or booms.

4.19 WINDSCREENS

The most common **windscreens** (sometimes referred to as **blast filters** or **pop filters**) are ball-shaped foam accessories that can be placed over the head or front of the microphone to help reduce the chance of a plosive sound. Not only do they prevent popping, but they also help keep dust out of the internal elements of the mic and can provide some cushion if the mic is accidentally dropped. Windscreens can also be built into the grill of the microphone, as shown in Figure 4.15. Another design consists of a porous, film-like material that is suspended within a circular frame. This windscreen apparatus is then attached to the microphone stand and positioned in front of the microphone rather than placed on the mic.

Announcing words that emphasize the *p*, *b*, or *t* sounds naturally produces a sharp puff of air and can produce a pop or thump when hitting the mic (especially when a dynamic mic is closely worked). The pop filter, however, eliminates or reduces this problem.

4.20 SHOCK MOUNTS

A **shock mount** is often employed to isolate the microphone from any mechanical vibrations, or shocks, that may be

FIGURE 4.15 This microphone design includes a built-in windscreen. (Image courtesy of Shure Incorporated.)

transmitted to the mic through its stand. The mic is physically suspended (usually by an arrangement of elastic bands) and isolated from the stand or boom to which it is attached (see Figure 4.16). If the mic stand is accidentally bumped, the sound of this thud will not be passed on and amplified by the mic.

4.21 MIC STANDS AND BOOMS

Mic stands consist of two chrome-plated pipes, one of which fits inside the other. A rotating clutch at one end of the larger-diameter pipe allows the smaller pipe to be adjusted to any height desired. At the other end of the larger pipe is a heavy metal base (usually circular) that supports the pipes in a vertical position. Some mic stands utilize a single pipe that's at a fixed height. In either case, the mic is attached to the top of the pipe by a standard thread and mic-stand adapter (see Figure 4.17A). **Floor stands** adjust for the announcer in a standing position, and **desk stands** are used for the seated announcer.

A **boom stand** is a long horizontal pipe that attaches to a floor stand (see Figure 4.17B). One end of the boom is fitted with the standard thread (for the mic), and the other end is weighted to balance the mic. The horizontal pipe

FIGURE 4.16 The microphone shock mount isolates the microphone from the mic stand. (Image courtesy of beyerdynamic.)

FIGURE 4.17   Microphone stands: (A) desk stands; (B) boom stand; (C) boom arm. (Images courtesy of Atlas/Soundolier.)

Production Tip #4—
"Microphone-to-Mouth Distance"

You see it every day on MTV; your favorite singers practically "eating" the microphone as they perform their latest hits. *Don't* emulate this! "Swallowing" the microphone is *not* good mic technique. When using a microphone in the standard studio setup, keep in mind two basic rules concerning distance from the microphone and position of the microphone. First, the announcer's mouth should be about 6 inches away from the mic. That's about the length of a dollar bill—a good way to remember mic-to-mouth distance. This is a good starting point for using a mic. You may find that you need to be closer or farther away because of the strength of your voice or the vocal effect that you're trying to achieve. Second, position the microphone so that you are not talking directly into it. Postion the mic level with your nose and tilted down toward your mouth, and talk beneath the front of the mic or place the mic below your mouth with the front of the microphone tilted up toward your mouth, allowing you to talk across the top of the mic.

allows the boom stand to be away from the announcer and positions the mic in a workable relationship to him or her. A **boom arm** (see Figure 4.17C) is a mic stand especially designed for use in the radio studio. It consists of metal rods and springs designed somewhat like a human arm; the mic attaches to one end, and the other end goes into a mounting base. The whole unit can then be attached to production studio furniture so that the mic can be placed in close proximity to the audio console.

4.22 MICROPHONE USAGE

An understanding of the microphone types, pickup patterns, and other mic characteristics is only useful if you can apply this knowledge to everyday radio production use. It seems reasonable to assume that the microphone in a broadcast studio will be a dynamic mic because that's the most commonly used mic in broadcasting, but it could also be a condenser mic. Perhaps the more important consideration is its pickup pattern. In the studio, we mainly want to pick up the announcer's voice and some ambience of the studio. A cardioid pickup pattern, with its pickup of front and side sounds, works best to accomplish this but not pick up unwanted sounds from the rear, such as the announcer moving papers or turning on and off various switches.

In radio production work, it's not uncommon to leave the studio to record an interview. Certainly the radio news person does this frequently. In a remote location interview, the dynamic microphone would probably be used because of its ruggedness, good quality, and the fact it does not need a power supply. In most cases, at a remote site you *want* to pick up the ambience of the location and various voices (particularly the announcer and the interviewee). The omnidirectional pickup pattern, with its ability to pick up sound equally well in all directions, provides a solution for this situation. If there's likely to be a great deal of background noise, a cardioid mic might be better, but it will have to be carefully placed so that it picks up both voices well.

Interviews (and some other broadcast situations) may require you to mic a group of people in the studio seated around a table. You could use a single omnidirectional mic in the center of the table, or you could use a separate cardioid mic for each individual at the table. Another option is to use the PZM, or pressure zone microphone.

Sportscasters are commonly out of the studio to broadcast games and other sports events. The sportscaster's headset provides both earphones and a microphone in a single unit, leaving the announcer's hands free (see Figure 4.18). The mic is usually a dynamic mic with either a cardioid or an omnidirectional pickup pattern. If a cardioid mic is employed, the sportscaster may want to have an additional mic for picking up crowd and sports action noise.

4.23 CONCLUSIONS

We said earlier that there is no one correct microphone to use in radio production. When using mics in any produc-

Headphone Section

Microphone Section

FIGURE 4.18 The sportscaster's headset combines headphones and a microphone. (Image courtesy of Telex Communications, Inc.)

tion, don't be afraid to experiment in each particular situation. The bottom line in any production should be how it sounds. It's good to be flexible in radio production because often you won't have a wide variety of microphones available. If you use what you've learned in this chapter, you should be able to obtain clear appropriate sound under a variety of circumstances.

Self-Study

■ QUESTIONS

1. Another name for the dynamic microphone is _____.
   a) condenser
   b) pressure
   c) capacitor
   d) PZM

2. The dynamic mic's sound-generating element is constructed of a diaphragm, a permanent magnet, and a voice coil. Into which of these is a small electrical current induced during use?
   a) diaphragm
   b) magnet
   c) coil
   d) none of the above

3. The condenser mic differs from the dynamic mic in that _____.
   a) the condenser mic needs a power supply, and the dynamic mic doesn't
   b) the dynamic mic has a diaphragm, and the condenser mic doesn't
   c) the dynamic mic has better sound quality than the condenser mic
   d) the condenser mic is bidirectional, and the dynamic mic is omnidirectional

4. Which kind of mic is most likely to be found in a broadcast-quality audio cassette recorder?
   a) dynamic
   b) ribbon
   c) wireless
   d) condenser

5. The mic that picks up sound on all sides is _____.
   a) hyper-cardioid
   b) cardioid
   c) omnidirectional
   d) bidirectional

6. Which mic would be most appropriate for conducting an interview on the sidelines at a football game?
   a) unidirectional
   b) omnidirectional
   c) bidirectional
   d) hyper-cardioid

7. Which mic would be most appropriate for picking up a sportscaster announcing at a baseball game?
   a) cardioid
   b) nondirectional
   c) bidirectional
   d) omnidirectional

8. Most broadcast-quality microphones are _____.
   a) low cost
   b) high-impedance
   c) low-sensitivity
   d) low-impedance

9. Which of the following is most likely to exaggerate the bass sounds of a person's voice?
   a) feedback
   b) proximity effect
   c) multiple-microphone interference
   d) bass roll-off

10. The purpose of a shock mount is _____.
    a) to reduce plosive sounds
    b) to keep the announcer's head at least 12 inches away from the mic
    c) to isolate the microphone from mechanical vibrations
    d) to prevent static electricity discharges

11. Which type of mic stand can be farthest away from a person and still allow the person to be close to the microphone?
    a) boom stand
    b) floor stand
    c) desk stand
    d) shock mount

12. Which stereo miking technique uses two microphones crossed (like swords) at a 90-degree angle to each other?
    a) split-pair miking
    b) mid-side miking

    c) M-S miking
    d) X-Y miking

13. Which type of microphone uses small multiple sound-generating elements within a single mic housing?
    a) ribbon mic
    b) wireless mic
    c) stereo mic
    d) boundary mic

14. A microphone's pickup pattern is exactly the same thing as a microphone's polar response pattern.
    a) true
    b) false

15. Which microphone has a permanently charged capacitor as part of its sound-generating element?
    a) condenser mic
    b) regulated phase mic
    c) electret mic
    d) ribbon mic

16. Which microphone would be best at picking up sound when the sound source is a considerable distance from the mic?
    a) lavalier mic
    b) PZM mic
    c) RF mic
    d) shotgun mic

17. Sound picked up from the rear of a microphone is 90 degrees off-axis.
    a) true
    b) false

18. Which microphone pickup pattern describes a mic with the narrowest scope of on-axis sound pickup?
    a) cardioid
    b) ultra-cardioid
    c) hyper-cardioid
    d) super-cardioid

19. Microphone impedance refers to a microphone's ability to create an output signal.
    a) true
    b) false

20. A "screech" that occurs when sound is picked up by a microphone, amplified, fed back through a speaker, and picked up again over and over is called _____.
    a) proximity effect
    b) multiple-microphone interference
    c) feedback
    d) bass roll-off

21. Which of the following is *not* a way that microphones are commonly classified?
    a) a mic's sound-generating element
    b) a mic's size
    c) a mic's pickup pattern
    d) a mic's impedance

22. Which stereo miking technique requires exact placement of two cardioid microphones?
    a) ORTF miking
    b) stereosonic miking
    c) X-Y miking
    d) A-B miking

23. Which microphone has a wire spiral embedded in a circular diaphragm as part of its sound-generating element?
    a) dynamic mic
    b) electret mic
    c) moving coil mic
    d) regulated phase mic

24. Multiple microphone interference can be avoided if the mics are at least three times as far from each other as they are from the sound source.
    a) true
    b) false

25. Which of the following is *not* another term for a wireless microphone?
    a) FM microphone
    b) RF microphone
    c) radio microphone
    d) PZM microphone – boundary mic

■ ANSWERS

If You Answered A:

1a. No. This is a different type of microphone. (Reread 4.3 and 4.4.)

2a. Wrong. The diaphragm feels the pressure. (Reread 4.3.)

3a. Right. The condenser mic power supply is needed to charge the backplate and diaphragm.

4a. No. While the dynamic mic is often found in the broadcast studio, it is not the correct response here. (Reread 4.3 and 4.4.)

5a. No. Hyper-cardioid mics pick up mainly from the front. (Reread 4.7 to 4.10.)

6a. Wrong. As a cardioid mic, it picks up in mainly one direction, so it would not pick up much of the crowd ambience. (Reread 4.7 to 4.10.)

7a. Yes. It would pick up the sportscaster without much of the background noise.

8a. No. Most broadcast studio mics cost $300 to $500. Although remote mics may be less, they are usually not inexpensive. (Reread 4.12.)

9a. No. Feedback is a howling noise caused by having open mics near speakers. (Reread 4.14 and 4.15.)

10a. No. A pop filter is used to reduce plosive sounds. (Reread 4.19 and 4.20.)

11a. Right. This is the best selection.

12a. No. This is a different stereo miking technique. (Reread 4.18.)

13a. No. As the name implies, a ribbon mic employs a thin metallic ribbon as part of a single sound-generating element. (Reread 4.5 and 4.6.)

14a. Wrong. A pickup pattern is the three-dimensional shape around the mic in which it hears the sound best; a polar response pattern is the two-dimensional representation of this. (Reread 4.11.)

15a. You're close to the correct response, but normal condenser mics require a power supply to charge the capacitor. (Reread 4.4.)

16a. Wrong. Lavalier mics are designed to be attached to the announcer's clothing. (Reread 4.6.)

17a. No. Sound that is 90 degrees off-axis would be coming from the side of a microphone. (Reread 4.7.)

18a. All cardioid microphones pick up sound mainly from the front, but this is not the correct answer. (Reread 4.10.)

19a. This is not correct. Impedance is an electrical characteristic similar to resistance. (Reread 4.12 and 4.13.)

20a. No. Proximity effect is a characteristic of microphones that accents the bass response of the mic. (Reread 4.14 and 4.15.)

21a. No. Microphones are categorized by their sound-generating elements. (Reread 4.2.)

22a. Correct. The mic heads are spaced 6.7 inches apart and form a 110-degree angle.

23a. Wrong. Dynamic mics do have a wire coil as part of their sound-generating element, but it's not configured like this. (Reread 4.3 and 4.5.)

24a. Yes. This is a true statement.

25a. No. FM microphone is another term for a wireless microphone. (Reread 4.6)

If You Answered B:

1b. Correct. The dynamic mic is also called the pressure mic or the moving-coil mic.

2b. Wrong. The magnet sets up the field. (Reread 4.3.)

3b. No. Both mics have a diaphragm. (Reread 4.3 and 4.4.)

4b. No. This is a professional-quality mic that is not used much anymore. (Reread 4.3, 4.4, and 4.5.)

5b. Wrong. The cardioid picks up sound on all but one side—usually the one right behind the mic. (Reread 4.7 to 4.10.)

6b. Correct. It would pick up from all sides, thus easily miking the interview and some crowd noise.

7b. No. The crowd noise would tend to drown out the announcer. (Reread 4.7 to 4.10.)

8b. No. Consumer-quality mics are usually high-impedance, but not broadcast quality. (Reread 4.12.)

9b. Right. When an announcer gets too close to the mic, the bass may be exaggerated.

10b. No. For one thing, the announcer's head should be about 6 inches away, not 12 inches away. (Reread 4.20.)

11b. No. A person must stand right beside a floor stand. (Reread 4.21.)

12b. No. This is a different stereo miking technique. (Reread 4.18.)

13b. No. Wireless mics employ a transmitter (part of the mic) and a receiver, but this is not a description of this system. (Reread 4.6.)

14b. Right. This is the correct response.

15b. No. The regulated phase microphone doesn't require phantom power, nor does it have a capacitor as part of its sound-generating element. (Reread 4.4 and 4.5.)

16b. Wrong. PZM mics are designed to be placed on a flat surface, such as a tabletop. (Reread 4.6.)

17b. Yes. This statement is false. Sound that is picked up from the rear of a microphone is 180 degrees off-axis.

18b. This is the correct response.

19b. This is the right answer because mic sensitivity refers to a microphone's ability to create an output level.

20b. No. This is not correct. Multiple microphone interference is a phase problem that creates peaks and cancellations in the sound. (Reread 4.15 and 4.16.)

21b. Correct. While microphones come in a wide variety of sizes, they are not usually categorized by size.

22b. Wrong. For one thing, stereosonic miking utilizes bidirectional mics, not cardioid mics. (Reread 4.18.)

23b. No. The electret mic is a type of condenser mic that uses a capacitor as its sound-generating element. (Reread 4.4 and 4.5.)

24b. You're incorrect. The statement is true. (Reread 4.16.)

25b. No. RF microphone is another term for a wireless microphone. (Reread 4.6)

If You Answered C:

1c. No. This is another name for the condenser mic. (Reread 4.3 and 4.4.)

2c. Correct. The current is in the coil.

3c. No. The condenser mic has slightly better quality than the dynamic mic. (Reread 4.3 and 4.4.)

4c. No. You're way off base here. (Reread 4.4 and 4.6.)

5c. Yes. An omnidirectional mic picks up on all sides.

6c. Wrong. It could pick up the interview, but wouldn't get much crowd noise. (Reread 4.7–4.10.)

7c. No. A bidirectional mic picks up on two sides, and the sportscaster would only be on one side. (Reread 4.7 to 4.10.)

8c. No. Condenser mics are high sensitivity, and dynamic mics are medium sensitivity. Neither is low sensitivity. (Reread 4.12 and 4.13.)

9c. No. This will create a distorted signal. (Reread 4.14 and 4.16.)

10c. Yes. This is a special type of microphone holder that suspends the mic.

11c. No. A desk stand has to be right in front of the person. (Reread 4.21.)

12c. No. This is a different stereo miking technique. (Reread 4.18)

13c. Yes. This is the correct answer.

15c. Yes. A type of condenser mic, the electret mic, has a capacitor that is charged during manufacture.

16c. Wrong. RF mics are wireless mics, but they don't have exceptional distance pickup characteristics. (Reread 4.6.)

18c. While the hyper-cardioid does have a narrow, unidirectional pickup pattern, this is not the best response. (Reread 4.10.)

20c. Correct. That screeching, howling sound is feedback.

21c. No. Microphone pickup patterns are used to categorize mics. (Reread 4.2.)

22c. Wrong. This is a similar miking technique, but there are distinct differences. For example, the angle formed by crossed mics can vary from 90 to 140 degrees with X-Y miking. (Reread 4.18.)

23c. No. This is not correct. The moving coil mic is just another name for the dynamic mic. (Check the response to 23a; reread 4.3 and 4.5.)

25c. No. Radio microphone is another term for a wireless microphone. (Reread 4.6)

If You Answered D:

1d. No. A PZM mic does not indicate a type of construction. (Reread 4.3 and 4.6.)

2d. Wrong. (Reread 4.3.)

3d. No. Both dynamic and condenser mics can have omnidirectional or bidirectional pickup patterns. (Reread 4.3, 4.4, and 4.8 to 4.10.)

4d. Yes. Most broadcast-quality cassette recorders have a built-in condenser mic.

5d. No. A bidirectional mic picks up sound from the front and back of the mic. (Reread 4.7 to 4.10.)

6d. No. This is a type of cardioid mic with a very narrow one-direction pickup pattern. Although it might be useful to pick up one specific section of the crowd, it wouldn't provide full background crowd noise. (Reread 4.7 to 4.10.)

7d. No. This is another term for nondirectional. (Reread 4.7 to 4.10.)

8d. Right. Low-impedance is what most broadcast equipment is.

9d. Wrong. Bass roll-off is an electronic "turn down" of bass frequencies. (Reread 4.14.)

10d. No. This is not the correct answer. (Reread 4.20.)

11d. No. Although this is often used in conjunction with a mic stand, it won't determine the distance between announcer and mic stand. (Reread 4.21.)

12d. Correct. This is a description of X-Y stereo miking technique.

13d. No. Boundary mics employ a single sound-generating element in conjunction with a sound-reflecting plate. (Reread 4.6.)

15d. No. The ribbon mic doesn't require a power supply, nor does it have a capacitor as part of its sound-generating element. (Reread 4.4 and 4.5.)

16d. Right. Shotgun mics are designed with a narrow tube that can be aimed at and will pick up sound from some distance away.

18d. While the super-cardioid does have a narrow, unidirectional pickup pattern, this is not the correct response. (Reread 4.10.)

20d. No. Bass roll-off is a switch on some microphones that electronically turns down the lower frequencies. (Reread 4.14 and 4.15.)

21d. No. Mic impedance is used to categorize microphones. (Reread 4.2 and 4.12.)

22d. Not correct. For one thing, A-B miking uses omnidirectional microphones. (Reread 4.18.)

23d. This is the correct response.

25d. Yes. The PZM is a type of boundary microphone that is designed to be placed on a flat surface, such as a tabletop.

PROJECTS

■ PROJECT 1

Position microphones in various ways to create different effects.

Purpose

To enable you to experience proximity effect, feedback, multiple-mic interference, and the differences in sound quality that occur when a microphone is placed at different distances and angles from an announcer.

Advice, Cautions, and Background

1. You have not yet read Chapter 5, "Digital Audio Players/Recorders," or Chapter 6, "Analog Audio Players/Recorders," so you may need some help from your instructor or the engineer in setting up the equipment.

2. For the proximity effect, try to find a mic that doesn't have a bass roll-off switch, or make sure it's switched off if it does.

3. Don't allow feedback to occur for too long. It can be damaging to all the electronic equipment—and your ears. You may have to plug the mic into something other than the audio board if the board automatically shuts off the speakers when the mic is turned on.
4. For the multiple-mic interference, make sure the mics are closer than 3 feet. Omnidirectional mics will demonstrate the effect the best.
5. Use a cardioid mic for the distance and angle experiments because it will demonstrate the points better.

How to Do the Project

1. Set up an audio board so that two microphones are fed into it and so that the sound of those two mics can be recorded on an audio recorder.
2. Put the recorder in record mode and activate one of the microphones. Start talking about 2 feet away from the mic, and keep talking as you move closer until you are about 2 inches from it. As you talk, say how close you are to the mic, and mention that you're experimenting with the proximity effect. Stop the recorder.
3. Position a microphone so that it's close to an activated speaker. Turn on the audio recorder, and talk into the mic. Record a short amount of the feedback, and turn off the recorder.
4. Position two mics in front of you that are less than 3 feet apart. Put the audio recorder in record mode, and talk into the microphones, saying that you're testing for multiple-microphone interference. Turn off the recorder.
5. Position one mic in front of you. Put the audio recorder in record mode. Position yourself 12 inches from the mic and talk into it. Then position yourself 6 inches from the mic and talk directly into it. Then talk across the top of the mic. Move 6 inches to the side of the mic, and talk into it with your mouth positioned to speak across the top of it. Get behind the mic, either by moving behind it or by turning it around, and talk from about 6 inches away. Describe each action as you do it.
6. Listen to the recording to hear the various effects and to see that you have, indeed, recorded all the assignments. If some of them didn't turn out as well as you would have liked, redo them.
7. Turn in a tape of your recording to your instructor for credit for the project. Make sure you put your name on the tape and label it MICROPHONE PLACEMENT.

■ PROJECT 2

With several other students, make a recording using stereo miking techniques.

Purpose

To give you experience utilizing standard microphones to employ various stereo miking techniques.

Advice, Cautions, and Background

1. Which technique you employ will depend on the microphones that are available at your facility.
2. Since this project requires several people, your instructor may assign it as a class project.
3. The "How To" section that follows uses X-Y techniques for illustration purposes; you can adjust it for any of the other techniques.

How to Do the Project

1. At one end of your studio (or room) arrange at least three students in a "left"–"center"–"right" configuration. This could also be three groups of students or even a small musical group, as long as they're arranged so that specific sections can be identified as being left, center, or right.
2. Set up two cardioid microphones to record onto an audio tape recorder.
3. Arrange the microphones in an X-Y position as described in the text, in line with the "center" of the students or group.
4. Begin recording and have the students or group do the following:
    a. have the "left" say something
    b. have the "right" say something
    c. have the "center" say something
    d. have all three sections say something different, but at the same time

    e. have just the "center" say something

    f. have the "left" and "right" say something

    g. have all three sections say something

5. As you are recording the above, make sure to identify what each segment is by having one student say something like, "This is just the 'left' group," before the group says anything.

6. Rewind and play back the tape. Are you able to "hear" the stereo image correctly? Does the left group "appear" to be located left? Make some observations about the recording results and write them down.

7. Repeat the same recording, but use a single microphone; that is, record in mono.

8. Listen to the second recording. What differences do you hear between the two recordings? Write down your observations again.

9. Turn in your tape and the observation sheet labeled STEREO MIKING to your instructor to receive credit for this project.

■ PROJECT 3

Compare sound from different types of microphones.

Purpose

To enable you to know the differences between dynamic and condenser mics and between cardioid and omnidirectional mics.

Advice, Cautions, and Background

1. You have not yet read Chapter 5, "Digital Audio Players/Recorders," or Chapter 6, "Analog Audio Players/Recorders," so you may need help from your instructor or engineer in setting up the equipment.

2. Don't be concerned if you can't discern differences between the dynamic and condenser mics. The pop and hiss effect doesn't occur for all voices.

3. If your facility has mics with other sound-generating elements (such as ribbon or regulated phase) or other pick-up patterns (such as bidirectional or ultra-cardioid), add those to the exercise.

How to Do the Project

1. Select a dynamic mic and a condenser mic from those at your facility.

2. Attach the mics to an audio recorder. You can put both mics through an audio console and use them one at a time, or you can attach each mic into the recorder in its turn.

3. While you're recording, say the following into the dynamic mic: "Peter Piper picked a peck of pickled peppers," and "She sells seashells by the seashore." Turn the recorder off.

4. Repeat step 3, but use the condenser microphone.

5. Select a cardioid mic and an omnidirectional mic from those at your facility.

6. Attach the microphones into an audio recorder as in step 2.

7. Position the cardioid mic on a stand, and, while recording, walk totally around the mic, saying where you are as you move: for example, "Now I'm right in front of the mic; now I'm ninety degrees to the right of the front of the mic." Turn the recorder off.

8. Repeat step 7, using the omnidirectional microphone.

9. Listen to the recording, and write down any observations you have about the differences among the various mics.

10. Turn in the paper and a tape of your recording to your instructor for credit for the project. Be sure to include your name on both and call the assignment MICROPHONE COMPARISONS.

CHAPTER FIVE

Digital Audio Players/Recorders

Information

5.1 INTRODUCTION

Digital technology continues to replace conventional technology in various applications around the radio production studio. For example, since the advent of the compact disc, turntables have steadily lost favor as a necessary piece of production equipment. Other analog mainstays, such as reel-to-reel tape recorders and cart machines, are also found in fewer and fewer production facilities. This chapter looks at the digital studio equipment that is both increasing the choice of available formats to work with and, in many cases, bringing on the demise of older analog equipment.

5.2 THE CD PLAYER

The compact disc player was the first piece of digital equipment to be embraced in radio production and broadcast work, and today the CD player is one of the main sources for playing back prerecorded material. Because CDs are often aired one right after the other, there are usually at least two CD players in each production room or on-air studio. In this way, one can be cued while the other is playing on-the-air.

The CD player shown in Figure 5.1 is typical of a unit designed specifically for broadcast use. Many radio stations and production facilities just use consumer CD players, but these often require special interfaces to be compatible with other broadcast equipment and are not really designed for day-in and day-out use. Good production practice dictates the use of broadcast-quality CD players rather than consumer models.

One of the main features of many broadcast-quality units is a **cue wheel** that allows the operator to "rock" the CD back and forth, much like cueing a record. In this manner the exact start point of the music can be found, and then the player can be paused at that spot, ready for play. Most CD players will also automatically cue to the start of the music when you cue up to any specific track on the CD or cue to an index point within an individual track. Other normal CD controls include a play button to start the CD, several controls to select or program specific tracks (or

songs) on the CD, and an open/close control to load the CD into the machine. Regardless of the exact design, the CD ends up in a **tray** or **well**, where it spins so the laser can read it.

The internal structure of the CD player centers around a laser beam system that reads the encoded data on the surface of the CD. A **laser diode** generates a laser light beam, and a **prism system** directs it toward the disc surface. Different types of lenses focus the laser beam exactly on the pits of data encoded on the disc. Reflected light is directed back through the lens and prism to another wedge lens and a **photodiode,** which provides the data signal that will be converted to an audio signal.

A different design approach to CD players has been to build them so that the CD must be put into a plastic housing before it can be played in the unit (see Figure 5.2). This is similar to the old audiotape cartridge concept rather than the turntable-based design most CD players use. Special broadcast features of this type of CD player include the ability to select one track while another is playing (so two songs can be played back-to-back from the same CD) and a countdown timer (so the operator knows exactly how much time remains on the song currently playing). The plastic cartridge increases the cost of this system, but it also affords the CD extra protection from dirt and damage.

Another type of compact disc player is the **multiplay** CD player. With an ability to hold up to 300 CDs and with interfacing capability, this type of unit has been used as a music source in automation systems. Not only does the operator have random access to thousands of individual songs, but also all the CDs can be secured under lock and key.

As noted earlier, regardless of the type of CD player utilized, some compact discs seem to display an overly bright, metallic, or even harsh sound—a distinctive "digital sound." The problem actually has nothing to do with the CD player or even the CD process. It occurs in some CDs because the original recording was intended for vinyl playback. Engineers often added equalization to compensate for sonic limitations of vinyl recording. Many early CDs were mastered with this same equalization applied rather than removed for transfer to the CD medium, thus the bright, or shiny, sound. Material that has been recorded essentially for CD does not display this problem, nor should

FIGURE 5.1 The professional-quality CD player is built for rack-mounting, heady-duty use, and may have features not available on consumer units. (Image courtesy of Denon Electronics)

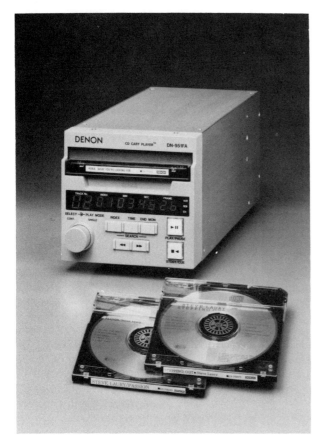

FIGURE 5.2 A compact disc must be put into a plastic housing before it can be played in a cart-style CD player. (Image courtesy of DENON America, Inc.)

older material that has been carefully prepared for transfer to CD.

5.3 ADVANTAGES OF THE CD PLAYER

The advantages of the CD player far outweigh any perceived problems. The CD player offers the superior sound quality of any piece of digital equipment—greater frequency response, better signal-to-noise ratio, improved dynamic range, and almost no distortion—when compared to an analog component. In addition, there is no physical contact between the player and the actual CD. Unlike the stylus, which rides the grooves of a record, the CD is read by a laser light, and there is no wear or degradation of the CD.

The CD format also offers the convenience of random access to the material stored on the disc. Unlike tape-based formats that require winding through the tape to move from one point to another, CD players can instantly move from one track on the disc to another track anywhere on the disc in a second or two. Another plus of the CD player, from a production viewpoint, is its ability to "cue to music." Whether using a cue wheel or an auto-cueing feature, CD players allow the announcer to find the exact beginning of the music and start the CD instantly at that point. CD timing information (elapsed/remaining time and track length) is helpful for production work, and the ability to select and play segments of music or to automatically fade-in at any point of the music can be a creative production tool.

The ease of cueing and the consistently high quality obtained makes the use of CDs and the CD player an important part of the production process in the modern studio.

5.4 COMPACT DISCS

The **compact disc (CD)** is a small plastic disc 4.7 inches in diameter. On one side of the disc, the music is stored as a spiral of microscopic pits and lands (or flat areas) that contain the encoded information about the sound. In addition to music information, data encoded on the disc tells the CD player where each track begins and ends, how many tracks are on the disc, and other timing and indexing information.

A CD stores music as 16-bit digital words, going from the center hole to the outside rim of the disc. With the standard digital sampling rate, 44,100 of these digital "words" are required for each channel every second! In fact, there are over 5 billion bits of data stored on a CD just to produce about an hour of music. A thin aluminum reflective coating (some CDs use a gold-coated reflective surface) less than 70 millionths of a millimeter makes it possible for the **laser** light to read the encoded data, and a layer of clear polycarbonate plastic protects the encoded information. The reverse side of the CD is made up of the label and a protective lacquer coating (see Figure 5.3).

CDs were originally designed to hold 60 minutes of recorded material; however, many are released that contain about 74 minutes of music and that has become the "standard" CD length. CD singles (3-inch CDs) were developed capable of holding about 20 minutes of music, but these never really caught on and are not frequently seen today.

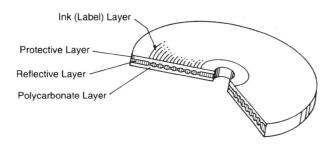

FIGURE 5.3 A compact disc is made up of several layers as this cutaway view shows.

Production Tip #5— "CD Information and Codes"

The number of tracks and timing information about songs have always appeared on the display of CD players, but why not other information, such as song titles? Although it has been technically possible to provide such information, such provisions were not put into the original CD "standards." If the codevelopers of the compact disc, Sony and Philips, revise the CD standard so that information about the artists, albums, and songs can be included with the music, then a text-capable audio CD player will be required. Computer CD-ROMs are text-capable players and some music CDs do contain additional information that can be accessed with a PC or with CD players manufactured to read it.

The Society of Professional Audio Recording Services (SPARS) developed a code for CD packaging to show just how "digital" the CD was. The code told whether the recording was from a digital or analog master and whether it was mixed and mastered in analog or digital. For example, an AAD disc was recorded and mixed in "analog" but mastered in "digital." Many AAD or ADD coded CDs didn't appeal to digital purists looking for that completely digital CD, labeled DDD, so the code was dropped for a few years. However, in 1995, SPARS recommended the code's return, and many of today's CDs again show this code, although it is not required on CD packaging.

5.5 CARE OF CDS

The compact disc is not as indestructible as it was once promoted to be. Practical use in the radio studio has shown that CDs do require some care. Some CD players can be mistracked by dust or fingerprints on the CD surface, and serious scratches can also render the CD unplayable.

CDs can be cleaned by wiping the aluminum side (opposite the label) with a lint-free cloth gently from the center hole of the CD directly out toward the CD rim. Do *not* use a circular cleaning motion because this could cause a scratch that follows the spiral data on the disc, causing the disc to mistrack.

When removing a CD from its jewel box case, put your thumb on the center spindle of the jewel box and your index or middle finger on the rim of the disc. Press down with your thumb and gently pull up on the disc until it is free of the case. When handling a disc, continue to hold only the outer edges or inside hole, and avoid bending the CD in any manner. Oily fingers or flexing a disc can damage the CD's protective coating and ultimately allow oxidation of the aluminum layer, which can ruin the CD. If your CD player has a tray that opens and closes, be sure to stop the CD *before* you open the tray. Hitting the open (eject) button while the CD is still playing can cause damage to the CD as it continues to rotate while the tray is opening.

5.6 DVD-AUDIO

The next generation of audio disc may well be the **Digital Versatile Disc (DVD)** or a variation of it. Originally designated as Digital Video Disc, the DVD was designed to hold a feature-length movie on a compact disc-sized medium. Primarily a video format, it also has applications for computer data and music. Physically, the DVD is the same size as a compact disc; however, it can have two data layers that can both be read from one side of the disc by refocusing the laser in the DVD player. The data information is spaced much closer than on a compact disc, so by using a data compression scheme (around 2:1) and a two-sided, dual-layer disc, the DVD could hold up to 17 gigabytes of data, or the content of about 25 current compact discs!

In addition to greater storage capacity, the DVD-Audio specifications offer a wide variety of possible formats of better quality than the CD. An audio-only DVD can have sampling rates of 44.1, 88.2, 176.4, 48, 96, and 192 kHz, plus 16-, 20-, and 24-bit quantizing compared to the CD's 44.1 kHz/16-bit standard. Most broadcasters prefer a DVD-Audio standard of 96 kHz/24-bit. DVD-Audio also offers the advantage of multichannel sound—up to a maximum of 6 channels. As this text is being written, DVD-Audio players are making their first appearance in the audio market place. Whether consumers or the broadcast industry embraces this technology is subject to speculation. Competing audio formats and even new technologies are also appearing that could bypass DVD-Audio.

5.7 THE CD RECORDER

CD recorders are finding a home in the broadcast studio. Although the first CD players were merely turntables for prerecorded CDs, shortly after their development, manufacturers produced a recordable CD. The high price of first-generation CD recorders kept broadcast studio use to a minimum, but falling costs over the years have made the CD recorder (see Figure 5.4) very affordable now. Broadcast companies like Tascam, Marantz, Fostex, and HHB all offer **CD recorders** that work in the **CD-R** and/or **CD-RW** format.

CD-R (CD Recordable) is a WORM (write once, read many) design. The CD consists of a photosensitive dye layer and a gold reflective layer, encased in the normal protective polycarbonate. When heated by high-power laser pulses, the recording layer melts, creating bumps (and pits) similar to those of a regular CD. The recording laser follows a preformed spiral track so the data can be played back on any standard CD player. Actually, the CD-R recorder allows you to record over several different sessions or until the disc is full (99 separate tracks, up to 74 minutes total); however, you may not be able to play the disc on a regular CD player until you "finalize" the disc and permanently write the Table of Contents of the disc. Partially recorded CD-Rs *will* play on the CD-R recorder at any time. The biggest drawback to the WORM design is the inability to record over and over; if you make a mistake in the recording process, you have ruined that disc or at least a section of the disc, and once you finalize the disc you cannot add any new material to it.

The CD-RW (CD Rewritable) disc is used in a similar fashion; however, the last track recorded can be erased (before the disc has been finalized), and the space on the disc can be re-used for recording other material. CD-RW discs that have been finalized can also be totally erased and rerecorded. The CD-RW format uses a phase-change technology; the material in the recordable CD surface goes from crystalline to amorphous when heated during the recording process, which changes its reflectivity. During playback, the laser light is reflected differently from opposite-phase areas, allowing the player to distinguish binary zeros and ones and thus reproduce a digital signal. An audio CD recorded in the CD-RW format may not play back correctly on all CD players, although it will play on its own recorder, which will also play standard CDs.

Even though there is intense competition with other digital recording media (such as the MiniDisc), the CD recorder is finding a place in the digital production studio. Some stations record jingles, commercials, custom sound effects, and other production elements on CD. Other sta-

tions might prerecord a block of programming onto CD for later playback, perhaps through an automation system. In addition, most sound effect and production music libraries that used to be available on vinyl record are now produced on compact disc.

5.8 THE MD RECORDER/PLAYER

MiniDisc (MD) recorders and players of different styles and applications have seen moderate success for a number of years, but recently the MD format has found a stronger presence in the radio production studio. Originally developed by Sony as a digital replacement for the cassette, the MiniDisc can be a handheld, tabletop (see Figure 5.5), or rack-mount system and has seen more success in the broadcast studio as a replacement for the audio cart. Employing a tiny 2.5-inch computer-type disk, the MD can still hold up to 74 minutes of music because of a data compression scheme. The MiniDisc is *not* actually CD quality, but extremely high-quality audio. The MD also features a "shock absorber" system that uses a memory buffer to store music that can continue to play for a few seconds if the

FIGURE 5.5 The MiniDisc recorder has replaced the old tape cart machine in many production studios. (Image courtesy of Denon Electronics.)

FIGURE 5.4 Most CD recorders found in the broadcast production studio can record in both the CD-R and CD-RW format. (Image courtesy of HBB Communications.)

player mistracks until the pick-up can return to its correct position.

The portable MD recorder as shown in Figure 5.6 is a serious competitor for standard cassette and DAT recorders for news gathering or any production situation that requires recording in the field. The stand-alone unit offers recording, playback, and editing tracks on the move.

Another development in the MiniDisc area is a small, single component (see Figure 5.7) that combines an MD recorder with a small mixing console to provide recording, editing, and mixing features. The mixer section can handle up to eight microphone or line-level sound sources. The recorder section can easily move audio from track to track with no noise buildup or quality loss, produce seamless

FIGURE 5.6   A portable MD allows recording and editing on the move, as well as all the other features of the MiniDisc format. (Image courtesy of Superscope Technologies, Inc.)

FIGURE 5.7   The MD multitrack recorder functions as a mini-studio and records on either MD Data discs or standard MiniDiscs. (Image courtesy of Yamaha Corporation of America; MD Data and MiniDisc are registered trademarks of Sony Corporation.)

edits with MiniDisc's cut and paste features, and support the full range of MIDI synchronization functions. Using an MD Data disc, which can hold 140 MB of data, 37 minutes of 4-track, or 18 minutes of 8-track digital recording/playback time, is available. Stereo or mono recording times on a standard MiniDisc range from 74 to 148 minutes.

5.9 THE MINIDISC

The MD is permanently sealed in a plastic cartridge (see Figure 5.8), so it can be handled without worrying about dust, dirt, or fingerprints getting on the disc. The MiniDisc comes in a prerecorded and recordable format. The actual disc is much smaller than a compact disc—about 2.5 inches in diameter—but otherwise shares many of the CD characteristics, including its digital data in a spiral of microscopic pits. The MiniDisc, like a computer disk, has a sliding protective shutter that automatically opens when the disc is put into a recorder/player.

FIGURE 5.8 The MiniDisc is housed in a plastic case to keep it free from scratches, dust, and fingerprints.

Recordable MDs utilize a **magneto-optical design**. A magnetically active layer of the disc is heated (by a laser) to the point where its magnetic orientation can be changed by a magnetic recording head. As the heated spot moves out of the laser beam, it rapidly cools, "freezing" its magnetic polarity according to the data applied to the recording head corresponding to a digital zero or one. During playback, the laser senses variations in reflected light in relation to the magnetic orientation. New material is recorded directly over the old with the MiniDisc format.

5.10 DATA COMPRESSION

In order for the MiniDisc to record the tremendous amount of necessary digital data and still employ its small disk recording medium, the MD recording process uses a data **compression** system developed by Sony known as **ATRAC** (**Adaptive Transform Acoustic Coding**) to provide digital-quality sound. Like any other data compression scheme, data compression occurs because only audible sounds are encoded. In other words, sound below the threshold of hearing or too soft to hear, and sounds masked by louder sounds heard at the same time, are excluded, according to a "perceptual coding" model. In addition, those sounds that are encoded use only the number of data bits necessary for near-CD quality sound. This allows the MiniDisc recording to cut down the amount of data that must be recorded by about one-fifth with no apparent sound quality change or loss.

There is no standard method of data compression, and other digital equipment utilizes other types of audio data reduction schemes. There has been some concern about the audible effects on sound that has been compressed more than once. For example, a MiniDisc could be played through a signal processor that also uses data compression. Some tests have shown a degradation of the audio signal with some combinations of data compression; however, this doesn't appear to be a major problem.

5.11 OTHER DIGITAL "CART MACHINES"

Designed to replace the old analog cart machines, various **digital cartridge recorders** have been developed by several broadcast manufacturers (see Figure 5.9). Instead of an analog audio cart or a MiniDisc as the recording or storage medium, these machines use 2-MB computer floppy disks, 100-MB Zip disks, or gigabyte capacity Magneto-Optical disks. Depending on the configuration, recording time can range from about a minute to many hours. Most digital cart recorders offer selectable sampling rates, the usual operational controls, and can add an electronic "label" (through the use of a keyboard), which can show the cart "name" and "timing" information on an LCD (liquid crystal display) screen.

FIGURE 5.9   Digital cartridge recorders utilize various recording/storage media instead of the old analog audio cartridge. (Image courtesy of Studer Professional Audio Equipment.)

FIGURE 5.10   Portable hard-disk recorders are designed like other broadcast location recorders. (Image courtesy of Maycom A.S.)

5.12 HARD DISC RECORDERS

Some production recorders combine an internal hard-disk drive and a removable storage drive. In addition to providing multitrack capability and all the normal transport controls, these recorders feature a large LCD display screen for file manipulation and editing, and a jog wheel for scrubbing and marking edit points. Hard drives offer the greatest amount of storage space, extremely quick access time, and low maintenance. However, if a hard drive device "crashes," a huge amount of audio can be lost, which can disrupt a production or on-air studio.

Direct-to-disk recorders are also available in a portable design, as shown in Figure 5.10. Looking very similar to a portable cassette, MD, or DAT recorder, the hard-drive-based recorder utilizes either an internal drive or PCMCIA (Personal Computer Memory Card International Association) card. The input/output devices are standard broad-

cast connectors, and the front panel of the unit shows an LCD screen and typical recorder controls. Additional controls are used to set various digital parameters, such as sample rate or data compression. Once recording is complete, basic nondestructive editing can be accomplished by manipulating a waveform display on the LCD screen, or the audio files can be fed to a laptop or desktop PC for editing or archiving.

Another type of portable recorder is Nagra's handheld audio recorder, the ARES-P shown in Figure 5.11. Like other "RAM recorders," it uses a PCMCIA flashcard that can provide a maximum recording time of over three hours. A single button initiates recording, and overwrite protection prevents recording on top of any previously recorded audio files. The recorder automatically generates a file directory that shows each recording length, time and date, and type of data compression used. Pressing the PLAY button instantly replays the last recorded file. The immediate advantage of this type of recorder is the small size of the recorder. As the design concept matures, such recorders will become less expensive, as will the cost of the flashcard media. Radio reporters, or any field recordists, should look forward to the further development of these types of devices.

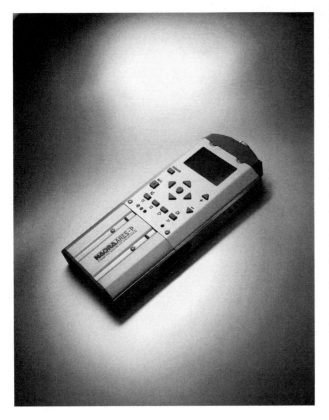

FIGURE 5.11   Some RAM recorders are designed to be held in your hand with all functional controls at your fingertips. (Image courtesy of Nagra USA Inc.)

5.13   DIGITAL REEL TAPE RECORDERS

A reel-to-reel digital format that is available for two-track and multitrack recorders is the **DASH (digital audio stationary head)** system. The two-track systems use specially formulated $\frac{1}{4}$-inch audio tape and standard digital technology. Sampling rates are either 48 Khz at standard tape speeds of 7.5 IPS (inches per second), 15 IPS, and 30 IPS, or 44.1 Khz at slightly slower tape speeds (6.9 IPS, 13.8 IPS, and 27.6 IPS). The reduced speed allows the same density of digital data to be put on the tape even at the lower sampling rate. The multitrack systems have found frequent use in the recording studio, but a very high price tag (even the audiotape for the DASH format is very expensive) has kept almost all broadcast stations away from the DASH machines.

5.14   THE DAT RECORDER

One tape-based digital format, DAT, has found some broadcast application, but has never been widely used. The **DAT (digital audio tape)** recorder, also known as **R-DAT (rotary head digital audio tape)**, uses technology that is part VCR, part traditional cassette recorder, and part CD player. As shown in Figure 5.12, the tape cassette, although it has the normal tape recorder controls (play, record, rewind, etc.), goes into a slide-out drawer (operated with an open/close control) like many CD players. The DAT unit, like the CD, has several controls for selecting specific songs on the tape. An **AMS (Automatic Music Sensor)** button allows the operator to skip forward or backward to the start of the next recorded track. Subcodes can be recorded along with the audio on a DAT tape so that the operator can select any individual track by entering in that track's "start ID" or "program number."

A DAT system records with rotating heads, putting digital data on $\frac{1}{8}$-inch tape in a series of diagonal tracks as does the VCR (see Figure 5.13). This is unlike the analog

FIGURE 5.12   The DAT recorder has never gained the wide use that some of the other digital recorder formats have. (Image courtesy of Fostex Corporation of America.)

FIGURE 5.13 Digital data is put on the DAT audio tape in a diagonal track configuration.

FIGURE 5.14 The DAT cassette is similar in design to a small VCR tape. (Image courtesy of TDK Electronics Corporation.)

cassette system, which records with a stationary head that puts data on the tape in a straight-line (linear) fashion. Tape speed for the DAT recorder is not a factor in the quality of the recording, since only binary data is recorded on the tape; however, with its rotary head drum spinning at 2,000 RPM, the DAT records at an effective tape-to-head speed of over 120 IPS. This high "recording speed" makes it possible to get all the necessary binary data on the tape. The result is the outstanding digital sound quality.

5.15 DAT CASSETTES

The actual DAT cassette tape is similar to a small VCR tape and consists of two little reels encased in a plastic housing about the size of a small pack of playing cards (see Figure 5.14). The audio tape is permanently attached to the two reels, and the longest DAT tapes are capable of recording over 2 hours. While cueing time for any track on a CD player is only 1 to 2 seconds, cueing time from one end of the DAT tape to the other is about 40 seconds. This slower access time is of some concern to broadcasters and would probably necessitate more available DAT sources than CD sources in practical use. On the other hand, cueing a DAT deck from any position to another position ten minutes either side of the current position can be done in 10 seconds or less, which compares with the normal run-out time on the audio tape cartridge, making DAT another possible replacement for the cart machine.

5.16 ADVANTAGES OF THE DAT RECORDER

The DAT recorders have the same superior sound quality associated with CDs—exceptional frequency response and signal-to-noise ratio, wider dynamic range, and virtually no wow, flutter, hiss, hum, or distortion. In addition, the DAT has been developed with recording capability, and the material recorded can be dubbed almost endlessly without degradation of quality. Even with recordable CDs now available, the DAT has the advantage of a longer recording time—2 hours, or about twice as long as the CD. Perhaps DAT's biggest advantages are its convenience of handling (similar to working with a cassette) and the relative compactness of its portable units. However, DAT's future use in the broadcast studio is unsure because it faces stiff competition from other digital recording equipment.

5.17 CONCLUSIONS

With the advent of digital equipment and the advantages in quality and convenience it offers, the use of some older analog equipment continues to diminish. Being comfortable working with various kinds of digital equipment will be a necessary skill for most radio production people. It's also probable that new types of digital-based equipment will continue to be developed in the future.

Self-Study

■ QUESTIONS

1. Digital cartridge recorders use the same audio carts as the older analog machines, but record in a digital format.
    a) true
    b) false

2. The MiniDisc recorder uses a _____ as its recording and storage medium.
    a) standard audio cassette
    b) 2.5-inch computer-type disk
    c) 3.5-inch computer-type disk
    d) DAT cassette

3. One reason for using a professional-quality CD player rather than a consumer model in the radio production studio is _____.
    a) the professional-quality CD player uses a higher-powered laser to read the CD than a consumer model
    b) the professional-quality CD player offers a better signal-to-noise ratio and less distortion than the consumer model
    c) the professional-quality CD player offers a greater frequency response and better dynamic range than the consumer model
    d) the professional-quality CD player is build for heavy-duty, continuous operation, and the consumer model isn't

4. The lacquer coating on a compact disc makes it virtually indestructible in normal broadcast use.
    a) true
    b) false

5. The CD/CD-player format is an improvement over the vinyl record/turntable format because _____.
    a) CDs reproduce analog sound more accurately than records
    b) CD players are more durable than turntables
    c) CD players don't wear out discs as turntables wear out records
    d) CD players have better cartridges than records

6. A DAT recorder _____.
    a) uses a stationary head
    b) places data on the tape in a linear fashion   *diagonal*
    c) cues up any track in two seconds
    d) uses an AMS function to skip forward or backward to the next track   *Auto Music Sensor*

7. ATRAC (Adaptive Transform Acoustic Coding) is used for _____.
    a) auto-reverse on a DAT recorder
    b) synchronization of CD-R and CD-RW discs
    c) data compression
    d) recording audio on a DVD disc

8. A CD recorder that can record a blank CD only once is using a _____ format.
    a) CD-RW
    b) DASH
    c) WORM
    d) DVD

9. Compact discs can be easily cleaned with a cloth wiped in a circular motion over the playing surface of the disc.
   a) true
   b) false

10. Most digital recorders allow the user to add to the recording an electronic label that can show track name, timing, and other information on an LCD screen.
    a) true
    b) false

11. The DVD-audio disc can utilize music encoded at each of the sampling rates and bit lengths shown. Which one is also shared with the CD?
    a) 44.1 kHz/16-bit
    b) 48 kHz/24-bit
    c) 96 kHz/24-bit
    d) 192 kHz/16-bit

12. Once a CD-RW disc has been "finalized" it *cannot* be erased and rerecorded.
    a) true
    b) false

13. Which type of digital player features a memory buffer that helps prevent mistracking if the player is bumped during playback?
    a) DAT
    b) CD
    c) MD
    d) CD-R

14. Which of the following is *not* an advantage of the CD player?
    a) random access to material on the CD
    b) lack of physical contact between player and CD
    c) large signal-to-noise ratio
    d) bright, shiny sound

15. Which recording medium would provide the longest recording time under normal stereo recording conditions?
    a) MD
    b) DAT
    c) CD-R
    d) CD-RW

■ ANSWERS

If You Answered A:

1a. No. Some digital cart machines use standard 3.5-inch computer disks; others use Zip disks, but none utilize the old analog carts. (Reread 5.11.)

2a. Wrong. The audio cassette is the recording and storage medium for the analog cassette recorder that MiniDisc was designed to replace. (Reread 5.8.)

3a. No. Both professional and consumer-model CD players use a similar laser system. (Reread 5.2.)

4a. No. Although the lacquer coating helps protect the CD, it is far from indestructible—fingerprints, dust, and scratches can damage CDs. (Reread 5.4 and 5.5.)

5a. Wrong. CDs use digital, not analog technology. (Reread 5.2 to 5.5.)

6a. No. The DAT recorder uses a rotary head. (Reread 5.14)

7a. No. This is not a feature found on DAT recorders. (Reread 5.10 and 5.14.)

8a. No. This is a recordable/erasable format. (Reread 5.7.)

9a. Wrong. CDs should only be wiped in a straight line from the center hole toward the outer rim. (Reread 5.5.)

10a. Correct. This is a feature of most digital recorders.

11a. Yes. This is the standard CD format that can also be used by DVD-audio.

12a. Wrong. CD-RW discs can be completely erased and rerecorded even after they have been finalized. (Reread 5.7)

13a. No. This is not the correct answer. (Reread 5.8 and 5.14.)

14a. No. Being able to instantly move from one track to another on the CD is a big advantage. (Reread 5.2 and 5.3.)

15a. Wrong. MD is limited to 74 minutes of stereo recording time. (Reread 5.8 and 5.15.)

If You Answered B:

1b. Correct. There are several formats of recording media for the digital cart machines, but none are the same as the analog carts.

2b. Yes. MiniDisc recorders utilize a small CD-type disc encased in a plastic housing similar to a computer disk.

3b. Wrong. All CD players have similar S/N and distortion characteristics. (Reread 5.2 and 5.3.)

4b. Yes. CDs require careful handling even though the lacquer coating helps prevent problems.

5b. Wrong. Both professional-quality CD players and turntables are durable. (Reread 5.2 to 5.5.)

6b. Wrong. The tracks on a DAT are diagonal. (Reread 5.14.)

7b. No. This answer doesn't really make any sense. (Reread 5.7 and 5.10.)

8b. No. DASH is a digital reel-to-reel system. (Reread 5.7 and 5.13.)

9b. Correct. While a circular cleaning motion works for vinyl, it can damage a CD.

10b. Wrong. Most digital recorders do offer this operational feature. (Reread 5.11.)

11b. No. This is a DVD-audio format, but it is not used by CDs. (Reread 5.6.)

12b. Correct. CD-RW discs can be erased even after they have been finalized.

13b. No. This is not the correct answer. (Reread 5.2 and 5.8.)

14b. No. Since the CD is read by laser there is no wear on the CD and this is a big advantage. (Reread 5.2 and 5.3.)

15b. Yes. DAT tapes are available that can record two hours.

If You Answered C:

2c. No. You're close, but the regular computer disk is used in another type of digital "cart" recorder, not the Mini-Disc. (Reread 5.8 and 5.11.)

3c. No. All CD players have similar frequency response and dynamic range characteristics. (Reread 5.2 and 5.3.)

5c. Right. Since there is no physical contact between CD and CD player, the CD doesn't wear out as a record's grooves will.

6c. Wrong. It takes longer than that to cue, especially if you're moving from one end of the tape to the other. (Reread 5.15.)

7c. Correct. This is Sony's data reduction scheme, which allows a long recording time on a small recording medium.

8c. Yes. This is the write once, read many format used by CD-R machines.

11c. No. This is a DVD-audio format, but it is not used by CD. (Reread 5.6.)

13c. Yes. MiniDisc uses a memory buffer as a shock absorber against bumps.

14c. No. The larger the S/N ratio the better, so this is an advantage. (Reread 5.2 and 5.3.)

15c. No. CD-R, like CD-RW, is limited to 74 minutes of recording time. (Reread 5.7 and 5.15.)

If You Answered D:

2d. No. DAT tapes are only used in DAT recorders and players. (Reread 5.8 and 5.15.)

3d. Yes. Most consumer-model CD players can't stand up long to the daily use of the broadcast facility.

5d. No. CD players do not contain a cartridge. (Reread 5.2 to 5.5.)

6d. Correct. AMS stands for Automatic Music Sensor and allows the operator to skip to the beginning of tracks.

7d. Wrong. Although there are different data compression schemes for recording onto digital media, ATRAC is associated with the MiniDisc. (Reread 5.6 and 5.10.)

8d. No. DVD is a different type of format. (Reread 5.6 and 5.7.)

11d. No. This is a DVD-audio format, but it is not used by CD. (Reread 5.6.)

13d. No. This is not the correct answer. (Reread 5.7 and 5.8.)

14d. Correct. For some, the clear CD sound is too bright or harsh, but this is a subjective judgment.

15d. Wrong. CD-RW, like CD-R, is limited to 74 minutes of recording time. (Reread 5.7 and 5.15.)

Projects

■ PROJECT 1

Play and record several compact disc selections.

Purpose

To familiarize you with the operation of CD players.

Advice, Cautions, and Background

1. You will have to do this exercise in conjunction with a microphone, audio board, and audio recorder, so you may need help from your instructor to operate the pieces of equipment that you haven't yet learned.
2. Different brands of CD players have slightly different features, so you will need to learn the particular characteristics of your player.
3. You can play several selections from one CD or use several CDs. If you only have one CD player, you would be advised to use three cuts from one CD as you will probably not have time to change discs. If you have two CD players, you would be better off playing selections from at least two CDs.

How to Do the Project

1. Make sure your CD player is connected so that it can be faded out and will record onto an audio recorder.
2. Make sure a microphone is available so that you can announce the title of the selections you choose.
3. Examine the CD player and practice with it so that you can cue, play, and pause it.
4. When you feel familiar with the player and have decided on three selections to play, start the recorder.
5. Complete the project by doing the following:
   a. Announce the name of the first musical selection, bring it in, and then fade it out after about 30 seconds.
   b. Announce the name of the second selection, bring it in, and fade it out after about 30 seconds. (If you have two CD players, you can cue the second one while the first is playing. If not, you'll need to cue a second selection while you are introducing it. This is not particularly difficult because most CD players enable you to cue easily.)
   c. In the same manner, announce the name of the third selection, bring it in, and then fade it out.
6. If you didn't record directly onto an audio cassette, dub the exercise from the recorder to a cassette.
7. Label the tape with your name and CD RECORDING.
8. Turn in the tape to your instructor to receive credit for the project.

■ PROJECT 2

Write a report on a digital player/recorder that is not discussed in this chapter.

Purpose

To keep you up-to-date on what is happening in this field.

Advice, Cautions, and Background

1. Technological developments in this field are changing rapidly. Undoubtedly there will be new products available by the time you read this text that were not available when it was written. It behooves anyone in the audio production field to keep up-to-date. However, audio equipment also comes and goes, so don't be surprised if the player/recorder you write about today is no longer available a year from now.
2. You can select equipment that does more than play and/or record. For example, some of the current recorders also allow for editing or mixing.

3. The Internet is an excellent place to find this information. The major manufacturers place a great deal of material about their products on their Web sites. Companies that are particularly active in this field include 360 Systems, Fidelipac, Enco, Fostex, Otari, and Tascam. All their Internet addresses begin with *www.*, followed by the company name, then *.com* (e.g., www.enco.com).

How to Do the Project

1. Find a piece of equipment that qualifies as a digital player/recorder. As suggested, you can do this on the Internet or you can write to companies for their catalogues.
2. Research the characteristics of the piece of equipment. If you know a facility that has this equipment, talk with the engineer or an operator who uses the equipment. You could also call a distributor who sells the equipment for additional information.
3. Organize your report, taking into consideration some of the following points:
   a. What is the primary purpose of the piece of equipment?
   b. How does it operate—with regular transport controls (play, record, stop, etc.); attached to a computer; with the use of a rotary dial?
   c. Is it designed to replace an older piece of equipment or is it designed for a new application?
   d. What compression format does it use, if any?
   e. What type of recording medium does it use—tape, computer disk, specially designed material?
   f. When was it first introduced to the market?
   g. What does it cost? Are there additional options?
   h. What is your assessment of whether or not this will be a successful product?
4. Write your report; remember to include your name and DIGITAL PLAYER/RECORDER as a title on it.
5. Turn the report in to your instructor to receive credit for this project.

■ PROJECT 3

Record a public service announcement that uses a "sound effect."

Purpose

To develop your skill in creating a radio spot that incorporates a sound effect to provide a transition.

Advice, Cautions, and Background

1. This project assumes you have enough familiarity with your studio equipment to accomplish basic recording and production techniques.
2. The production incorporates a single announcer voice, two distinct music beds, and a sound effect to provide a transition between the music beds.
3. You will need to write a simple script that can be read in about 20 seconds. Write the copy about an environmental concern, such as water pollution, littering, or forest fire prevention. The spot should follow a "problem-solution" format.
4. There are many ways to accomplish this project, so don't feel you must follow the production directions exactly.

How to Do the Project

1. Select music beds that are appropriate for the style of the spot. You should use a more "somber" sounding bed for the "problem" and a more "upbeat" sound for the "solution." The CD-ROM contains a variety of musical styles that may provide what you need or you can find your own music on another CD.
2. You can play back the music beds directly from the CD.
3. Record the music bed and script (voice) onto a recorder, such as a reel-to-reel or digital recorder. First record the "problem" part of the spot, putting a "serious" tone to your voice and mixing the appropriate music bed with it. Then record the "solution" with a "lighter" vocal delivery, slightly faster pace, and more up-tempo music.

4. Begin recording the music bed at full volume. Start the vocal track and simultaneously fade the music bed slightly so the vocal track is dominant.

5. Now, find an appropriate sound effect. It will be used to separate the two music beds and provide a transition between the "problem" and "solution" parts of the spot.

6. Record the sound effect onto another recorder.

7. Set correct playback levels for the vocal/music bed tracks and the sound effect. Then cue both to the beginning sound.

8. Record your completed spot onto an audio cassette, so set your cassette recorder to record mode.

9. It may take you several attempts to get the spot to come out correctly. If you need to "do it over," just recue everything and try again.

10. On the finished commercial tape, write your name and SOUND EFFECT RADIO SPOT, and turn it in to your instructor to receive credit for this project.

CHAPTER SIX

Analog Audio Players/Recorders

Information

6.1 INTRODUCTION

In most production and broadcast studios you'll still find a combination of analog and digital equipment. However, some equipment that was once a mainstay of audio production is now relegated to secondary status. For example, many facilities still employ the turntable for playback of specialty material that is not available on CD.

Three basic kinds of **audio tape recorders** found in the radio production facility—reel-to-reel, cartridge, and cassette recorders—are in a similar position as the turntable. In most audio studios, they're gathering more dust than use.

6.2 BROADCAST TURNTABLE FUNCTIONS

In a radio production facility, the **turntable** has two basic functions: to spin a record at the precise speed at which it was recorded, and to convert the variations in the grooves of the record to electrical energy (utilizing the cartridge/stylus/tone arm assembly). A turntable designed for professional use requires some means of amplification. Usually the signal is first sent into a preamplifier to increase the level of the signal produced by the cartridge/stylus and then to the audio console for further amplification.

Professional-grade turntables are different from consumer-grade turntables in that the former are designed for heavy-duty use, to maintain precise speeds, for quick speed buildup, to backtrack the platter for cueing, and to be housed in a sturdy base or cabinet.

6.3 BASIC TURNTABLE PARTS

The basic parts of the broadcast-quality turntable, as shown in Figure 6.1, include a platter (a heavy metal plate about 12 inches across covered by a felt or rubber mat), a motor to turn the platter, a tone arm, a cartridge/stylus, and a preamplifier. Additionally, most production turntables have an on/off switch and speed selector switch that work in conjunction with the motor. Some broadcast turntables also offer the option of a pitch control.

The on/off switch and the **speed selector switch** work with the motor to rotate the **platter** at a precise speed. Most broadcast turntables use only the 45 RPM and 33⅓ RPM speeds. Even though a speed may be selected, if the turntable is off the operator can move the turntable in either direction by hand for cueing. The majority of broadcast turntables use a **direct-drive** system in which the platter sits on top of the motor. In fact, the shaft of the motor may be the spindle of the turntable.

6.4 TONE ARM/CARTRIDGE/STYLUS ASSEMBLY

A **tone arm** is usually a metal tube attached to a pivot assembly near the back of the turntable. At the front is a **headshell**, which allows installation of the cartridge/stylus assembly. The function of the tone arm is to house the cartridge and stylus and allow them to move freely across the record as it is played. This is a very sensitive piece of equipment and should be handled carefully. Most tone arms have small handles on the headshell, next to the cartridge that should be used to pick up the arm and place it on the record. This needs to be done carefully to avoid damage to the cartridge/stylus and to avoid changing the weight and angle of the tone arm. The cartridge/stylus assembly is the working end of the tone arm that actually picks up the signal from the record (see Figure 6.2). The **cartridge** receives the minute vibrations from the **stylus** and converts or transduces them into variations in voltage. It acts similarly to the sound-generating element in a microphone (another transducer) and sends the signals to the control board. The stylus is a very small, highly compliant strip of metal. The end that touches the record groove is made of a hard material, usually diamond. It may be called a needle by the home consumer or beginning broadcaster, but stylus is the professional term.

FIGURE 6.1 The turntable gets limited use in the modern production studio. (Image courtesy of Pana-sonic Company.)

FIGURE 6.2 The cartridge/stylus assembly picks up the signal from the record grooves. (Image courtesy of Audio-Technica U.S., Inc.)

Styli are either spherical or elliptical; spherical styli are preferred for broadcast use because they allow backtracking of the record (for cueing up) with a minimum amount of damage to the vinyl grooves. The stylus should not be touched with the fingers. If it's necessary to remove dust from the stylus, do this by blowing lightly on it, or use a special fine-hair stylus brush.

6.5 CARE OF VINYL RECORDS

Vinyl records are thin plastic discs either 7 inches (the 45 RPM single) or 12 inches (the $33\frac{1}{2}$ RPM LP) in diameter. Some broadcast "singles" are produced on the 12-inch disc but are recorded at the 45 RPM speed. Beginning broadcasters have often played records at the wrong speed

because they automatically assumed the 12-inch disc was a $33\frac{1}{3}$ RPM record. **RPM** stands for revolutions per minute and is just that: the number of times the record goes around in a minute. The music, or audio signal, is represented in an analog fashion by tiny wiggles in the walls (or sides) of the record groove. The 45 was originally designed to hold about $4\frac{1}{2}$ minutes of music, and the LP could contain about 30 minutes of music on each side. By spacing the grooves closer, these times have been expanded slightly.

Dust is probably the biggest problem for records and turntables. Dust in record grooves causes undue record and stylus wear. Ultimately, dust develops permanent pops and scratches on the record. The static electricity produced by playing a record compounds the problem by attracting more dust. Use a good-quality record cleaner before playing records to help minimize the dust problem. Unlike CDs, records can be wiped with a cloth and record cleaning fluid (to remove dust or fingerprints), using a circular motion following the record grooves. Records should be handled by the edges to avoid getting fingerprints on the grooved surface, and, unless they're being played, keep records in their paper/plastic inner sleeve and cardboard jacket to keep dust off them. Both LPs and 45s should be stored in a vertical position to prevent them from warping.

6.6 CUEING RECORDS/"WOW"

In most broadcast and production situations, you'll want the sound to begin immediately when playing a record.

Broadcasters cue the record to avoid any silence (**dead air**) between the start of the record and the first sound heard. To cue a record, gently place the stylus in the outer groove of the record. Rotate the turntable platter clockwise until the first sound is heard, then backtrack the platter enough to avoid wowing the record—usually one-eighth turn for 33 $\frac{1}{3}$ RPM records and one-quarter turn for 45 RPM records. Make sure the speed selector switch is set to the proper speed and turn the on/off switch to on just before you want actual sound to begin.

Another way to cue a record is known as **slip cueing** because you hold the edge of the record with a finger with enough force to keep it from spinning when the on/off switch is turned to *on* (the turntable platter will be spinning below the record) and you release the record when you want the actual sound to begin. You can only attempt to slip cue if the turntable has a felt-type mat. The typical rubber mat on some professional ones doesn't allow the platter to continue to spin as you hold the record edge. Slip cueing allows tighter cueing than conventional cueing, but it takes some practice to become proficient at it.

Both methods for cueing records cause some deterioration, known as **cue burns**, of the outer grooves of the record as the stylus moves back and forth.

A common problem with turntables is improper playback speed, which results in a distorted reproduction of the original sound signal. **Wow** refers to changes in pitch caused by slow, regular variations in the playback speed, and the term is somewhat descriptive of the actual sound heard. It's commonly caused by not backtracking far

enough when cueing a record, so the record wows as it builds up to speed when the turntable starts to play. Wow can also be heard because of a record defect (warp or off-center hole) or a turntable defect (worn motor bearings or idler-wheel dip). In any case, wow should be avoided and never heard on the air.

6.7 RECORDERS

Prior to the advent of digital recorders, analog audio tape recorders were the workhorse of the production room. Most of the next few sections of this chapter deal with the reel-to-reel recorder, although many of the general concepts are equally true for both the cartridge and cassette recorders. Often the term "recorder" is used, even though some of the machines can only play back. The basic "parts" of a typical reel-to-reel recorder consist of the tape recorder heads, the tape transport, and the electronics of the recorder.

6.8 HEAD ARRANGEMENT

Tape recorders are devices that rearrange particles on magnetic tape so that sound impulses can be stored on the tape and played back later. This rearranging of particles is done by the recorder's **heads**. You'll learn more about audio tape in Chapter 7, "Audio Editing," but for now it's useful to understand that the magnetic layer of tape consists of metallic particles. When a tape is unrecorded, the magnetic particles are not aligned and are on the tape in a random pattern (see Figure 6.3).

Usually, professional-quality recorders have three heads: one to erase, one to record, and one to play. The erase head is always before the record head so that old material can be erased and new material recorded at the same time. It is erased an instant before the new material is recorded on the audio tape. With the play head behind the record head, it's possible to monitor what you've just recorded. When the machine is just in play, the erase and record heads are disengaged. The easiest way to remember the arrangement of heads in an audio tape recorder is to remember: "Every recorder plays," or "ERP"—erase, record, play.

If the recorder appears to have a single head, it may be because the erase head has been combined into the same case with a record/play head. However, some playback-only machines truly have just a single play head. Less expensive recorders (and many home recorders) have only two heads: one for erase and another for both play and record. Regardless of the possible head arrangements, ERP is the most common one for audio tape recorders found in the radio production room.

6.9 SEL SYNC

One feature often found on audio tape recorders is **sel sync** (selective synchronization), also known as sound-on-

---

Production Tip #6—"Dead Rolling"

In production work it's frequently important to end a piece of music at an exact time. For example, at the end of a program you might want the music and closing narration to end at exactly the same time, or a radio show's musical theme to end right at the top of the hour so that a newscast can begin. Regardless of the situation, you won't often find music that fits exactly the time that you have to fill. One method of dealing with this is the **dead roll**. To dead roll means to begin playing a CD, record, or any sound source with the volume turned down. For example, if you had a piece of music 4:30 minutes long but needed to fill 3:00 before the top of the hour, you would dead roll the music starting at 55:30, and then fade in the music at 57:00. In other words, the first 1:30 of the music would not be heard, but because you dead rolled it, the music would end exactly as desired at the top of the hour. Obviously you usually dead roll music that's instrumental, so it isn't noticeable that you have cut out part of the song, but you can also dead roll some vocal music.

FIGURE 6.3 Tape recorder heads align the metallic particles of audio tape in a pattern analogous to the original sound.

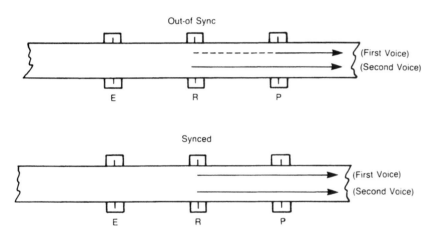

FIGURE 6.4 During sel sync recording, the record head also acts as the play head so previously recorded material can be heard as you're recording new material.

sound. Because of the ERP head arrangement, you can't record one track in synchronization with a previously recorded track. For example, if you record one voice on one track and want to record another voice on another track on the same tape, you run into the following problem. As the previously recorded voice is playing, the sound signal is coming from the play head, but the second voice is recording at the record head. Because of the small distance between these two heads, you hear the previously recorded material a split second before you can record the second voice and therefore the two tracks would be out-of-sync when played back. To overcome this problem and allow this type of recording, the sel sync feature makes the record head also act as the play head. Now you're hearing the previously recorded material at the same time as you're recording the new material, so there is no time difference between them, and you can easily synchronize the two recordings (see Figure 6.4). This can be an important production tool, especially when you're doing multi-voice spots.

6.10 TAPE RECORDER FUNCTIONS—ERASE, RECORD, AND PLAY

The erase, record, and play heads are very similar. Each head consists of a laminated metal core (see Figure 6.5) that is wound with an extremely fine wire coil at one end. At the other end of the core is a gap between the two magnet poles of the head. Tape recorder heads are merely small electromagnets; an electrical current through the coil creates a fluctuating magnetic field at the head gap.

When recording, the audio tape is pulled across the head gap at a right angle. The sound signal is delivered to the record head from the record amplifier in the tape recorder and is transformed or converted from an electrical signal to a magnetic signal. This magnetic signal jumps the head gap and magnetizes the iron oxide layer of the audio tape (remember, the tape was just erased), passing by in a pattern analogous to the original sound signal (refer to Figure 6.3).

Internal View

FIGURE 6.5 Audio tape recorder heads function as small electromagnets.

Unfortunately, because the oxide coating on audio tape responds to magnetization differently at low and high input signal levels, it won't record an exact analog of the original sound source at normal levels and could be severely distorted at lower levels. To compensate for this, a bias current is added during the recording process. **Bias** is an inaudible, high-frequency (at least 100,000 Hz) tone that, when mixed with the audio signal, raises the overall level to a point where the audio tape records sound more evenly.

The addition of bias improves the frequency response of the recording and provides a distortion-free signal. If the recording sounds too bright and fuzzy, there may be too little bias used; too much bias can result in the loss of the audio recording's high frequencies. Proper bias settings are accomplished by the recorder manufacturer or station engineer and are usually set for one particular brand of audio tape. As a radio production person, avoid using a hodgepodge of different audio tapes, and stick to the brand that your tape recorders have been set to, for best recording results.

During play, the recording process is reversed. A recorded (magnetized) tape is drawn across the gap of the play head. The magnetic field of the tape (at the gap) passes into the core and then into the coil, creating an electrical current. This current is sent to a play amplifier in the recorder and is an exact reproduction of the original sound signal. Audio tape reproduces low and high frequencies at a softer level than the middle frequencies, and for that reason **equalization** is often used. Equalization affects the amount of amplification that is given to the highs and lows of the sound signal. Generally, the highs are boosted during recording and slightly decreased during playback; the low frequencies are increased during playback. The ultimate goal is a flat signal response. Like bias, equalization adjustments are often handled by the engineer, although some tape machines do have controls that can be adjusted by the radio production person.

The erase head is on during the recording process. A magnetic field is produced at the erase head gap that is so powerful, it demagnetizes the audio tape as it passes by. During the erase process, the random pattern of metallic particles on the unrecorded audio tape are arranged in a pattern that makes them ready to be recorded again (see Figure 6.3).

6.11 TAPE RECORDER SPEEDS

Most reel-to-reel tape recorders found in the production studio can record at different speeds, ranging from $^{15}/_{16}$ IPS (inches per second) to 30 IPS. The most common are $3^{3}/_{4}$ IPS, $7^{1}/_{2}$ IPS, and 15 IPS. Of course, you must play back the tape at the same speed at which it was recorded. If you don't, it will have a speeded up "Donald Duck" sound or a slow "groggy" sound.

A tape machine operating at $7^{1}/_{2}$ IPS means $7^{1}/_{2}$ inches of recording tape go past the head each second. The more tape that goes past the head, the better the recording because an audio signal with greater frequency response can be put on the tape with a better signal-to-noise ratio. Most radio production work is done at $7^{1}/_{2}$ IPS or 15 IPS. You'll find that if you are editing audio tape, the faster the tape recorder speed, the easier it is to edit. (Obviously, the pauses between words, etc., will be longer at the faster speed.) A tape recorder speed of $3^{3}/_{4}$ IPS is usually acceptable for recorded material that is voice only. To get high-quality music recordings, avoid the slower speeds. However, one advantage of the slower speed is that you can get more material on the tape.

6.12 TAPE COUNTERS/TIMERS

Most audio tape recorders have a built-in timer or tape counter. Modern machines have a digital timer that gives an accurate minutes and seconds count. Some machines have a mechanical counter that counts up from "0000," but the numbers have no relationship to time and are merely a gauge as to where you are on the tape. Most timers and counters also have a "zero set" that allows you to rewind to an exact location. For example, at the beginning of a voice track you're recording, you set the timer (or counter) to

Supply Reel

Take-Up Reel

Pinch Roller

Heads

Capstan

Controls

FIGURE 6.6 The tape recorder transport is that part of the recorder involved with the actual motion of the audio tape as it passes the heads. (Image courtesy of TASCAM Division, TEAC America, Inc.)

"00:00" and enable the zero set button. When you complete the recording, just push the rewind or memory button on the recorder, and it will rewind to the point where you set the "00:00." Timers are also useful to get a timing of a longer radio program. You don't have to listen to the program in real time since most timers work in the fast forward mode of the recorder. An accurate timing of a half-hour radio show may only take a few minutes in fast forward; just reset the timer to "00:00" at the first sound at the beginning of the tape, fast forward to the last sound at the end of the tape, and look at the timer reading.

6.13 TAPE RECORDER TRANSPORT

Figure 6.6 shows the face of a typical reel-to-reel recorder that is found in the production studio. The labeled parts in this diagram are referred to as parts of the **tape transport**. As the name suggests, the tape transport is that part of the recorder that's involved with the actual motion of the audio tape as it passes the tape recorder heads. Starting with the tape reels, since the audio tape threads on a recorder from the left to right, the left reel is the **supply reel,** or the **feed reel** (the reel that has audio tape on it as you begin to use the recorder). The right reel is the **take-up reel**, which starts out empty. Behind each reel (inside

the tape recorder) are motors that help drive the tape from one reel to the other and help maintain proper tape tension.

The three standard reel sizes used in radio production facilities—5-inch, 7-inch, and 10½-inch—are shown in Figure 6.7. The 10½-inch reel shown in the diagram has an NAB hub (center) that requires an adapter when used with most recorders. It's important that both the feed reel and the take-up reel be the same size for keeping the audio tape at the proper tension. There is often a reel-size switch on the recorder that the operator should set properly. The small reel setting generally refers to 7-inch or smaller reels, and the large reel setting is for the 10½-inch reels.

The audio tape is kept in line with the tape heads by various tape guides and tension arms. The **tape guides** are usually just stationary pins that provide a track or groove the width of the audio tape. The **tension arms** are generally movable. As the audio tape threads through them, they provide some spring, or tension, against the tape. There is often a tension arm on each side of the tape heads. One of these tension arms is usually an **idler arm**. In addition to providing proper tension on the audio tape, if the tape breaks, this arm drops down into an off position, and the reel-to-reel recorder stops running, so the tape doesn't spill off the feed reel and all over the studio floor.

FIGURE 6.7 Reel sizes of 5-inch, 7-inch, and 10½-inch are used on reel-to-reel recorders. (Image courtesy of Ampex Recording Media Corporation.)

FIGURE 6.8 The audio tape recorder electronics include recording and playback volume controls. (Image courtesy of Studer Revox America, Inc.)

The heart of the tape transport is the capstan and pinch roller. Normally located just to the right of the tape heads, the **capstan** is a metal shaft, and the **pinch roller** is a rubber wheel. The audio tape must pass between these two components. When the recorder is running, the pinch roller holds the tape against the revolving capstan. The capstan controls the speed of the tape as it passes the heads.

The final components of the tape transport are the actual controls of the audio tape recorder. Most recorders have an on/off button, rewind and fast forward buttons, a play button, a stop button, a pause button, a cue button, and a record button. Most of these functions are obvious and merely control the direction and speed of the audio tape through the transport. The cue button allows the tape to stay in contact with the tape heads during rewind and fast forward or even the stop position, so you can aurally find a certain spot on the tape. Usually the tape is lifted away from the heads in the rewind or fast forward position to save wear and tear on the heads. Some tape recorders require the operator to depress both play and record to put the machine into the record mode, but some will go into record when just the record button is pressed.

6.14 TAPE RECORDER ELECTRONICS

The other half of the face of the audio tape recorder involves the electronics of the recorder (see Figure 6.8). These controls include record-level and play-level pots, VU meters, and a source/tape switch. The **record-level pot** (pots, if stereo) adjusts the volume or level of the incoming sound signal. If the signal is being fed from an audio console, there

is a pot, or channel, on the console that also controls the incoming volume. The best recording procedure is to make sure the level indicated on the audio board VU is near 100 percent, and then fine-tune the volume with the record-level pot on the audio tape recorder. The **play-level pot** controls the volume of the sound signal as it's being played from the audio tape. Again, there is also a volume control that adjusts the output volume of the recorder as it plays through the audio console. These pots should adjust closely together so that you don't have the tape recorder pot turned way down and then need to turn the audio console pot for the tape recorder way up to get a good signal level.

The VU meter indicates the signal level, just like the VU meters on the audio console that were presented in Chapter 3, "The Audio Console." What signal you see on the audio tape recorder VU meter is dependent on where the **source/tape switch** is set. The source position is sometimes labeled "record," "input," or "source" and the tape position is sometimes labeled "play," "reproduce," "output," "tape," or "monitor." In the source position, the VU meter shows the volume of the incoming signal at the record amplifier, usually just before the bias current is added. If this switch is set at the tape position, the VU meter shows the output level of the reproduced signal at the playback head, so it only shows an indication of level when you are actually recording.

You can use the source/tape switch to make comparisons between the two levels. If the tape recorder is properly calibrated, there should be very little level change as you switch between the source and tape positions. Some machines, however, have an output level control that isn't calibrated with the input level control, or dirty record or playback heads, so that you shouldn't always expect the two levels to be exactly equal.

Also associated with the electronics of the audio tape recorder are the inputs found on the back of the recorder. Most tape recorders have provisions for plugging other electronic equipment, such as mics and CD players, into them. The main concept to understand for this is the concept of **preamplification**. Some electronic devices, such as CD players and tape recorders, have provisions within them for amplifying their electrical impulses. Others, mainly microphones, do not. If a CD player is plugged into a tape recorder, it should be plugged into the **line-level** input because it has already been preamplified in the CD player. In this way the tape recorder won't amplify the sound again, causing distortion. A microphone, on the other hand, should be plugged into a **mic-level** input that allows the tape recorder to amplify the signal.

Most recorders also have a line-out connector so that the sound from the recorder can be fed to other electronic equipment, such as an audio console. Some recorders also have a speaker-out position so that the sound can be transferred to speakers located away from the recorder. Normally in the radio production facility, the audio tape recorders are patched or wired to the other equipment through the audio console, and the operator doesn't have to worry about the various inputs and outputs.

6.15 REEL-TO-REEL TRACK CONFIGURATION

Another thing to understand about tape recorders is the recording patterns ("tracks") on the audio tape. Various audio tape recorders record differently by using different portions of the tape. There are four different track configurations that conventional reel-to-reel recorders use. They differ in the number of signals put on the $\frac{1}{4}$-inch tape and the placement of the signals. Some recorders are **full-track**; that is, they essentially use the whole $\frac{1}{4}$-inch space to record one signal. This was the first tape recording method developed, and since it is one signal on the whole width of the tape, it's a monophonic recording. Also, full-track recording can occur in only one direction (see Figure 6.9A). In general, the more tape that is used in the recording process, the higher quality the recording will be, so full-track is a high-quality recording method.

There is also **half-track mono** recording on $\frac{1}{4}$-inch tape. In this instance, the tape is recorded on twice. The top is recorded on as the tape moves from left to right. Then the tape is flipped over, what was the bottom half becomes the top half, and it's recorded on. The two signals go in opposite directions because the tape has been flipped (see Figure 6.9B). In no instance is the back of the audio tape recorded on.

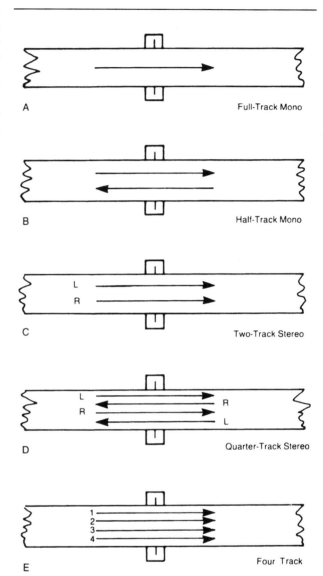

FIGURE 6.9 The reel-to-reel track configurations include: (A) Full-Track Mono; (B) Half-Track Mono; (C) Two-Track Stereo; (D) Quarter-Track Stereo; and (E) Multitrack (Four-Track, shown here).

Most recorders used in radio production today are stereo or multitrack. Stereo can use $\frac{1}{4}$-inch tape, but it requires two tracks for each recording—one for the right channel and one for the left channel. When recording in **two-track stereo** (sometimes called **half-track stereo**), each of the two tracks uses half the tape, and both go in the same direction. One track is for the right channel, and one track is for the left channel (see Figure 6.9C). Recording can only be done in one direction on this tape because the two tracks use the entire width of the audio tape. This is probably the most common recording method found in the radio production facility.

Many home recorders (and some professional ones) use a **quarter-track stereo** recording method. Tracks one and three (the top one and the next-to-bottom one) are used for the first side, going from left to right. Then the tape is flipped and tracks two and four become one and three and are recorded. The two recordings go in opposite directions (see Figure 6.9D). The track widths naturally have to be narrower, since four actual tracks have to fit on the $\frac{1}{4}$-inch audio tape.

Multitrack recorders are becoming more and more common in the radio production facility. For example, a **four-track recorder** uses four separate tracks all going in one direction (see Figure 6.9E). Although a few machines use $\frac{1}{4}$-inch tape for the four tracks, most multitrack recorders use $\frac{1}{2}$-inch or wider audio tape. Multitrack recorders used in radio are normally four- or eight-track, and the recording studio may employ recorders with sixteen, twenty-four, thirty-two, and more tracks. Obviously, at some point in the production process the multitracked signal is mixed down to stereo or mono for broadcast. Multitrack recording will be discussed further in Chapter 10, "Multitrack Production Techniques." Four-track recording should not be confused with quarter-track recording. Both use four tracks, but a review of each description will show they are quite different.

6.16 CROSSTALK AND COMPATIBILITY

All the stereo and multitrack recording heads have **guard bands**—spaces between each track that provide small portions of blank tape between each track and at the edges to prevent crosstalk. **Crosstalk** occurs when the signal from one track is picked up simultaneously with the signal from an adjacent track. For example, if the record and play-

back heads on a quarter-track recorder were misaligned, you might hear part of side 2 (playing backward) when listening to side 1 because the right channel tracks are adjacent to each other, and the misalignment is causing crosstalk.

Another important consideration is compatibility. Quarter-inch tapes recorded on one machine can play on a different machine. In other words, a tape recorded on a quarter-track stereo machine can be played on a full-track mono recorder. All the tracks will be heard. However, there will be recorded material going both forward and backward, and the resulting sound will be a garble. If the stereo tape were recorded only on one side, then playback on the mono full track would be intelligible, but, of course, it would not be stereo and probably would have some hiss noises from nonrecorded sections. Certainly the best production practice would be not to mix track configurations, even though some are compatible to a degree.

6.17 THE CARTRIDGE TAPE RECORDER

Another type of tape recorder is the **cartridge recorder** shown in Figure 6.10. The cart machine gained favor in broadcast use because it cued up automatically. For years, many commercials, public service announcements, station promos, and jingles that you heard on the radio were being played from tape cartridge recorders. For some radio stations, even the music was transferred from record or CD to cartridge.

A tape cartridge recorder requires no threading; you simply slip the audio tape cartridge into a machine. Cart machines operate at $7\frac{1}{2}$ IPS and use $\frac{1}{4}$-inch tape. The track configuration of the cartridge recorder is similar to some that you're now familiar with; when cartridge tape is recorded, however, a cart tape head can put a **cue tone** on the tape that can't be heard. This primary cue tone is just in

FIGURE 6.10 The cartridge recorder and player once played a major role in delivering the commercials, PSAs, promos, jingles, and music heard on radio. (Image courtesy of International Tapetronics Corporation.)

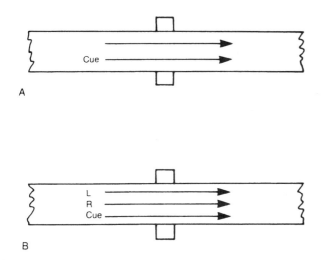

FIGURE 6.11 Mono and stereo audio cartridge tape track configurations.

FIGURE 6.12 The audio cartridge contains an endless loop of audio tape within a plastic shell. (Image courtesy of Fidelipac Corporation.)

front of the recorded information so that when the machine is running (in play), the special tone signals the machine to stop before it repeats itself. This automatic re-cueing also allows for putting several different spots on one cartridge and playing one without fear of playing another before stopping the machine. Most cart machines can also put secondary and tertiary cue tones on the cartridge that can be used to indicate the end of a spot, to start another cart machine, to engage warning lights in the studio, and to activate other programming features often found in automated situations.

A mono tape cartridge recorder has two tracks—one for the recorded material and one for the cue tones (see Figure 6.11A). A stereo tape cartridge has three tracks—one for the left and right channel and one for the cue tones (see Figure 6.11B). Mono and stereo tape cartridges are not compatible. Although you may be able to play a cartridge recorded in stereo on a mono machine or vice versa, it's likely that the tracks will be misaligned, and you won't hear all of the audio signal, or there will be problems in picking up the cue tone. Good production practice dictates that mono and stereo cartridges are clearly labeled and not mixed between various tape decks. Tape carts record in only one direction. Tape cartridge machines can be either record/play or play-only. The play-only machines still have two heads in them, but one is a dummy that merely keeps the tape tension correct as the audio tape passes the heads.

It's also very important to notice that cartridge tape recorders don't have erase heads in them. Tape carts must be erased using a bulk eraser, or **degausser**. This is merely a strong electromagnet that radiates a magnetic field that erases any audio tape brought near it when it's turned on. More will be said about the degausser in a later chapter (see section 8.18, Tape Degaussers, in Chapter 8, "Monitor Speakers, Cables, Connectors, and Studio Accessories).

6.18 AUDIO TAPE CARTRIDGES

The audio tape cartridge is constructed as a plastic container with an endless loop of tape. The tape is wound onto the center spool with the end next to the spool sticking up so that when the tape is cut from the master reel, it can be spliced to that end, thus making a continuous loop (see Figure 6.12). The tape pulls from the inside and winds on the outside of the spool. Some carts employ tape guides that the tape goes past and pressure pads to control tension and alignment; others use a design that eliminates the need for pressure pads.

The recording tape used in a cartridge machine is $\frac{1}{4}$ inch wide, but it's a special type that has a lubricant on both sides rather than just the oxide side. The tape is wound on the spool so that the oxide side is facing out, away from the spool. To see if the tape on the cartridge is good, simply look at the oxide side of the tape through the holes on the front side of the cartridge. If the tape is shiny, it's worn (little oxide on it), but if the tape is dull, it probably has quite a bit of oxide left. Often before the tape gives out, the **pressure pads** will. To check the pressure pads on a tape cartridge, just press in on them (go under the tape so that oil from your fingertips doesn't get on the tape); if they tend to stay down and don't spring back, the tape cartridge won't play the tape properly because the pressure pads keep the tape pressed against the tape heads.

FIGURE 6.13 Of all the analog tape recorders, the broadcast-quality cassette recorder is the most useful in the production studio today. (Image courtesy of TASCAM Division, TEAC America, Inc.)

6.19 THE CASSETTE TAPE RECORDER

The **cassette recorder** has found its way into the broadcast facility mainly because of its portability and ease of use, but also because the modern, high-quality cassette recorder offers recording quality that often exceeds that of reel-to-reel recorders. Tape machines like the one shown in Figure 6.13 are commonly found in the radio studio. Portable units are also used, primarily in the news area, to record events or conduct interviews. From time to time, however, a cassette recorder is also handy for production work. For example, you might not have a sound effect that you need on record or CD, but you can easily record your own on a portable cassette.

One of the reasons the cassette tape became popular is that it doesn't have to be threaded onto the machine as the reel-to-reel does. Just pop the audio tape cassette in the machine, and you're ready to record. Cassette tape is $^1/_8$-inch wide, so it can never be played back on a $^1/_4$-inch reel-to-reel recorder. There are two basic cassette tape recording methods. One is half-track mono, which is like half-track mono on a $^1/_4$-inch tape except that it records the bottom of the tape first (see Figure 6.14A). The other recording method for cassettes is quarter-track stereo. This is not the same as $^1/_4$-inch quarter-track stereo (review Figure 6.9D); rather, the bottom two tracks are used for one side going in a left-to-right direction. When the tape is turned over, the top two tracks are the bottom two, so they're recorded going in the opposite direction (see Figure 6.14B). Cassettes were designed this way so that mono and stereo cassettes would be compatible.

There are numerous cassette recorders available. Many are only suitable for home use and not the broadcast studio. Most portable cassette recorders have a built-in microphone. Avoid using this mic for broadcast work because it often picks up as much internal noise (tape recorder motor, etc.) as the sound you want. Use a good-quality mic like those mentioned earlier in Chapter 4, "Microphones." Some other features that should be part of a professional-quality cassette machine are a VU meter, three heads (rather than two), standard mic inputs, and durable construction.

FIGURE 6.14 Cassette track configurations for mono and stereo recording.

FIGURE 6.15 The internal structure of an audio cassette tape.

6.20 CASSETTE TAPES

The **cassette** tape is a small $^1/_8$-inch reel-to-reel tape housed in a plastic case (see Figure 6.15). A short **leader tape** is attached at each end, and both ends of the tape are permanently attached to the reels. When recording onto cassettes, it's important to remember the leader tape, because if you're at the very beginning of the cassette, the actual recording will not begin for a few seconds, until you are past the leader tape.

Another feature of the cassette is the knock-out tabs on the back edge of the cassette shell. These two little plastic tabs (one for each side of the cassette) allow the recorder to go into the record mode. If you wish to save an important cassette and be sure no one records over the tape, you can knock out the tab. If at a later date you want to record on this cassette, you can put a small piece of cellophane tape over the hole where the tab was, and it will work just as if the tab was there. The audio tape in a cassette is often quite thin so that 30, 60, and 90 minutes of recording time (both sides) can be fit into the plastic shell.

6.21 TAPE RECORDER MAINTENANCE

Most tape recorder maintenance that a production person might be expected to handle is related to the heads themselves. The most common problem is, simply, dirty heads. Tape heads can become dirty just from day-to-day use, and, as you'll see in Chapter 7, "Audio Editing," editing audio tape can put unwanted grease-pencil marks on the heads. It's good production practice to clean the tape heads before you begin any production work. The production studio usually has a supply of cotton swabs and head cleaner or denatured alcohol to gently clean any residue off the tape recorder heads. If in doubt about what you're doing, ask for help.

One reason for keeping the tape path clean is to prevent wow and flutter. Both wow and flutter are tape recorder problems that are related to changes in the speed of the tape as it passes through the tape transport. **Wow** refers to slow variations in tape speed, and **flutter** refers to rapid variations. Both problems result in off-pitch sounds that are reflected in their names.

A final tape recorder maintenance concern is a buildup of magnetism on the tape recorder heads. After extended use, the tape heads will tend to become magnetized permanently. This could result in the heads actually erasing part of the signal that you don't want erased. Usually it will affect the high-frequency signals first. To prevent this, a **demagnetizer** is used to get rid of any built-up magnetism. Usually this is part of the general maintenance done by the engineer, but in some production facilities this type of maintenance, along with cleaning of the heads, is left to the operators. A demagnetizer is brought near to (but not in contact with) the heads, guides, and other metallic parts in the tape path. Since it operates like a bulk eraser, you must be sure to turn it on and off away from the heads.

6.22 CONCLUSIONS

Turntables and audio tape recorders were the primary workhorses in most radio stations for years. With the advent of digital equipment and the quality and convenience they offer, older analog equipment's use continues to diminish. However, many studios still use some of this equipment, and a good solid background about the main analog components will not hurt your future production studio work.

Self-Study

■ QUESTIONS

1. Which of the following could be a proper head arrangement for an audio tape recorder, assuming the tape goes from left to right?
   a) erase–record–play
   b) record–erase–play
   c) play–record–erase
   d) erase–play–record

2. If you put a 5-inch reel of tape on a reel-to-reel recorder at $7\frac{1}{2}$ IPS, another 5-inch reel on a recorder at 15 IPS, and a third 5-inch reel on a recorder at $3\frac{3}{4}$ IPS, and start all the recorders at once, which one will run out of tape first?
   a) the reel at $3\frac{3}{4}$ IPS
   b) the reel at $7\frac{1}{2}$ IPS
   c) the reel at 15 IPS
   d) they would all run out of tape at the same time

3. Which of the following prevents crosstalk?
   a) sel sync
   b) the pinch roller
   c) leader tape
   d) guard bands

4. A sel sync feature in an audio tape recorder _____.
   a) makes the record head act as a play head
   b) places the erase head after the play head
   c) converts a two-head recorder to a three-head recorder
   d) converts a two-track recorder to a quarter-track recorder

5. Of the tapes in the diagram below, tape B would probably be used on a _____.
   a) cassette recorder
   b) reel-to-reel recorder
   c) cartridge recorder
   d) none of the above

6. The erase head _____.
   a) rearranges the iron particles, so they're in a random pattern
   b) is on during the recording process
   c) closes the gap on the metal core, so the signal jumps to magnetic energy
   d) rearranges the iron particles analogous to the original sound

7. Which of the following represents half-track mono recording?

8. Which of the following is an adjustment that changes the amount of amplification given to highs and lows of the sound signal?
   a) digital
   b) bias
   c) equalization
   d) sel sync

9. Which of the following represents quarter-track stereo recording?

10. Referring to Figure 6.6, which of the following controls the speed of the tape as it passes the head?
    a) feed reel
    b) tape guide
    c) capstan
    d) take-up reel

11. What would happen if a two-track stereo tape were played back on a half-track mono recorder?
    a) both stereo tracks would be heard, but one would be going backward
    b) the tape would be intelligible, but the lower track's material would be missing
    c) four sounds would be heard—two going forward and two going backward
    d) no sound would be heard

12. If the source/tape switch on a tape recorder is in the source position, the VU meter shows _____.
    a) a zero signal
    b) the outgoing signal that has been recorded
    c) the signal that was erased
    d) the incoming signal that is being recorded

13. Which of the following represents half-track mono cassette recording?

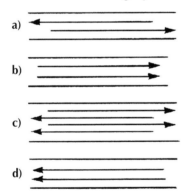

14. What would happen if a stereo cassette recorded on both sides were played on a mono cassette recorder?
    a) two sounds would be heard, one going forward and one going backward
    b) the stereo tape would be intelligible but would not be stereo
    c) there would be a garbled sound
    d) there would be no sound since they're not compatible

15. One difference between a cassette recorder and a cartridge recorder is _____.
    a) a cartridge recorder needs to be threaded
    b) only cassette recorders are used in radio stations
    c) the cartridge tape has no actual beginning or end
    d) only cassette recorders have separate record and play heads

16. Which type of tape must be erased with a degausser?
    a) reel-to-reel
    b) cassette
    c) cartridge
    d) DAT

17. If a tape has a cue tone on it, it will _____.
   a) start automatically
   b) stop automatically
   c) repeat itself
   d) not record

18. To begin a record (or any sound source) with the volume control turned down is to _____.
   a) cue the record
   b) wow the record
   c) dead air the record
   d) dead roll the record

19. Which of the following is a function of the turntable?
   a) spinning a record at the proper speed
   b) allowing the cartridge/stylus to move freely across the record
   c) amplifying the signal
   d) none of the above

20. Which part of the turntable changes vibrations into variations in voltage?
   a) cartridge
   b) stylus
   c) diamond tip
   d) tone arm

■ ANSWERS

If You Answered A:

1a. Right. And this is the most common head arrangement for broadcast recorders.
2a. No. (Reread 6.11.)
3a. Wrong. (Reread 6.9 and 6.16.)
4a. Right. This feature allows you to hear previously recorded material that matches with what you are recording.
5a. Yes. It is $\frac{1}{8}$-inch wide, so it would be used on a cassette.
6a. No. It rearranges them into an orderly pattern. (Reread 6.10.)
7a. No. The signals must go in opposite directions. (Reread 6.15.)
8a. No. This is a recording technique using binary technology. (Reread 6.10.)
9a. Right. You figured the tracks correctly.
10a. Wrong. This is the reel that the tape is placed on, but it doesn't really control tape recorder speed. (Reread 6.13.)
11a. No. At first glance, this looks logical, but it's not. A half-track mono only plays back half a tape at a time. If it played back the full track, it would play back both sounds of its own tapes. All that is played back is the top half of the tape. (Reread 6.15 and 6.16.)
12a. No. There would be a reading on the VU meter. (Reread 6.14.)
13a. Correct. This is the same configuration as $\frac{1}{4}$-inch half-track mono.
14a. No. (Review Figure 6.14; reread 6.19.)
15a. No. Neither needs to be threaded. (Reread 6.17 to 6.20.)
16a. No. A reel-to-reel recorder has an erase head that can erase right before new material is recorded. (Reread 6.17.)
17a. No. It must be started by hand. (Reread 6.17.)
18a. No. To cue a record is to prepare it for air play, but this doesn't describe what's happening here. (Reread 6.6 and the Production Tip for this chapter.)
19a. Correct. This is a function of the turntable.
20a. Right. It's the cartridge that converts vibrations into voltage.

If You Answered B:

1b. No. Erase must be before record. (Reread 6.8.)
2b. No. (Reread 6.11.)
3b. Wrong. (Reread 6.13 and 6.16.)

4b. No. You can't move the heads, and you wouldn't want that configuration. (Reread 6.8 and 6.9.)

5b. No. (Reread 6.15 and 6.20.)

6b. Right. It is on so that the tape can be erased before it's recorded on again.

7b. No. This is, if anything, backward full-track. (Reread 6.15.)

8b. No. Bias improves frequency response and provides a distortion-free signal. (Reread 6.10.)

9b. No. (Reread 6.15. Pay particular attention to which tracks are used in which direction.)

10b. No. This guides the tape through the recorder mechanism but not at any particular speed. (Reread 6.13.)

11b. Your answer is correct; half-track mono only plays back the top half of the tape.

12b. No. The tape position would do that. (Reread 6.14.)

13b. No. This is like two-track stereo on ¼-inch tape. (Reread 6.15 and 6.19.)

14b. Right. Cassette mono tape and stereo tape can each be played on the other recorder and be understood.

15b. No. In fact, cart machines are more common in radio stations than cassettes. (Reread 6.17 to 6.20.)

16b. No. A cassette recorder has an erase head that can erase right before new material is recorded. (Reread 6.17.)

17b. Right. Because of the cue tone, it will stop automatically before whatever is next can play.

18b. Wrong. Wow is an off-speed problem associated with records, but it's not this situation. (Reread 6.6 and the Production Tip for this chapter.)

19b. You're close. The tone arm (which is part of a turntable) houses the cartridge/stylus and allows them to move across the record. (Reread 6.2 and 6.4.)

20b. No. The stylus picks up vibrations. (Reread 6.4.)

If You Answered C:

1c. No. Erase must be before record. (Reread 6.8.)

2c. That's right. It goes through the recorder the fastest and so would finish first.

3c. Wrong. (Reread 6.16 and 6.20.)

4c. Wrong. Adding a head is a much more complex process. (Reread 6.8 and 6.9.)

5c. No. (Reread 6.15, 6.18, and 6.20.)

6c. Wrong. This answer really doesn't make sense. You are probably confused about many of the terms in this chapter. (Reread the entire chapter.)

7c. Good. Your answer is correct.

8c. You are correct.

9c. No. (Reread 6.15. Pay particular attention to which tracks are used in which direction.)

10c. Right. This, in conjunction with the pinch roller, pulls the tape through at a uniform speed.

11c. No. There are only two tracks on two-track stereo, so it couldn't play back four. (Review Figure 6.9; reread 6.15 and 6.16.)

12c. No. Nothing shows the signal erased. (Reread 6.14 very carefully.)

13c. No. You are way off; this has four tracks. (Reread 6.15 and 6.19.)

14c. No. (Review Figure 6.14; reread 6.19.)

15c. Right. The cartridge tape is a continuous loop.

16c. Right. A cartridge machine has no erase head.

17c. No. The purpose of the cue tone is to prevent the tape from repeating itself. (Reread 6.17.)

18c. Wrong. You're close because dead air equals silence, but it's not this situation. (Reread 6.6.)

19c. No. A turntable itself doesn't amplify. Amplification is done through the preamplifier and audio console. (Reread 6.2 and 6.3.)

20c. No. This is part of the stylus. (Reread 6.4.)

If You Answered D:

1d. No. This is not a common head arrangement. (Reread 6.8.)

2d. You might be confused because they all have the same size reel, but you're not correct. (Reread 6.11.)

3d. Right. Guard bands prevent crosstalk.

4d. Wrong. Some recorders do have a switch to accomplish this, but it has nothing to do with sel sync. (Reread 6.9 and 6.15.)

5d. Wrong. One of the other answers is correct. (Reread 6.15, 6.18, and 6.20.)

6d. No. You're getting this confused with the record head. (Reread 6.10.)

7d. No. You're not correct. (Reread 6.15.)

8d. Wrong. This allows you to record one track in synchronization with a previously recorded track. (Reread 6.9 and 6.10.)

9d. No. This is multitrack recording, in this case four-track. (Reread 6.15.)

10d. No. As the tape goes past the heads it is taken up by this reel, but it doesn't really control the speed. (Reread 6.13.)

11d. Wrong. Although there is not full compatibility between two-track stereo and half-track mono, some sound would be heard. (Reread 6.15 and 6.16.)

12d. Correct. "Source" shows the source.

13d. No. This is not the correct track configuration. (Reread 6.15 and 6.19.)

14d. No. Stereo and mono cassettes are compatible. (Reread 6.19.)

15d. Wrong. Both cartridge and cassette recorders can have separate play and record heads. (Reread 6.17 to 6.20.)

16d. Wrong. DAT tape is erased during the recording process. (Reread 6.17.)

17d. No. A cue tone would not prevent a tape from being recorded. (Reread 6.17.)

18d. Yes. This describes a dead roll.

19d. No. There is a function of the turntable listed. (Reread 6.2.)

20d. No. (Reread 6.4.)

Projects

■ PROJECT 1

Dub taped material between cassette and reel-to-reel recorders.

Purpose

To make sure you are able to do even, clear dubbing, which is a common task in production work.

Advice, Cautions, and Background

1. The material you are to dub (which can be taken from the CD-ROM that accompanies this text) was *not* recorded properly in that it is not all at the same level. You are to make it as much at the same level as possible. On professional equipment, there are sophisticated meters to help you. On less expensive equipment, you will have to do this by practicing a few times and getting the feel of it.

2. If you're unsure of what you're doing, get help. Don't ruin the equipment.

How to Do the Project

1. Make sure you know how to operate your cassette recorder. If in doubt, ask the instructor.

2. In the same way, make sure you know how to operate the reel-to-reel recorder.

3. Transfer the material from the CD-ROM to your reel-to-reel recorder without making any level adjustments. If you have difficulty with this, ask your instructor for help.

4. Listen to the material, noting where the level changes are, and decide on a strategy for dubbing it so that it's all at one level.

5. Rewind the tape, and connect the cable from the proper audio output on the reel-to-reel to the proper audio input on the cassette recorder. If your equipment is already connected through an audio console, just be sure the switches and knobs are set properly so that you can record from reel-to-reel to cassette.

6. Place a tape in the cassette recorder.

7. Put the reel-to-reel recorder in play. Monitor the recording, and, at the same time, adjust the volume on one of the recorders so the level will be even.

8. Rewind the reel-to-reel recorder, and set the cassette recorder so that it will record and the reel-to-reel recorder so that it will play. The sound will then go from the reel-to-reel to the cassette recorder.

9. Practice your dub several times, adjusting levels until you get the feel of how much you need to vary the volume. Then make the dub.

10. Now you're ready to make your dub from cassette back to the reel-to-reel recorder. Place a different tape on the reel-to-reel recorder.

11. If necessary, change cables so that one goes from the proper audio output on the cassette to the proper audio input on the reel-to-reel. (Again, you may just have to set the proper switches and knobs on your audio console.)

12. Decide on a volume for both recorders, and put the cassette recorder in play and the reel-to-reel recorder in record.
13. Make your dub. This time you shouldn't have to adjust levels. Listen to the dub to make sure it recorded properly.
14. Label the tape with your name and TAPE DUB. Turn it in to the instructor to get credit for this project.

■ PROJECT 2

Record several generations of an audio signal, using analog and digital recording processes.

Purpose

To enable you to hear the loss of signal quality inherent in the analog recording process, but not in digital.

Advice, Cautions, and Background

1. This project assumes that you have a DAT or other digital recorder in your production facility. If you don't, you can still do the exercise, using only analog recorders. Compare the dubbed sound with the original CD sound.
2. As you make the analog recordings, watch the levels and other elements that might introduce a poor quality recording due to operator error.

How to Do the Project

1. Review the material on digital recorders and recording in Chapter 5, "Digital Audio Players/Recorders."
2. Use a CD as your original sound source or use music on the accompanying CD-ROM.
3. Make a dub of the music onto an analog audio tape recorder. This will be the first-generation recording.
4. Now, using *the tape that you just made* as the sound source, make another analog tape recording. This will be the second-generation recording.
5. Now, using *the second-generation recording* as the sound source, make another dub, or a third-generation recording.
6. Listen to and compare the three recordings you just made with the original sound source (the CD). You should notice a loss of sound quality plus increased noise and distortion, among other things.
7. Repeat steps 2 through 6, using a digital audio recorder.
8. Listen to and compare the digital recordings with the original sound source.
9. Write a one-page report that summarizes what you feel are the differences between the analog and digital recordings.
10. Turn in your report labeled ANALOG/DIGITAL RECORDING and both the analog and digital recordings to your instructor to receive credit for completing this project.

CHAPTER SEVEN

Audio Editing

Information

7.1 INTRODUCTION

From creating a music bed to adding sound effects to editing out vocal "fluffs," or mistakes, audio editing is a day-to-day part of radio production work and it's one of the more important skills you need to learn as a radio production person. Because of the use of digital equipment, the techniques for audio **editing** are changing, but an understanding of *both* digital audio editing and "old-fashioned" audio tape splicing is important. And lest you think you're learning outdated skills, many of the basic procedures of audio tape editing are the same, whether you're using "cut and splice" methods or manipulating a mouse.

7.2 REASONS FOR EDITING

Why edit audio tape? The answers are relatively obvious. For example, rarely will you produce the vocal track for a commercial exactly the way you want it on the first try. Editing gives you the ability to eliminate mistakes. While you could record a script over and over until you got it perfect, it's more likely you'll get part of it great on one take, part of it great on another, and so on. The best take will probably be bits and pieces from various takes that you edit to take out fluffs and bad segments and keep only the exact words and phrases you want. Other production work may require you to edit out excessive pauses or "uhs" from an interview or language not allowed by the FCC from a piece of news tape.

In addition to eliminating mistakes, editing allows you to decrease the length of production work. Radio requires exact times for commercials, news stories, and other programs, and editing can keep your work to the exact lengths required. You can either manually edit out excessive pauses in a vocal track or, in some instances, utilize digital audio editing software to automatically "time compress" a vocal segment to the exact length you need.

Audio editing also allows you to record out of sequence. For example, you might be putting together a commercial that uses the testimonial of several customers, and the one that you want to use first in your commercial may not have been recorded first. Editing allows you to easily rearrange the order or use just a portion of what you actually taped.

7.3 TYPES OF EDITING

There are traditionally two terms associated with audio editing: splicing and dubbing. **Splice editing** normally

---

**Production Tip #7—
"Destructive Vs. Nondestructive Editing"**

The two most common methods for manipulating audio once it has been brought into a digital or computer system are **linear** and **nonlinear**. The linear mode is a "destructive" form of editing because the software makes physical changes to the data as the editing is accomplished. Each editing action is performed on the original soundfile in sequential order, writing the processed data to a new soundfile that represents the edited audio. With a linear or destructive system, the edited audio can be heard only after the audio has been processed and written to the hard drive. Destructive is a little misleading, for although the original audio data is ultimately altered, these editing systems do have an UNDO feature that lets data be restored. To do so, however, requires copying and saving large amounts of the original data during the editing process. This not only eats up lots of computer storage space on the hard drive, but also requires more time to accomplish the edits.

Nonlinear or nondestructive systems use pointers to tag the original audio and mark where the edits take place. To edit out a portion of an audio soundfile, a pointer at the beginning and end of the edit would instruct the software program to skip the deleted section of audio during playback. Essentially, you manipulate the pointers that are linked to the original data. Playback occurs immediately and the audio on the hard drive remains intact.

refers to physically cutting audio tape, taking a portion out, and splicing the remaining pieces back together. It's almost always done with a reel-to-reel recorder because the tape in other recorders, such as a cart or cassette, is essentially inaccessible. **Dub editing** refers to editing in which portions of one tape are copied onto another tape. Although splicing and dubbing have been the standard ways to edit audio tape, digital audio editing is the most common form of editing in the modern production studio. **Digital audio editing** refers to any system that uses computer software to manipulate audio with either a PC computer or proprietary editing equipment.

7.4 DIGITAL AUDIO EDITING

In Chapter 2, "Digital Audio Production," you became familiar with various types of digital editing equipment from desk-top editing systems to digital audio workstations. Editing normally begins after you've recorded some audio into whichever type of system you're using. There are many different systems currently available for digital editing; however, there is no one standard technique for doing so. To gain an understanding of digital audio editing, we'll look at one system (see Figure 7.1) that uses a PC compatible computer, digital sound card, and a multitrack digital editor program—*Cool Edit Pro.*

To illustrate the basic audio edit, let's record three words—*dog, cat, banana*—into our system. To begin recording, click on FILE from the "Options Menu," select NEW, click the appropriate recording specifications (for example, sample rate = 44,100, channels = stereo, resolution = 16-bit), and then click on OK. We'll assume you have a microphone plugged directly into your sound card or the output of your audio console feeds into the sound card. Click on the RECORD button (red circle) on the "Transport" controls and speak the three words into the mic, pausing slightly between each word. Finally, click on the STOP button (gray square) on the "Transport" controls. The audio you recorded will appear as a green waveform (see Figure 7.2) on the black background in the "Waveform Display" area of the screen. Silence (the pauses) will be shown as a flat green line.

Even though some procedures and some terminology will be different, many of the basic principles would apply to any equipment that's capable of digital audio editing. Much like dealing with the audio console, an understanding of one editing program will give you a good idea for the operation of most of the other available programs.

If you wanted to edit out the word *cat*, you would click an edit point just to the left of the waveform for the word *cat* and then drag the mouse to the right, stopping just before the waveform for the word *banana*. Including the "pause" after the word maintains the natural pacing of the

FIGURE 7.1 With the digital audio editor you can instantly cut, paste, copy, and otherwise manipulate audio with a few mouse clicks. (Image courtesy of Syntrillium Software Corporation.)

FIGURE 7.2 The waveform display of the digital audio editor shows a visual representation of the audio. (Image courtesy of Syntrillium Software Corporation.)

audio. Selecting edit points just before and immediately after the word *cat* would increase the pause between *dog* and *banana*. In a similar manner, selecting edit points just after the word *dog* and just before the word *banana* would eliminate any pause between those words, creating an unnatural flow to the words. The area you have selected will become "highlighted" in white (refer to Figure 7.2). You can hear the audio segment you've highlighted by clicking on the PLAY button (single, green forward triangle). If you need to adjust either edit point, hold down the SHIFT key and click on the edit point. Move the edit point left or right as required. Most editor programs have a function to zoom in on the segment of audio you're working on to fine-tune any adjustments and get the mark exactly where you want it. To complete the edit, click on EDIT on the "Options Menu" and select CUT or click on the appropriate "Toolbar" icon. The selected audio will be cut to a clipboard and the remaining audio will automatically "heal" or be joined together leaving the words *dog* and *banana*. It takes a lot longer to explain this process than it does to accomplish—as you'll quickly learn!

Suppose you now want to put the word *cat*, which we just edited out, in front of the word *dog*. Simply click a single edit point just to the left of the waveform of the word *dog*, then click on EDIT on the "Options Menu" and select PASTE. The audio from the clipboard will be edited back in at that point so the word order is now *cat*, *dog*, and *banana*. Should you decide you don't really want to do this, you can click on FILE and select an UNDO command that will cancel or undo your last action. Normally, UNDO can be repeated to back out of several actions if necessary.

You'll find that regardless of what audio editor you're using, it's capable of a lot more than these few simple operations. We've only touched the surface of what a digital audio editor can do, but it should be obvious, when comparing this procedure with the steps involved in traditional

splicing explained later in this chapter, that digital audio editing is the more accurate, quicker, and easier technique. The best way to learn what an editor can do is to try different things and, of course, reading the manual or HELP screens doesn't hurt either. Most digital audio editors also feature multitrack and signal processing capabilities, which we'll look at in Chapter 9, "Signal Processing Equipment" and Chapter 10, "Multitrack Production Techniques."

7.5 SPLICE EDITING: TOOLS OF THE TRADE

The basic tools of the trade for splicing are a grease pencil, a splicing block, a razor blade, and splicing tape. A white or yellow **grease pencil**, or **china marker**, is used to physically mark on the tape the points where you're going to cut. The side of the audio tape that is marked is the back (outside) or unrecorded side. When marking, make sure none of the grease pencil gets on the tape recorder heads or on the front (recorded) side of the tape, because the crayon-like substance in a grease pencil can clog the head gap.

A **splicing block** is a small metal or plastic block (see Figure 7.3) with a channel to hold the audio tape and two grooves to guide the razor blade when cutting the tape. The channel has tiny lips at its edges so that the audio tape snaps down into it. The tape can easily be slid in the channel by the operator, but it won't move on its own. The cutting grooves are usually at 45-degree and 90-degree angles to the audio tape. For almost all production work, you'll use the diagonal cut. Although broadcast supply companies offer industrial-grade razor blades, almost any standard *single-edged* razor blade will work for cutting audio tape. Be careful! Razor blades are sharp and will cut your fingers as easily as they cut audio tape.

Splicing tape is commercially available and is specially designed so that its adhesive material does not soak through the audio tape and gum up the heads of the tape recorder. Never use cellophane tape or other office tape to do editing work. Splicing tape is slightly narrower than audio tape ($^7/_{32}$ inch versus $^1/_4$ inch) so that any excess adhesive material will not protrude beyond the edge of the audio tape. In addition to rolls of splicing tape, you can get splicing tabs—precut pieces of splicing tape on applicator strips, designed to make the splicing process easier.

7.6 MARKING EDIT POINTS

Audio tape editing is really a two-step process: marking the edit points and then splicing. Since audio tape passes through the recorder from left to right, sounds are recorded on the tape in the same manner. For example, the phrase "editing is really a two-step process" would be recorded on audio tape in this manner: "ssecorp pets-owt a yllaer si gnitide." The sounds of the letters would appear on the tape just as they do on this page, looking at them left to right, but the rightmost word ("editing") would be recorded first. If we wanted to edit out the word "really" in this phrase, we would make two edit points, one on each side of the word. The edit point is always made in front of the word (or sound) that you wish to edit out on the one side and in front of the word (or sound) that you're leaving in on the other side. It's important that you always mark in front of words to maintain the proper phrasing of the speech, as we explained previously.

You already know (from the previous chapter) that the heads in an audio tape recorder and their functions are signified by "ERP" or "erase-record-play." For marking purposes, you are only concerned with the playback head, because this is where you'll make your marks. Look at the

FIGURE 7.3 A splicing block is one of the tools used in audio tape editing. (Image courtesy of Xedit Corporation.)

heads on the recorder that you'll be doing your editing on (see Figure 7.4). Find the playback head, and then find the dead center of that head. Remember that audio tape will be covering the actual head gap, so look for some kind of reference above and below this portion of the head that will allow you to find this spot consistently. Now take "AIM." Every time you make an edit mark, make it slightly *to the right* of dead center. (Marking to the right compensates for the split second it takes you to actually press the stop button when listening to the audio tape to find where to make an edit.) You can also cue to your edit point by manually rocking the tape reels back and forth with the recorder in the stop position—that is, "scrubbing" the tape to find an exact sound. What you are doing is establishing an "*actual indicator mark*"! Your AIM will be exactly the same time after time, and that means your edits will be the same time after time. Your goal should be to make the same edit over and over and have each one sound the same. That is uniformity in editing, and that's a skill you want.

7.7 STEPS IN SPLICING TECHNIQUE

If you've marked the audio tape at two points, it's time to perform the actual splice. Normal splicing technique follows these steps:

A. *Position the tape at the first edit mark in the splicing block.* (See Figure 7.5A.) Remember, the unrecorded side of the tape should be facing up in the splicing block, and the edit mark should be exactly at the 45-degree cutting groove. The diagonal groove is used for splicing for two reasons. First, it provides more surface for contact with the splicing tape at the point of the edit, and thus a stronger bond or splice is made. Second, and more importantly, the diagonal cut provides a smoother sound transition. For example, if you are splicing together two pieces of music, rather than an abrupt change from one piece to another at the edit (such as a 90-degree splice would produce), you have a short blend of the music pieces at the edit.

B. *Cut the tape at your first mark.* (See Figure 7.5B.) It isn't necessary to saw away with the razor blade or apply excessive downward pressure. A simple slicing motion with the blade through the groove should cut the tape

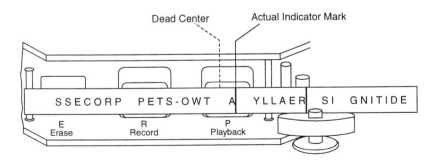

FIGURE 7.4 Audio tape editing requires marking the tape at the play head.

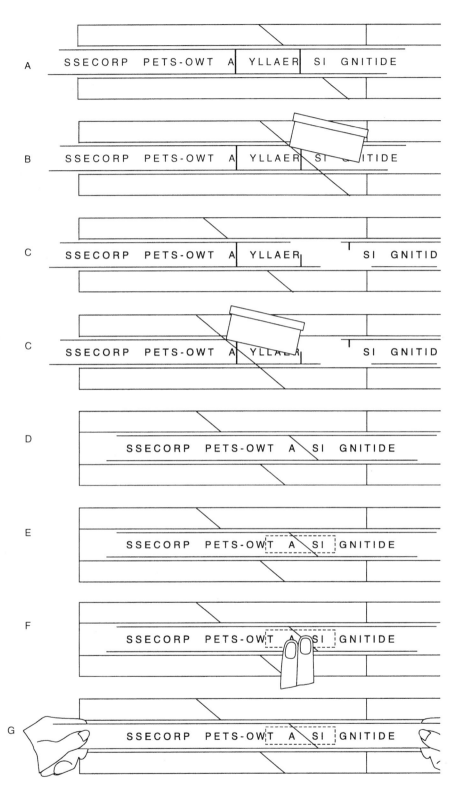

FIGURE 7.5 To edit audio tape: (A) Position tape at first edit mark. (B) Cut tape at first mark. (C) Position and cut tape at second edit mark. (D) Butt tape ends together. (E) Apply splicing tape. (F) Smooth out splicing tape. (G) Remove tape from splicing block.

cleanly. If a razor blade doesn't slice cleanly through the audio tape, it's already dull and you should get a new one. A ragged cut makes it difficult to align the tape for a good splice. Frequently changing razor blades will also prevent them from becoming magnetized. Because the metal blade cuts through the magnetic layer of the audio tape, over a period of time it will become magnetized, and continued use may put a click on the audio tape or degrade the recorded signal at the point of the edit.

C. *Repeat steps A and B at the second edit mark.* (See Figure 7.5C.) Remove the unwanted piece of audio tape, *but don't discard it yet.* It's good production practice to hang on to cut-out tape until after you're sure the splice has been accomplished as you want it. If you've erred in your AIM, it's possible (although difficult) to splice the cutout piece of tape back in and try the splice again.

D. *Butt the remaining tape ends together.* (See Figure 7.5D.) Move both pieces of the tape slightly left or right so that you don't butt them together directly over the cutting groove.

E. *Apply the splicing tape on the edit.* (See Figure 7.5E.) If you're using splicing tape from a roll, a piece about $3/4$ inch in length is ample. Splicing tabs are precut at the appropriate length. The splicing tape should be centered at the edit. Make sure it's positioned straight along the channel of the splicing block. Remember, the splicing tape is narrower than the audio tape, so it should not protrude over either edge of the audio tape.

F. *Smooth out the splicing tape.* (See Figure 7.5F.) Be sure to get air bubbles out from under the splicing tape for a strong bond. Rubbing your fingernail over the splice will usually take care of this.

G. *Remove the audio tape from the splicing block.* (See Figure 7.5G.) Never remove the audio tape from the splicing block by grasping one end and lifting. The lips on the edges of the channel will damage the audio tape. The proper procedure for removing audio tape from the splicing block is to grasp both ends of the tape just beyond the splicing block, apply slight pressure to the tape by pulling your hands in opposite directions, and lift straight up. The tape will pop out of the block, and you will have completed your splice.

It's best not to fast rewind the tape until you've played it to help secure the splice, so manually wind the tape on the feed reel until you're past the splice. Then, thread the tape on your recorder, and listen to the edited tape. If it came out as you wanted, you can discard the unwanted tape section. Sometimes you may find it necessary to shave a piece of the edit by splicing off one edge or another of the tape. If you've made a good edit mark, you'll rarely have to do this.

7.8 SPLICE DEFECTS

Beginning audio tape editors often encounter problems with their first few splices. These are usually overcome with practice and experience, but it's not uncommon to see splicing errors in manipulating the splicing tape itself and in manipulating the audio tape. (See Figure 7.6 for examples of common splicing problems.) One of the most common problems with splicing tape manipulation is using too much; a piece of splicing tape that's too long is difficult to position properly on the audio tape and makes the tape too stiff at the edit, which prevents proper contact with the tape recorder heads. On the other hand, a piece of splicing tape that's too short may not hold the audio tape together during normal use. Another cause of an edit not holding is the splicing tape being poorly secured on the audio tape. For example, air bubbles or dirt or grease (from fingerprints or excessive marking with the grease pencil) may be under the splicing tape, preventing it from adhering to the audio tape. Other problems arise when the splicing tape is put on crooked; a portion of the splicing tape hangs over the edges of the audio tape, making it impossible for the tape to glide through the tape recorder transport properly.

One of the most common problems with audio tape manipulation during the editing process is leaving a gap as you butt the two tape ends together. Obviously, a gap at the edit point will be heard as an interruption of sound or too long a pause. On the other hand, if you overlap the two tape ends as you butt them together, you'll get the same effect as if you had mismarked the edit point; in other words, the splice won't occur where you thought it would.

7.9 PHYSICAL MAKEUP OF AUDIO TAPE

Audio tape for a radio production person is like paper to a writer. In other words, it's the storage medium on which various ideas are put down and then manipulated. Both the writer and the radio person can erase unwanted segments or edit long segments into shorter, workable concepts, but for the radio person it all starts with getting something onto tape first.

Although we see audio tape as merely a thin ribbon of tape, its physical makeup actually consists of three basic layers: a **plastic base** sandwiched between a **backing layer** and a **magnetic layer** (see Figure 7.7). The back coating provides traction as the audio tape moves through a tape recorder transport, and it also provides protection from tape breakage and print-through.

Print-through is defined as the transfer of the magnetic signal on one layer of tape to the magnetic signal on the next layer of tape either above it or below it on the reel. Think of the sandwich concept again, and visualize a jelly sandwich stacked on top of a peanut butter sandwich. If the jelly soaks through the bottom piece of bread and onto the top piece of bread on the peanut butter sandwich, print-through has occurred. It's most audible when one of the tape layers contains a very loud sound and the adjacent layer contains a soft sound. Although most modern audio

WITH THE AUDIO TAPE

(TAPE ENDS NOT BUTTED TOGETHER LEAVING A "GAP")

(TAPE PIECES "MISALIGNED")

(TAPE PIECES "OVER-LAPPED")

WITH THE SPLICING TAPE

("TOO MUCH" SPLICING TAPE USED)

("TOO LITTLE" SPLICING TAPE USED)

(A GOOD SPLICE)

("AIR BUBBLES" OR "DIRT" TRAPPED UNDER THE SPLICING TAPE

(SPLICING TAPE "MISAPPLIED")

(SPLICING TAPE "UNSECURED")

FIGURE 7.6 Splicing problems occur with improper manipulation of either the splicing tape or the audio tape.

tape is not very susceptible to print-through, you can help prevent it by recording at normal levels (i.e., avoid recording "in the red") and by avoiding using thin (less than 1.5 mil) tapes.

Are digital tapes, such as DAT, subject to print-through? Yes, they are, but the digital playback system simply ignores it. As noted above, on analog tapes, the print-through signal may be clearly audible when it's loud, and the original audio signal is soft. However, in digital recording systems, the playback electronics detect only the presence of the digital signal at any given time and when the signal is too low (such as print-through would be); then the playback system doesn't detect it at all.

The plastic base (the middle of our sandwich) in modern audio tape is polyester or mylar. This produces a strong tape that rarely breaks; however, it will stretch if pulled too hard. Often, polyester audio tape is **tensilized**, or pre-stretched, to prevent stretching problems during day-to-day use. Early audio tape used an acetate base that broke cleanly, but it was susceptible to temperature and humidity effects. Acetate tapes also became weak or brittle after long-term storage, while polyester or mylar tapes were less susceptible to this problem.

The top of the audio tape sandwich is an iron-oxide coating. This coating is composed of tiny slivers of magnetic oxides that are capable of storing an electromagnetic signal that's analogous to the original sound made during the recording process. Instead of an iron-oxide coating, modern audio tape offers different magnetic coatings, such as chromium dioxide, for better recording characteristics.

Audio tape thickness is measured in mils, or thousandths of an inch. Most tape used in radio production work is either 1 mil or 1.5 mil; the latter is preferred by broadcasters. There are thinner audio tapes available, such as those used in audio cassettes. The advantage of thinner tape is that you can get more tape on a reel, which gives you more playing time. But thin tape also stretches more easily, is more susceptible to print-through, and is very difficult to handle in splicing. Tape specifically designed for digital recording is usually thinner than standard audio tape because it only has to store digital data on it.

The other physical dimension of audio tape that concerns production people is its width. The standard width for reel-to-reel audio tape is $1/4$ inch. Cassette tape is usually considered to be $1/8$-inch wide (actually .15 inch), and some multitrack recorders found in the radio production studio use $1/2$-inch tape. Most wider audio tape (1- and 2-inch) is only found in the recording studio.

7.10 CASSETTE TAPE TYPES

Audio cassettes are classified according to the kind of tape formulation used in the cassette. The magnetic material used in standard cassettes is ferric oxide ("rust" in its natural form), and these cassettes are designated as **Type I** tapes. **Type II** tapes use a chromium-dioxide or a chrome-

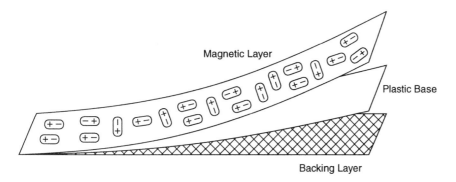

FIGURE 7.7 The basic "layers" of audio tape are the magnetic layer, the plastic base, and the backing layer.

equivalent formulation. A **Type III** cassette tape, which was a dual-layer ferri-chrome tape, existed briefly but is no longer available. Cassette tapes that use a pure metal magnetic material rather than an oxide compound are known as metal or **Type IV** tapes.

Each of the cassette tapes requires different amounts of **bias** (during recording) and **equalization** (during playback). Type I tapes are called "normal bias" tapes because they use a bias current near the usual level for reel-to-reel tapes. Type II tapes are "high bias" because they use a bias level about 50 percent greater than Type I tapes, and Type IV tapes use an even higher bias. Cassette recorders usually employ one of two kinds of playback equalization: 120-microsecond ("normal" equalization) for Type I tapes, and 70-microsecond for Type II and Type IV tapes. Some cassette decks automatically set the bias and equalization, using special sensing cutouts on the plastic cassette shell, but many require the operator to set the correct tape type.

Type I and Type II tapes are most frequently found in the radio production studio situation. Although there isn't a huge quality difference between them, Type II tapes should produce a slightly better recording. Metal tapes (Type IV) actually provide the best quality but are expensive for day-to-day broadcast use.

7.11 AUDIO TAPE DEFECTS

Although audio tape has proven to be an excellent working medium for radio production, it's not perfect. Perhaps the biggest problem with audio tape is signal loss due to drop-out. **Drop-out** is a defect in the oxide coating (see Figure 7.8) that prevents the signal at that point from being recorded at the same level—or at all. Drop-out is a problem that occurs in the manufacturing process of audio tape, but it can also be caused by flaking of the oxide coating due to heavy use or abuse of the tape.

Other tape defects or problems that you're likely to encounter during production work include adhesion, scat-

FIGURE 7.8 The biggest audio tape problem is drop-out, which is caused by flaking of the oxide coating.

tered winds, curling, and cupping. **Adhesion** occurs when tape has been stored on reels for some time, and one layer sticks to another as it's unreeled. Tape stored in humid conditions is more likely to experience adhesion problems. Occasionally tape will wind unevenly onto a reel, leaving some edges of the tape exposed above the rest of the tape on the reel. This is known as a **scattered wind**, and you must be careful not to damage the exposed tape strands. Both **curling** (tape twisting front to back) and **cupping** (tape edges turning up) are problems due to a poor binding between the plastic base and the oxide coating. Almost every tape problem can be avoided by using high-quality tape for all your radio production work.

7.12 LEADER TAPE

Leader tape is often used in the editing process. Leader tape is plastic or paper tape that does *not* have a magnetic layer. It is sometimes clear plastic, but more often it's colored as well as marked, or timed, in 7$\frac{1}{2}$-inch segments. This timing enables the operator to use leader tape to accurately cue up an audio tape. Leader tape is usually put at the beginning of an audio tape to mark the exact start of the recorded sound. (In contrast with audio tape editing, leader tape is normally spliced onto audio tape using the 90-degree cutting groove.)

The beginning of a tape is called the **head** (tape is normally wound on a reel "**heads out**"), and white or green leader tape is commonly used to signify this. Another reason for putting leader tape at the beginning is to use it to thread the tape recorder and avoid wear and tear on the actual recorded portion of the audio tape. Leader tape can also be written on; titles or notes can be put at the beginning of a tape this way. The end of an audio tape is called the **tail**, and if leader tape is put on the end of a tape, it will usually be yellow or red (often the leader tape is actually white, with the timing marks being green, red, etc.). Some audio tape (especially that used for prerecorded programs) is stored on reels "**tails out**," or tails at the end of the recorded material. To play back a tape that is tails out, you would have to rewind the tape first.

In addition to being used at the beginning and end of an audio tape, leader tape is often used to separate various program segments. It's easier to cue up a tape when the operator can see the segments as they pass through the tape transport (even in fast forward) rather than having to listen for pauses between the segments.

As mentioned previously, cassette tapes also usually have leader tape at both ends of the tape reels. This keeps the actual audio tape within the plastic shell and not exposed at the open "head area" of the cassette. In addition, if the hub of the cassette (where the tape is attached) is slightly "out-of-round," it can cause sound quality problems at the beginning and end of the tape; however, the leader tape provides a cushion effect that helps prevent any adverse effect. Cassette leader tape is also used to activate an auto-stop or auto-reverse mechanism on some tape recorders.

process" from the master to the slave tape recorder. Dub editing requires a good deal of coordination because you manipulate the two machines so that they start at the same time. Usually dubbing produces a glitch at the edit point that can range from barely noticeable to terrible, depending on the tape recorders used. Straight dubbing is frequently used in radio production work for purposes other than editing. Often a master tape is dubbed onto a working tape before splicing so that the original tape isn't cut during the editing process. You can dub from one tape format to another. For example, you may have a news tape that was recorded on cassette, but you want to put it on reel-to-reel so that you can edit it down or perhaps equalize it to improve quality. Finally, dubbing can be used simply to make duplicate copies of any existing tape.

Editing—or, more correctly, dubbing—can also be done with audio tape cartridge recorders if the recorder has **cue defeat** capability. Many analog cart recorders have a switch that when set for cue defeat will not put a cue tone on the tape at the beginning of the recording. This would allow you to assemble several segments back to back on the cart by recording the first segment (with cue), stopping the cart, setting the cart in record mode again (with cue defeat), recording the next segment, and so on. When played back, the recording would sound like one continuous recording— and, of course, would stop at the beginning cue tone after playing.

7.13 DUB EDITING

Dubbing is another form of audio tape editing. This type of editing requires the use of two tape recorders. As you dub or copy from one to the other, the "master" tape recorder is in the play mode, and the "slave" tape recorder is in the record mode. Using our previous example ("editing is really a two-step process"), you would dub "editing is" from the master to the slave tape recorder, and then stop both. Next, you'd cue up the master tape recorder past the word "really" and then dub "a two-step

7.14 CONCLUSIONS

This chapter is an important one in your development as a radio production person. You might want to review it again before attempting the Self-Study or Projects sections. Audio editing, be it digital or razor blade, is a concept that is growing in importance as more emphasis is placed on sound bites and ear-catching commercials. The type of equipment or particular software that is used is not nearly as important as how this equipment is used to convey information in a meaningful way.

Self-Study

■ QUESTIONS

1. Which layer of audio tape provides traction as the tape moves through the tape recorder transport?
   a) backing layer
   b) plastic base
   c) magnetic layer
   d) oxide layer

2. Which of the following is the term for an unwanted effect of the magnetic signal involving adjacent layers of audio tape?
   a) tensilize
   b) drop-out
   c) adhesion
   d) print-through

3. Which type of audio tape is preferred by broadcasters?
   a) polyester
   b) acetate
   c) paper
   d) Type IV

4. Which thickness of audio tape is preferred by broadcasters?
   a) .5 mil
   b) 1.0 mil
   c) 1.5 mil
   d) 2.0 mil

5. Which of the following is a reason to edit audio?
   a) eliminate mistakes
   b) record out of sequence
   c) cut to exact length
   d) all of the above

6. In addition to specially designed reels of splicing tape, audio tape editing can be accomplished with _____.
   a) cellophane tape
   b) splicing tabs
   c) masking tape
   d) leader tape

7. In most production situations, which type of edit is preferred?
   a) diagonal cut
   b) vertical cut
   c) horizontal cut
   d) none of the above

8. The purpose of the UNDO function of a digital audio editing program is to _____.
   a) clear all the Transport controls
   b) bring up the Options menu
   c) cancel the last action you undertook
   d) bring up the Help screen

9. If you use splicing tape that is too long it will _____.
   a) be difficult to position it properly
   b) create a gap
   c) misalign the recording tape
   d) overlap the recording tape

10. Which term describes having the end of the material recorded on an audio tape at the outside of the reel?
    a) tails out
    b) tails in
    c) leader out
    d) none of the above

11. Which describes a colored or clear plastic or paper tape that has the same dimensions as audio tape and is often used in audio tape editing?
   a) splicing tape
   b) scotch tape
   c) cellophane tape
   d) leader tape

12. A recorder with *cue defeat* would be used for which type of editing?
   a) splice editing
   b) dub editing
   c) digital editing
   d) analog editing

13. Chromium-dioxide or chrome-equivalent cassette tapes are known as _____ tapes.
   a) Type I
   b) Type II
   c) Type III
   d) Type IV

14. Both splicing and dubbing can be easily accomplished with reel-to-reel, cassette, and cartridge tapes.
   a) true
   b) false

15. Which tape defect is a problem due to flaking of the oxide coating of the audio tape?
   a) print-through
   b) adhesion
   c) drop-out
   d) scattered wind

16. Audio tape that is made with an acetate base is often tensilized to prevent stretching problems.
   a) true
   b) false

17. Which type of audio cassette tape requires the highest bias current during recording?
   a) Type I
   b) Type II
   c) Type III
   d) Type IV

18. An audio soundfile that has been edited with a destructive system has been permanently altered so the original audio cannot be restored.
   a) true
   b) false

19. Which type of audio tape editing is the most accurate and easiest?
   a) splicing
   b) dubbing
   c) digital audio editing
   d) analog audio editing

20. Where would you place the edit marks to edit out the word *one* from the phrase *one . . . two . . . three*?
   a) just after letter *e* of *one* and just before letter *t* of *three*
   b) just before letter *t* of *two* and just before letter *t* of *three*
   c) just before letter *t* of *two* and just after letter *o* of *two*
   d) no correct way to mark this edit is shown here

■ ANSWERS

If You Answered A:

1a. Right. It's the bottom layer of the tape sandwich.

2a. Wrong. To tensilize is to prestretch audio tape. (Reread 7.9.)

3a. Right. Polyester tape is preferred because it's strong and little affected by temperature and humidity.

4a. No. Thinner audio tape stretches too easily and is more susceptible to print-through. (Reread 7.9.)

5a. Although this is one reason for editing audio, there is a better answer. (Reread 7.2.)

6a. Never. The adhesive material on cellophane tape will bleed through audio tape and gum up the heads of the tape recorder. (Reread 7.5.)

7a. Right. The diagonal cut or 45-degree cutting groove is used in audio tape editing because it gives a smoother sound transition and a stronger edit.

8a. Wrong. If you chose this answer, you don't understand the function of either the Transport control or UNDO. (Reread 7.4)

9a. Right. Shorter tape will make for better edits.

10a. Right. The end of an audio tape is called the tail.

11a. Wrong. Splicing tape is used in audio tape editing, but it does not have the same dimensions as audio tape. (Reread 7.5 and 7.12.)

12a. Wrong. Splicing refers to physically cutting the audio tape during the editing process and doesn't require a recorder with cue defeat. (Reread 7.3, 7.7, and 7.13.)

13a. No. These are standard ferric oxide tapes. (Reread 7.10.)

14a. Wrong. For all practical purposes, cassette and cart tapes can only employ dubbing techniques. (Reread 7.3 and 7.13.)

15a. No. Print-through is the transfer of the magnetic signal on one layer of tape to the magnetic signal on an adjacent layer. (Reread 7.9 and 7.11.)

16a. You're correct in thinking that to tensilize tape is to prestretch it, but acetate tape is not the type that is tensilized. (Reread 7.9 to find out what tape base is prestretched.)

17a. No. Type I tapes utilize "normal" bias current levels. (Reread 7.10.)

18a. You're not quite right with this answer. While audio edited with a destructive system is ultimately physically changed, most editing systems provide an UNDO function that can restore the original audio. (Reread 7.4 and the Production Tip for this chapter.)

19a. No. Splicing can be very accurate when done by a skilled operator, but it really isn't the easiest method. (Reread 7.3 and 7.4.)

20a. No. This would leave no space or pause between the words *one* and *three*. (Reread 7.6)

If You Answered B:

1b. Wrong. This is the part that mainly provides strength. (Reread 7.9.)

2b. Wrong. Drop-out is a defect in the oxide coating. (Reread 7.9 and 7.11.)

3b. Wrong. Acetate tape was once favored by broadcasters, but it breaks too often and is susceptible to temperature and humidity problems. (Reread 7.9.)

4b. You're close; 1-mil audio tape may be used by broadcasters, but it's not the best choice. (Reread 7.9.)

5b. Although this is one reason for editing audio, there is a better answer. (Reread 7.2.)

6b. Right. Splicing tabs are commercially available precut pieces of splicing tape on applicator strips specially designed for audio tape editing.

7b. No. The 90-degree cut is only used when putting leader tape on an audio tape. (Reread 7.5, 7.7, and 7.12.)

8b. No. It is possible that on some programs UNDO might be under the Options menu, but generally these two things have nothing to do with each other. (Reread 7.4.)

9b. No. The length of splicing tape has nothing to do with this. (Reread 7.8.)

10b. Wrong. (Reread 7.12.)

11b. No. Scotch tape should never be used in audio tape editing. (Reread 7.5 and 7.12.)

12b. Right. A form of dub editing requires using a cart recorder with a cue defeat feature.

13b. Yes. This is the correct answer.

14b. Right. For all practical purposes, cassette and cart tapes can only employ dubbing techniques.

15b. No. Adhesion is a problem associated with humidity when tape layers stick together. (Reread 7.9 and 7.11.)

16b. Correct. Polyester-based tape is tensilized, not acetate.

17b. No. Type II tapes do utilize a "high" bias current level, but there is a tape type that uses a higher level. (Reread 7.10.)

18b. Yes. Because most destructive editing systems have an UNDO function that enables edited audio to be restored.

19b. Wrong. Dubbing is neither a very accurate nor a very easy method of audio tape editing. (Reread 7.3, 7.4, and 7.13.)

20b. Yes. This would edit out the word *two,* but it would maintain the natural pause between *one* and *three.*

If You Answered C:

1c. Wrong. This is where recording occurs. (Reread 7.9.)

2c. Wrong. Adhesion is a problem of tape layers sticking together, usually due to humidity. (Reread 7.9 and 7.11.)

3c. No. Paper tape would most likely be leader tape. (Reread 7.9 and 7.12.)

4c. Yes. Audio tape that is 1.5 mil thick is most often used by broadcasters.

5c. Although this is one reason for editing audio, there is a better answer. (Reread 7.2.)

6c. No. Office tapes should not be used for audio tape editing. (Reread 7.5.)

7c. No. You're way off base with this choice. (Reread 7.5, 7.7, and 7.12.)

8c. Right. It cancels the last action, and can often cancel more than just that action, so you can UNDO several layers of actions.

9c. No. It shouldn't affect the position of the recording tape. (Reread 7.8.)

10c. Wrong. Although there may be leader tape at the end of the audio tape, this is not the correct term. (Reread 7.12.)

11c. Wrong. Cellophane tape (also known as Scotch tape) should never be used in audio tape editing. (Reread 7.5 and 7.12.)

12c. Wrong. Digital audio editing does not utilize a recorder with a cue defeat function. (Reread 7.3, 7.4, and 7.13.)

13c. No. This tape formulation no longer exists. (Reread 7.10.)

15c. Yes. Drop-out occurs when the oxide coating of audio tape flakes off; if there's no recording material on the tape, the audio signal drops out at that point.

17c. No. Type III cassette tapes are no longer in use. (Reread 7.10.)

19c. Of course. Digital audio tape editing is extremely accurate and easy to accomplish.

20c. No. This would lengthen the pause between *one* and *three* and sound unnatural. (Reread 7.6.)

If You Answered D:

1d. No. This is the magnetic layer where recording occurs. (Reread 7.9.)

2d. Right. Print-through occurs when the magnetic signal of one layer of audio tape affects an adjacent layer.

3d. No. This is a metal cassette tape not frequently used in broadcasting. (Reread 7.9 and 7.10.)

4d. No. This is not a standard thickness for audio tape. (Reread 7.9.)

5d. Right. All of these are good reasons for editing audio.

6d. No. You're quite confused. Leader tape is not an adhesive tape of any kind. (Reread 7.5 and 7.12.)

7d. No. There is a correct response. (Reread 7.5, 7.7, and 7.12.)

8d. No. UNDO, like other functions, will probably be defined in the HELP portion of the program, but it won't bring it up. (Reread 7.4.)

9d. Wrong. This wouldn't cause the recording tape to overlap. (Reread 7.8.)

10d. No. There is a correct response. (Reread 7.12.)

11d. Right. This accurately describes leader tape.

12d. You're close in that it is a form of analog editing, but there is a better answer with one of the other choices. (Reread 7.3 and 7.13.)

13d. No. These are metal tapes. (Reread 7.10.)

15d. Wrong. A scatter wind occurs when tape winds unevenly on a reel. Some of the tape edges become exposed as they wind higher or lower then the rest of the tape on the reel. (Reread 7.9 and 7.11.)

17d. Yes. Type IV or metal cassette tapes require the highest bias current during recording.

19d. No. Analog audio editing is what splicing and dubbing techniques are. They are no longer the most accurate or easiest methods for editing. (Reread 7.3 and 7.4.)

20d. No. One of the other answers is the correct way to mark this edit. (Reread 7.6.)

Projects

■ PROJECT 1

Make several edits utilizing a digital audio tape editor.

Purpose

To enable you to practice editing a vocal audio tape with a digital editing system.

Advice, Cautions, and Background

1. If you're not sure of what you're doing, ask the instructor for assistance. Don't take the chance of ruining the equipment.
2. Remember, you're to do several edits, not just one.
3. You'll be judged on the cleanness of your edits, so be sure you make your edit marks accurately.

How to Do the Project

1. Familiarize yourself with the operation of the digital editing system in your production studio. If you have questions, ask your instructor.
2. You may use the material on the CD-ROM enclosed with the text, or you may be allowed to record your own. If you can record your own, select some news copy or a weathercast from your news wire service, or write something similar and record it into your editing system. Label this soundfile as required by your system.
3. Do your edits as follows:
    a. Press the play "button," and listen to what is recorded.
    b. Select something you wish to edit. Write down on a piece of paper the part you plan to edit with a few words before and after it. Put parentheses around what you plan to take out. For example: "This is Mary Anderson (broadcasting from KZXY) bringing you the latest news."
    c. Stop playback so that it's at the exact place you wish to edit—in our example, just in front of "broadcasting."
    d. Make your beginning edit mark.
    e. Continue playing the audio until you get to the end of your edit—in our example, just before "bringing."
    f. Make your end edit mark just as you did before.
    g. If you can, preview the edit. You can probably adjust either edit mark so that you have accurately positioned them. If necessary, do so.
    h. Perform the actual edit, and listen to your edit. If you've made some type of error, "undo" the edit, and start it again.
4. Repeat the above steps for another edit. Do a few more similar edits.
5. When you've done several edits, record them all onto a disc or cassette tape.
6. Label the tape or disc with your name and DIGITAL AUDIO EDITING.
7. Turn in the tape or disc to your instructor to receive credit for the project.

■ PROJECT 2

Make two edits in an audio tape on a reel-to-reel recorder.

Purpose

To enable you to feel comfortable editing a vocal audio tape with analog reel-to-reel equipment.

Advice, Cautions, and Background

1. If you're not sure of what you're doing, ask the instructor for assistance. Don't take the chance of ruining the equipment.
2. Remember, you are to do two edits, not just one.
3. You'll be judged on the cleanness of your edits, so don't try to edit something that is too tight.

How to Do the Project

1. Familiarize yourself with the operation of the reel-to-reel tape recorder in your production studio. If you have questions, ask your instructor.
2. Assemble the editing tools and supplies that you will need, including splicing block, razor blades, grease pencil, and splicing tape.
3. You can use the material provided on the CD-ROM that accompanies this text, or you can record something of your own.
4. Do your edits as follows:
    a. Press the play button and listen to what is recorded.
    b. Select something you wish to edit. Write down on a piece of paper the part you plan to edit with a few words before and after it. Put parentheses around what you plan to take out. For example, for the CD material, you could write: "Today's weather calls for (sunny skies and) a temperature of seventy degrees."
    c. Stop the tape recorder so it's at the exact place you wish to edit—in our example, just in front of "sunny."
    d. You are hearing the tape on the play head (remember ERP). Just right of dead center on the play head, make your edit mark on the audio tape (remember AIM). Be careful *not* to get any grease pencil on the actual tape recorder heads.
    e. Continue playing the tape until you get to the end of your edit—in our example, just before "a."
    f. Using the grease pencil, make your edit mark just as you did before.
    g. Spool out enough tape so that your edit marks can be positioned in the splicing block. Cut the audio tape at the first edit point, according to proper splicing procedure. (You might want to review section 7.7.)
    h. Position the other edit mark in the splicing block, and cut the tape as before. You should now have a loose piece of tape (the unwanted words "sunny skies and") and two pieces of tape with diagonal cuts that are both connected to the two tape reels.
    i. Butt the two tape ends and apply a proper amount of splicing tape. Make sure there are no twists in the audio tape.
    j. Rethread the tape in the recorder, and rewind it a ways by hand. Push play and listen to your edit.
5. Repeat the above steps for your second edit. If using the CD material, you can edit out "seventy-two in Philadelphia" so that the voice says "it will be sixty-six in Chicago and seventy-six in New York."
6. Label the tape with your name and EDITED AUDIO TAPE.
7. Turn in the tape to your instructor to receive credit for the project.

■ PROJECT 3

Dub from one audio tape recorder to another, making two edits as you do so.

Purpose

To enable you to feel comfortable with the type of editing that can be done through dubbing.

Advice, Cautions, and Background

1. If you're not sure of what you're doing, ask the instructor for assistance. Don't take the chance of ruining the equipment.
2. The best way to do this exercise is to use the material provided on the CD-ROM that accompanies this text. You could also dub something off the radio.
3. You may have trouble getting the machines to operate so that the edit occurs where you want it to. It's better to make the edit too loose than too tight because one that's loose is easier to correct. You simply need to record

again, bringing in the material a little sooner. If your edit is too tight and cuts off the last part of what you had previously laid down, you'll need to lay that part down again.

4. Make sure you have access to two tape recorders and two audio tapes.
5. Remember, you are to do two edits, not just one.

How to Do the Project

1. Record the CD-ROM material (or radio material) to a cassette or reel tape. If you record from the radio, make sure you get a commercial and some other voiced material.
2. Connect one tape recorder to another so that the sound can be transferred electronically. You'll need to take a cable from the audio output on the "master" tape recorder to the audio input on the "slave" tape recorder. If your studio is already set up for two tape recorders, you can just go on to the next step.
3. Dub a small portion of what you have on the master tape to the slave machine, just to make sure everything is working correctly. You'll need to put the master tape recorder in play and the slave tape recorder in record. Adjust levels so that both tape machines are about the same. If you have access to "tone," set the machine's VU meters that way. (See Chapter 3, "The Audio Console.")
4. Play back what you have just recorded and make any necessary adjustments. If everything recorded well, you are ready to start the actual dubbing.
5. Dub what you recorded off the CD-ROM or the radio from the master to the slave until you come to a commercial break (on the CD-ROM it's the furniture commercial). Hit the pause control on the slave machine right before the commercials begin, and hit pause on the master machine right after the commercials begin. It's better to let both machines run longer than you really want than to cut everything off too short.
6. Play the master tape until you get to the end of the commercial break. Listen carefully so that you know exactly where you want the edit of the program material to begin. Be sure it makes sense, given what was said before the commercial. You may have to edit out some of the intro to the music. Back up at least 5 seconds from your desired edit point, and put the master machine in pause.
7. If you feel confident that the place where you pushed pause on the slave tape is where you want one portion of the program to stop and another to begin, leave it as it is. If you are not sure, listen to the tape again and find the correct point and put the machine in record and pause. Don't go past the point where you recorded, or you'll have an awkward period of no sound at all.
8. Play the master tape, and just as it gets to the spot where you want the edit to be, take the slave tape recorder out of pause. Let both recorders go until the next material you want to edit. For the CD-ROM, take out the last spoken sentence—the one that starts, "In other games . . ." and ends, "thirty-four to three."
9. At that point, pause both machines as you did for the previous edit.
10. Go back and listen to the edit you just made on the slave machine. If it is what you want, proceed with the second edit. If not, redo it.
11. To do the second edit, cue the master tape at the end of the sentence about Jeff McKenzie, and cue the slave tape close to where you stopped the recording, just as you did for the first edit.
12. Play the master recorder, and take the slave recorder out of pause, just as you did before. Continue recording to the end of the material; then stop both machines.
13. Listen to the edit you have just finished and make sure it was done correctly.
14. Label the tape with your name and TAPE DUBS.
15. Turn in the "slave tape" to your instructor so that you can get credit for the dub edits.

Monitor Speakers, Cables, Connectors, and Studio Accessories

Information

8.1 INTRODUCTION

This chapter looks at production studio items that are often treated as passive devices that simply exist in the studio, but they are actually quite significant. Monitor speakers (see Figure 8.1) are used to listen to the program (and also audition or auxiliary) sound in the radio studio. The sound that comes from them is the final product, so they are important in determining the quality of that product. What you hear on the monitor speakers is an accurate gauge of what the listener will hear.

The various pieces of equipment used in the radio production studio, including monitor speakers, are all interconnected. This chapter also looks at the **cables** and **connectors** used for this interconnection, as well as some of the accessories that make work in the production studio easier. Some accessories have been previously mentioned: microphone windscreens and audio cassettes, among others.

8.2 TYPES OF SPEAKERS

Speakers are transducers. They work in a manner opposite to that of microphones. Instead of converting sound waves into electrical energy, speakers produce sound from an electrical signal by converting the electrical signal into mechanical energy that produces an audible sound. The most common type of monitor found in the broadcast studio is a **dynamic speaker**. Also known as a **moving coil** or an **electromagnetic speaker**, its transducing element, called a "driver," consists of a paper diaphragm, or cone, suspended in a metal frame. Attached at the narrow end of the cone is a voice coil (a cylinder wound with a coil of wire), which is located between powerful circular magnets (see Figure 8.2). When an electrical current is generated in the voice coil, it creates another magnetic force that moves the

coil (and cone) in and out, according to the electrical signal entering the coil. The cone vibration causes the surrounding air to move in a like manner, which our ears pick up as sound.

Other speaker drivers, such as **electrostatic**, **ribbon**, or **planar-magnetic**, are usually considered too exotic for radio use, and you aren't likely to run across them in the production studio.

With the radio production facility becoming an all-digital environment, at least one manufacturer now offers a digital monitor speaker (see Figure 8.3). The speaker has a S/P-DIF digital input, in addition to analog inputs, which can identify a 16- to 24-bit digital signal with a sampling rate between 22 kHz and 55 kHz. When a digital signal is detected, the speaker's internal D/A converter is activated. Does the digital speaker sound better? There really isn't a monumental sound difference between an analog and a digital input; however, the convenience of attaching directly to the digital output of an audio console or digital audio workstation will become more important in the future.

8.3 BASIC SPEAKER SYSTEM COMPONENTS

The basic components of the typical speaker system (see Figure 8.4) are the woofer, tweeter, crossover, and speaker enclosure. **Woofer** and **tweeter** are names given to drivers or individual speakers used in a speaker system. Since no one speaker design can reproduce the entire frequency range adequately, different speakers were developed to handle different portions of it. A woofer is designed to be able to move the large volume of air that is necessary to reproduce lower frequencies. The cone should be large in size (usually in a range from 8 to 12 inches) or be able to make large movements, and often a woofer utilizes a combination of both. However, this bulk prevents the speaker

FIGURE 8.1 Studio monitor speakers help you judge the sound quality of your audio production. (Image courtesy of JBL Professional.)

from adequately reproducing the higher frequencies that require rapid cone movement. The tweeter uses a lighter and smaller design; often a convex dome (1 inch or less in diameter) replaces the cone. There are also midrange speakers with cones from 3 to 5 inches in diameter that are designed to reproduce higher-bass and lower-treble frequencies.

An individual speaker is really a speaker system in that most modern speakers use at least a woofer and a tweeter driver. To divide the audio signal and send the proper frequencies to the proper driver, another element of the speaker is used: the **crossover**. A crossover is a network of filters between the input to the speaker and the individual speaker drivers. In the two-way system, one filter would pass all audio below a certain frequency, sending it to the woofer. Another filter would pass all audio above a certain

frequency, sending it to the tweeter. Although there is no universal design for the crossover, most dividing points between the bass and treble frequencies are between 500 and 1,500 hertz. A speaker that has just a woofer, a tweeter, and a crossover is a **two-way speaker system**, like the one shown in Figure 8.4. Speakers that employ another driver (such as a midrange) are **three-way systems**.

8.4 SPEAKER SYSTEM ENCLOSURE DESIGNS

The speaker drivers and crossover are encased in a box (enclosure) that also plays a role in how the speaker sounds. Although there are different speaker system designs, each is intended to handle the rearward sound wave. Every speaker produces sound both behind and in front: The back

Cone

Frame

Voice Coil

Pigtail Leads (signal in)

Magnet

FIGURE 8.2 The most common type of speaker driver is the dynamic cone driver.

FIGURE 8.3 Digital monitor speakers offer a digital input for direct patching into a digital audio console or workstation. (Image courtesy of Genelec, Inc.)

sound wave is exactly opposite to the one that goes into the forward listening space. If the two sound waves are allowed to combine naturally, they would be acoustically out-of-phase (see section 8.7) and "cancel" each other out, producing no sound or very diminished sound in a good portion of the frequency range, especially the bass sounds.

The two most widely used speaker enclosure designs are the acoustic suspension and bass reflex systems shown in Figure 8.5. The **acoustic suspension** (or **sealed-box**) design puts the speaker drivers (and crossover) in a tightly sealed enclosure that produces an accurate, natural sound with strong, tight bass. By containing and absorbing the back wave in the enclosure, the acoustic suspension design prevents the rear sound from radiating and disrupting the

main sound of the speaker. Because half the sound energy is trapped and absorbed in the box, acoustic suspension speakers are less efficient than other designs and require a more powerful amplifier to drive them. The acoustic suspension design also requires a rather large, sturdily-built physical enclosure to insure accurate reproduction of the lowest bass notes.

On the other hand, the **bass reflex** (or **vented box**) design is quite efficient and produces a strong bass sound with less power required. The bass reflex speaker enclosure is designed with a vent, duct, or port—an opening that is tuned to allow some of the rear sound (mainly the lower frequencies) to combine in phase and reinforce the main sound from the speaker. Some bass reflex design speakers have been criticized for not having tonal accuracy that is quite as good as the acoustic suspension design and even adding a "boomy" quality to the sound. These problems, however, are often the fault of a particular speaker's tuning and construction, not caused by the bass reflex design.

There are many different vented box designs, and most modern bass reflex speakers produce clean, wide-ranging bass.

8.5 SPEAKER SOUND QUALITIES

There's a wide variety of speaker systems to choose from, and, as with some other radio production equipment, the differences between various models may be minimal. One of the important qualities that a good monitor speaker must have is excellent frequency response. We are able to hear sounds or frequencies in the range of 20 hertz to 20 kilohertz, although most of us don't hear quite that low or that high. Top-line broadcast monitors often provide a frequency response range from 35 to 45 hertz to 18 to 20 kilohertz. Increased use of CDs and other digital equipment will make speakers that produce as much of this range as possible necessary.

Another quality important for the broadcast monitor speaker is its ability to produce a **flat frequency response**. The speaker should be able to reproduce low, midrange, and high frequencies equally well to produce a natural sound. The speaker itself shouldn't add anything to the audio signal, such as a boosting of the highs.

Perhaps most important is merely how a speaker sounds. Among the combinations of driver types, speaker enclosure design, and crossover frequencies, there is no one speaker configuration that produces the "best sound." It is

FIGURE 8.4   The basic two-way speaker "system" consists of a tweeter, a woofer, and a crossover housed within an enclosure.

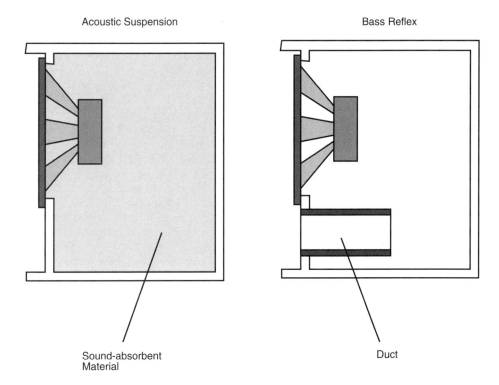

FIGURE 8.5   The two most widely used speaker enclosure designs are the acoustic suspension and bass reflex systems.

agreed, however, that a good speaker sound doesn't depend only on the speaker itself. How a speaker sounds is also dependent on the program (what is being played through it), the dimensions and acoustic properties of the room in which the speakers are heard, the location of the speakers (in relation to the listener), and the listener.

8.6 SPEAKER PLACEMENT

In the radio production room, there may not be many options as to where the monitor speakers are located. Usually they are positioned one on each side of the audio console, but exactly how they are positioned after that is open to various schools of thought. If nothing else, you should try to achieve an acoustically symmetrical layout. Don't put one speaker in the corner next to a glass window and the other speaker in the middle of a wall that's covered with acoustic tiles. That would be a mismatched acoustic environment for the two speakers, rather than a similar one.

One thought is to mount the speakers in the wall. As long as the speakers are isolated from the wall structure—using rubber shock mounts, for example—this flush mount creates an infinite baffle that prevents back wave problems. Large speakers can be built into the wall, providing a loud, clear sound with plenty of "heavy" bass; unfortunately, this type of installation is often not practical for a radio studio.

Some production people feel the ideal sound is obtained when speakers are at or a bit above ear level. This installation is called **near-field** or **close proximity monitoring** and can be accomplished by putting small speakers, such as those shown in Figure 8.3, on the audio console "bridge" or on short stands to the left and right of the console, about 3 feet apart. Keeping the speakers a couple of feet from the back wall will prevent any excessive bass boost. Since the speakers are so close to the listener, you hear mostly direct sound with very little worry about the effect from room acoustics. Toeing in the speakers (angling them toward the listener) or pointing them straight away from the wall will control the treble, with speakers pointing toward you providing the greatest high frequency response. Hearing a great amount of clear detail and excellent stereo imaging are characteristics usually associated with near-field monitoring setups. A new concern with monitor speaker placement, especially true of studios that employ near-field monitoring, has to do with the increased use of computer equipment in the broadcast studio. Unless the monitor speakers are magnetically shielded, they must be positioned far enough away from the screen of the computer equipment so that they don't distort the picture.

Perhaps the most practical monitor installation in many production studios is when the speakers are hung from the ceiling or attached to the wall behind the audio console. For the best sound dispersion, the speakers should be hung toward the upper corners of the production room. Keeping

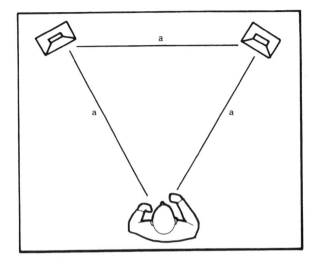

FIGURE 8.6 The most basic rule of speaker placement dictates that the distance between the speakers equals the distance from speaker to listener.

them close to the wall prevents a great deal of reflected sound and should produce a full bass sound at a higher sound level than other possible positions. When speakers are placed closer to a wall, there is more bass sound produced because the usual omnidirectional "soundfield" is cut down, and the sound is concentrated into a smaller dispersion area. Putting speakers totally into the corners of a room (such as the upper corners) may result in too much bass boost, but this is not an uncommon location. Hung speakers also keep counter space available for other production room equipment, and this is an important consideration in most broadcast settings.

Regardless of where the speakers are ultimately placed, the location of the operator in relation to the speakers also plays a role in how they sound, especially with stereo programming. Ideally, the operator is located directly between the two speakers and far enough back from them so that an equilateral triangle is formed if a line were drawn from speaker to speaker and from operator to speaker (see Figure 8.6). If the layout of the production room positions the operator closer to one speaker than the other, the source of all the sound appears to shift toward that one speaker. As a production person, you may not have any control over the speaker placement, but it's important that you realize the effects of speaker placement on the sound you hear.

8.7 PHASE AND CHANNEL ORIENTATION

The concept of **phase** was previously mentioned in Chapter 4, "Microphones." Miswiring monitor speakers can also cause phase problems. Each speaker is fed its sound signal from the audio console monitor amp (and sometimes an external amp) by a positive and negative wire. If the wires are reversed on one of the speakers (i.e., the positive wire is connected to the negative terminal), the two speakers will be out of phase. As the driver moves the cone of one speaker in and out, the driver on the other speaker is moving out and in, so that the two speaker sounds are fighting each other and tend to cancel out individual sounds, diminishing the overall sound quality. This would be especially noticeable if the speakers were reproducing a mono signal.

Another concern about speaker wiring is channel orientation. Most studio monitors are wired so that moving a balance control from left to right will shift the sound image from left to right as you *face the speakers*. In other words, while looking at the speakers, the left speaker is in line with your left hand. This is important for true stereo sound reproduction. For example, if you were listening to a classical music piece and the channel orientation was reversed, the violins would sound as if they were to the right of the "sound stage," which would be contrary to normal symphony orchestra arrangement.

However, since most speakers are wired by the station engineer, phase and channel orientation should not be a problem for the radio production person.

8.8 MONITOR AMPLIFIERS

As you've previously learned, the audio console has an internal monitor amp that provides the signal to drive the monitor speakers. Although this is adequate for many studio applications, some production rooms (and control rooms) are set up with external monitor amplifiers. This is merely a more powerful amplifier that provides higher volume levels and clearer reproduction of the sound signal. *Remember, the volume of the monitor speakers is only for the pleasure of the operator and has no relationship to the volume of the signal being broadcast or recorded.*

8.9 SPEAKER SENSITIVITY

A speaker's sensitivity is the amount of sound (output level) that a speaker can produce from a given input level, much like the sensitivity of a microphone studied in Chapter 4, "Microphones." It is measured in decibels of sound-pressure level (SPL), and a good quality broadcast monitor will usually have a sensitivity of more than 90 db SPL measured at one meter with 1 watt of input level. There are speakers that range from low-sensitivity to high-sensitivity, but, in reality, this characteristic of a speaker has little bearing on its quality. What it does mean is that a low-sensitivity speaker will need more power to drive it to any given volume level than a high-sensitivity speaker. There is also a relationship between speaker size, sensitivity, and bass response. To increase a speaker's low frequency response, its enclosure can be made larger, or its sensitivity

can be decreased. For most broadcast situations, a smaller speaker size offers a lot more flexibility in placement of the speaker and thus is preferred, even if it means a low-sensitivity speaker that perhaps requires a bit more powerful monitor amplifier.

8.10 HEADPHONES

Headphones are another type of monitor in that they are tiny speakers encased in a headset. Headphones are necessary in radio production because the studio monitor speakers are muted when the microphone is on, and the operator must be able to hear sound sources that are also on. For example, if you're talking over the introduction of a song or reading a commercial over the background of a musical bed, headphones allow you to hear the other sound and the mic sound so that you can balance the two or hit appropriate cues. Headphones are also portable, so sounds can be monitored when an actual monitor speaker might not be available.

Like regular monitor speakers, headphones come in a variety of designs, styles, and prices. The two main types of headphones found in the production studio are closed headphones and open-air headphones. **Closed headphones**, also known as **circumaural**, have a ring-shaped muff that rests on the head around the ear and not actually on the ear (see Figure 8.7). These headphones are probably the most common in radio since they usually provide a full bass sound and attenuate outside noise better than other styles. However, closed headphones are also heavier and more cumbersome than other styles.

FIGURE 8.7 Circumaural (closed) headphones have a ring-shaped muff that rests on the head around the ear. (Image courtesy of AKG Acoustics, U.S.)

Open-air headphones, also known as **supra-aural**, have a porous muff, instead of an ear cushion, that rests directly on the ear (see Figure 8.8). Often made of very lightweight material, this design can be very comfortable for the wearer. However, open-air headphones are subject to possible feedback because the audio signal can leak out if driven at high volume levels, so some broadcast production people avoid them.

Other headphone types include the tiny **earbud**, which is designed to fit in the ear; **electrostatic headphones**, which are extremely high priced and high quality and require external amplification and special couplers to hook up; and **wireless headphones**, which operate similarly to wireless microphones by transmitting an RF, or infrared, audio signal from the source to the headphones.

Unlike consumer headphones, many broadcast-quality headphones are purchased "barefoot"; that is, they have no end connector on them. Although most equipment that allows headphone use requires a standard $\frac{1}{4}$-inch phone connector, there are other situations, and the barefoot headphone allows the engineer to wire them as necessary.

Which headphone style is most appropriate is often merely the personal taste of the announcer using them; however, broadcast-quality headphones should feature large drivers and full (but comfortable) ear cushions and headband. *One note of caution for all headphone users: Listening at extremely high volume, especially for extended periods of time, such as in a broadcast situation, can damage your hearing permanently.* Good production practice (and common sense) dictates moderate volumes for headphone use.

8.11 HARD WIRING AND PATCHING

Audio equipment in the production studio is connected together by two methods: **hard wiring** and **patching**. Hard-wired connections are somewhat permanent (such as the CD player directly connected to the audio console) and are usually soldered or wired by the engineer. Equipment that may, from time to time, be moved from one production area to another (such as an audio recorder) is often connected by male and female connectors known as plugs and jacks. More will be said about the typical broadcast connectors in the next few sections of this chapter.

Many pieces of audio equipment and even two different production studios are often connected together through the use of a **patch panel** or **patch bay** (see Figure 8.9), as they are also called. The patch panel is located between the equipment and the audio console so that the input and output of each piece of equipment is wired to the patch panel. In a typical setup, the top row of sockets on the panel is where the audio signal is coming from, and the bottom row of sockets is where the signal is going to. Putting a patch cord into the correct holes in the panel allows you to interconnect and reconfigure the various pieces of equipment or studios. Patch cords are available as either a single-plug cord or a double-plug cord. A double cord works well for stereo patch bays since it has two plugs at each end. One side of the plug casing will be marked (usually with a serrated or ribbed edge), so you can keep left and right channels correctly aligned on both the input and output sockets of the patch panel. Of course, single cords work just as well—just remember to always plug in one cord from the top row right channel of the patch panel to the bottom row right channel before plugging in the left channel. That way you won't cross channels as you could if you plugged both left and right channels of the top row before plugging in the bottom row.

Figure 8.10A shows a portion of a patch bay in which a cassette recorder and CD player are linked to two channels on an audio console. With no patch cord put into the panel, CASS 1 is linked to Channel 3 and CD 1 is linked to Channel 4. In patch panels, the top row is internally wired to the bottom row, and the audio signal flows in that manner. When it is unpatched like this, it's known as a "normaled" condition. Figure 8.10B shows another portion of a patch panel that links the output of the audio console to audio recorders. When normaled, the PGM (program) output goes to REEL 1, and the AUD (audition) output goes to DAT 1. The PGM signal could be sent to DAT 1 (as shown) by putting a patch cord from the PGM position on the top row to the DAT 1 position on the bottom row. Now the signal flow has been changed, and that's the purpose of a patch panel—to allow flexibility in configuring the production

FIGURE 8.8 Supra-aural (open-air) headphones have a porous muff that rests directly on the ear. (Image courtesy of AKG Acoustics, U.S.)

FIGURE 8.9 The patch panel simplifies rewiring individual audio components into an audio console or studio. (Image courtesy of Gentner Broadcast Systems.)

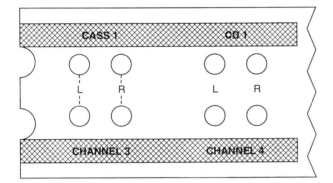

FIGURE 8.10A A portion of a patch panel that is "normaled."

FIGURE 8.10B A portion of a patch panel that has been "patched."

studio. In this way the audio signals from various pieces of equipment can be sent to the audio console, and the audio console output can be sent to various pieces of equipment.

An alternative to the patch panel is the **audio routing switcher**. The router operates like a patch panel by allowing several input sources to be switched to a single output (or sometimes multiple outputs); however, the switching is done electronically, by selecting the appropriate switches or buttons, rather than using patch cords.

In most broadcast situations, you'll be dealing with four types of connectors: RCA, XLR, phone, and miniphone. In general, the female, or receiving, connectors are called **jacks** and the male connectors are called **plugs**, but often the terms "plugs," "jacks," and "connectors" are all used interchangeably.

8.12 RCA AND XLR CONNECTORS

The **RCA connector** is also known as the **phono connector**. Notice that it is *phono*, not phone. Most home stereo equipment uses this type of connector. In broadcast facilities that have turntables, this connector is often used to connect the turntable tone-arm assembly to the turntable preamp, and many CD players utilize RCA connectors. This connector is always a mono connector, so two of them are needed for a stereo signal—the left and right channel output. The male plug consists of a thin outer sleeve and a short center shaft that plugs into the female jack (see Figure 8.11). Although there are female in-line jacks, the female end is most often enclosed in a piece of equipment (such as an audio recorder or preamp) so that the male end will just plug into the equipment. RCA connectors are used for unbalanced connections that sometimes pick up extraneous electrical noises, such as switch noise and hum.

The **XLR connector** is also known as the **Cannon connector** or **three-pin connector**. It's the most common microphone connector in broadcast production use. This connector attaches firmly and cannot be disconnected unless the latch lock is pressed. The three prongs of the male plug fit into the conductor inputs of the female jack. The guide pin on the female end fits into the slot for the guide pin on the male end so that the connector can't be put together improperly (see Figure 8.12). Like the RCA connector, the XLR connector is mono so that a stereo connection requires one XLR connector for the right channel and one for the left channel. The balanced three-conductor wiring of the XLR connector makes this a high-quality connection less likely to pick up noise through the cable. It's often used as the input and output connection on audio recorders in addition to connecting microphones.

8.13 PHONE AND MINIPHONE CONNECTORS

The **phone connector** is also known as the $\frac{1}{4}$-**inch phone**. Notice it is called *phone*, not phono. Most broadcast-quality headphones are connected to the audio console with a phone plug, and most patch bays consist of female phone jacks into which phone plugs are inserted. The **miniphone connector** (also called a **mini**) is most often required to connect portable cassette recorders to other pieces of production equipment. The output of many portable cassette recorders is a female minijack. As you would expect, the miniphone is a smaller version of the phone connector. Although there are various sizes of miniphone connectors, the one used most in broadcast production is 3.5 millimeters.

The phone and miniphone plug consist of a tip and a sleeve, which go into the female jack. Male mono plugs have one insulating ring that separates the tip from the sleeve, and stereo plugs have two insulating rings, which actually define the ring portion of the connector (see Figure 8.13). If the signal is stereo, both the female and male connectors should be stereo.

Again, the female end is often enclosed in a piece of equipment, but you can get in-line jacks if required.

Male
Plugs

Female
Jack

SLEEVE   TIP   SLEEVE   TIP

FIGURE 8.11 The RCA or phono plug is one of the common broadcast connectors. (Images courtesy of Switchcraft, Inc., a Raytheon Company and Mackie Designs, Inc.)

8.14 OTHER CONNECTORS AND CONNECTOR ADAPTERS

Most of the connectors mentioned so far are intended for analog inputs or outputs; however, much of the equipment in the broadcast studio today has both analog and digital connections. Some digital connections utilize standard broadcast connectors—specifically the XLR and RCA plugs and jacks—and other digital inputs and outputs use differ-

Lock Release

Conductors

Male Plug

Female Jack (In Chassis)

SHIELD   2
HOT
COLD   3   1

FIGURE 8.12 XLR connectors feature a locking latch that prevents them from being accidentally disconnected. (Images courtesy of Switchcraft, Inc., a Raytheon Company, and Mackie Designs, Inc.)

FIGURE 8.13 Phone and miniphone connectors can be either stereo or mono. (Images courtesy of Switchcraft, Inc., a Raytheon Company and Mackie Designs, Inc.)

FIGURE 8.14 Some digital input and output connections require the use of connectors not normally associated with the wiring of radio broadcast audio equipment. (Image courtesy of Neutrik® USA.)

ent types of connectors. Two that are often used for digital hookups include the BNC and Toslink connectors (see Figure 8.14). The Toslink connector was developed by Toshiba and is the most common optical connector for digital audio. The connectors are usually molded plastic with a fiber-optic glass cable and are more common in audiophile applications than broadcast. BNC connectors feature a locking design along the lines of the XLR and are designed for use with 75-ohm cable. Used extensively for years in video applications, BNC connectors are now being developed specifically for audio use with radio's digital equipment.

Instead of using the connectors previously mentioned, some equipment manufacturers use a nonstandard connector for the input and output signals. For example, some tape recorders use a multipin connector, similar to the one shown in Figure 8.15, that includes input and output, as well as remote start and cue functions.

Something else in the connector realm that is very handy to have in a radio production studio is a supply of **connector adapters**. These enable you to change a connector from one form to another. Let's say, for example, that you need to connect an RCA output to a phone connector input, but the only cable you can find has an RCA connector at both ends. You can convert one of the RCA connectors to a phone connector with an adapter. This is a single piece of metal, which in this case houses a female RCA input at one end and a male phone output at the other (see Figure 8.15). When the male RCA connector is inserted into the female end of the adapter, the signal is transferred from the RCA connector to the phone connector, and from there it can go to the phone input. Adapters usually come in most handy in emergency situations when some connecting cable fails, so having a variety of them around is good production practice.

FIGURE 8.15 Connector adapters allow you to change from one type of connector to another, and the multipin connector may replace some of the standard broadcast connectors.

FIGURE 8.16 Typical broadcast audio cable is designed for a balanced wiring scheme. (Image courtesy of Cooper Industries—Belden Division.)

8.15 BALANCED AND UNBALANCED LINES

The cable most often used in broadcasting consists of two-stranded-wire conductors that are encased in plastic insulation plus a third uninsulated shield wire, all encased in a foil wrapping and another plastic sheathing as shown in Figure 8.16. For most wiring practices, the inner wires are designated + (red) and – (black); the uninsulated wire is the ground wire. The audio signal is carried on the positive and negative conductors. This type of cable is referred to as three-wire, or **balanced cable**, and often requires the XLR connector, because that is the one designed to connect three wires and is also utilized by many types of broadcast equipment.

Another type of cable is two-wire, or **unbalanced**. In this configuration, the negative wire also acts as a ground. An unbalanced cable is not as good as a balanced cable because unwanted audio interference, such as that created by a

nearby electric motor, can creep into the two-wire system. Also, balanced cables can be longer than unbalanced cables without encountering degradation of the signal. Ideally, balanced and unbalanced cable should not be mixed in the same audio setup, but sometimes this can't be avoided because different pieces of equipment are built for different cabling.

Wiring digital equipment is going to bring some new cabling concerns to broadcasters. On the one hand, since the digital signal carries both stereo channels on a single data stream, wiring digital equipment will actually take less cable than a normal installation. However, except for fairly short runs, ordinary audio cable should not be used for digital applications. Cable designed to handle the correct impedance and bandwidth of the digital signal should be used whether wiring a balanced or unbalanced circuit.

8.16 MIC, LINE, AND SPEAKER LEVELS

Equipment inputs and outputs can be one of three levels: mic, line, or speaker. You can think of these levels as very low for mic level (which usually must be preamplified to be used further), normal for line level (most equipment will use line levels), and very high for **speaker levels** (designed to drive a speaker only). Problems arise when various levels are mismatched. For example, if you tried to feed an audio recorder from a speaker-level source, you would probably distort the recording because the speaker-level source is too loud, and there is no control to turn it down. Another problem would occur if you fed a mic-level signal into a line-level input. In this case, the signal would be too low to be usable because mic levels must be preamplified to a usable level. Most broadcast equipment inputs and outputs

FIGURE 8.17 A broadcast studio timer provides accurate timing for radio production work. (Image courtesy of Radio Systems, Inc.)

are clearly designated as mic, line, or speaker level, and good production practice sends only the proper output to the proper input.

Fortunately, most of the cabling of production room equipment has been done by the engineer, and all the connections of various pieces of equipment have been worked out so that everything matches.

8.17 STUDIO TIMERS

Timers have already been mentioned because some audio consoles have built-in timers, but it is not uncommon to find a separate studio timer in the radio production room (see Figure 8.17). Since the timing of radio production work is so important, an accurate timing device is crucial. Most studio timers are digital, showing minutes and seconds, and include at least start, stop, and reset controls. Many timers can be interfaced with other equipment (such as audio recorders and CD players) so that they automatically reset to zero when that piece of equipment is started. Shorter timers (10 minutes) are usually adequate for radio production work; however, 24-hour timers are often found in the studio.

8.18 TAPE DEGAUSSERS

The audio tape **degausser**, or **bulk eraser**, is merely a strong electromagnet used to erase audio tape in the production studio. Since equipment such as the reel-to-reel recorder and audio tape cart recorder is being used less and less in the production studio, the tape degausser will not be needed in the future. However, if you use a tape-based recording medium, it's good production practice to erase all audio tapes prior to use even though some recorders have built-in erase heads. Some bulk erasers are designed for tabletop use (see Figure 8.18), and others can be handheld.

FIGURE 8.18 As less tape-based equipment is used, the bulk eraser or degausser may be hard to find in the production studio. (Image courtesy of Audiolab Electronics, Inc.)

Erasing tapes is a simple operation, but it's often done improperly by beginning production people and studio pros alike. To erase an audio tape (reel-to-reel), do the following:

a. Extend the tape to be erased an arm's length away from the degausser and then turn the degausser on. (If the tape is already sitting on the degausser when you turn it on, the transient surge of turning the unit on will put a click on the audio tape that can't be erased by normal operation of the eraser).

b. Place the tape on the guide pin, and rotate it two or three revolutions.

c. Turn the tape over, and rotate it another two or three times.

d. Move the tape an arm's length away from the degausser, and turn it off.

Cartridge and cassette tapes are erased in a similar manner. Using a handheld degausser is similar, except that the tape is held still, and the degausser is moved. The important points to remember are to turn the degausser on and off with the tape away from it, and to keep the degausser turned on as you turn the audio tape from one side to the other. Since the degausser is a strong electromagnet, it's a good idea to keep your watch out of close contact with it when erasing tapes. Also, keep tapes (diskettes and Zip disks) you don't want erased away from the degausser when it is operating. Once a tape is erased, it can't be restored except by rerecording the material.

There is another type of cartridge eraser that resembles a cartridge machine in appearance. When a cart is inserted and the eraser is turned on, the electromagnet comes on gradually (to avoid the surge that would cause a click on the audio tape) and thoroughly erases the cartridge. This type of unit (called an **eraser/splice finder**) also finds the splice on the audio tape cartridge. As the tape runs in the machine, a sensor locates the splice (where the tape was joined together to form the endless loop) and stops the tape just past the splice, which is the point where you would begin to record. This is important, because you do not want to record over the splice if you can avoid it.

8.19 CLEANING SUPPLIES

Cleaning supplies are common broadcast accessories, many of which have to do with the care of CDs. The Discwasher CD Hydrobath (see Figure 8.19) cleans CDs of dust, finger-prints, and other forms of dirt using hydrodynamic princi-ples. The CD and cleaning solution are put in the cleaner/dryer case. In less than a minute, as the CD spins at high speed, the cleaning solution is directed on the CD surface, dirt is trapped and removed, and the CD is spun in the opposite direction to dry it. This type of "no contact" cleaning prevents any accidental damage to the disc surface that could happen with hand cleaning.

Other CD accessories include a laser lens cleaner, CD repair kits to remove scratches, and CD cleaning sprays and cloths.

With more and more computer equipment making its way into the radio production studio, cleaning supplies for the monitor screen and keyboard need to be included as a broadcast accessory.

Older basic supplies are cotton swabs and head cleaner, used to keep audio tape recorders clean. The swabs are not Q-Tips, but long wooden sticks with a cotton tip on one end. These are excellent for getting at hard-to-reach tape heads (like those in tape cartridge machines) and removing edit pencil grease, tape residue, and other dirt. Expensive head-cleaning solvents can be replaced by denatured alcohol, but avoid using lower-quality isopropyl, or rubbing alcohol, because of its water content. Record-cleaning and stylus-care systems are also useful aids in keeping the tools of audio production clean.

8.20 JEWEL BOXES

Broadcast suppliers offer empty plastic cases for CDs, known as **jewel boxes** or **jewel cases**. These are needed because many promotional CDs come to radio stations in paper jackets rather than cases, and regular CD cases do break from time to time. Good production practice dictates keeping the CD in its case when not in use to prevent scratches or problems from dust and dirt.

FIGURE 8.19 A CD cleaning system can help keep dust and fingerprints from the surface of a compact disc. (Image courtesy of Discwasher® a divi-sion of Recoton Corporation LIC, New York.)

FIGURE 8.20 The telephone interface allows mixing an audio signal and a telephone signal. (Image courtesy of Gentner Broadcast Systems.)

Production Tip #8—"Proper Vinyl Storage"

Most production facilities still have a stack of vinyl LP records around, such as an old sound effects library or production music bed library. Of course, some radio stations still have a collection of music on record. If you're looking to store your vinyl long-term, do it the right way. Use a conventional wooden enclosure, designed for record storage, that is appropriate for the size of your collection. The most important point about vinyl storage is to keep the records absolutely vertical. If you do, the only weight at the edge of the record will be the record itself. If you allow the records to lean to one side or the other, then the weight will be unequal and it could cause the disc to warp. Also be careful of storing records in either very dry locations, which will cause the paper record jackets to crumble, or very damp locations, which will cause mildew. A temperature between 65 and 70 degrees Fahrenheit with relative humidity between 30 and 40 percent offers the best environment for storing vinyl.

8.21 TELEPHONE INTERFACE

The **telephone interface**, or **telephone coupler** (see Figure 8.20), is a piece of equipment designed to connect telephone lines to broadcast equipment. In a basic configuration, the telephone goes through the interface and comes into the audio console on its own channel (just like a CD player, for example). The caller volume is controlled with that channel's fader, in addition to a caller volume control on the interface. Once a call is taken by the announcer and the interface is switched on, the announcer talks to the caller through the studio microphone, not the telephone instrument (which can be hung up at this point) and hears the caller through the headphones.

The interface electronically maintains an isolation between the studio "send" signal and the caller "return" signal, providing a high-quality, clear telephone signal. In addition, many radio stations have installed high-quality digital (ISDN) services that give a clearer signal than the older analog systems. Since the telephone becomes just another audio input, it can be easily recorded (and later edited), mixed with other sound sources, and otherwise manipulated for production use.

8.22 CONCLUSIONS

Often, monitor speakers and studio accessories are given little or no thought. Some production people are only concerned with making sure sound comes out of the speakers and some accessory item is available. But, as you now understand, the role of the monitor speaker in radio production is not as minor as one might initially believe. And although not every accessory used by the professional radio broadcaster has been mentioned in this chapter, you have been introduced to the most common items used in the production studio, so you're less likely to run across something that makes you ask, "What's this for?"

Self-Study

■ QUESTIONS

1. A two-way speaker system consists of _____.
   a) a tweeter, a woofer, and a midrange speaker
   b) a tweeter, a woofer, and a crossover
   c) a tweeter and a woofer
   d) a tweeter, a woofer, and two crossovers

2. The transducing element of a speaker is called _____.
   a) a tweeter
   b) a crossover
   c) a woofer
   d) a driver

3. Which speaker enclosure design utilizes a tuned port to provide a highly efficient system with a full bass sound?
   a) acoustic suspension
   b) bass reflex
   c) bass boom
   d) sealed box

4. The individual speaker designed to reproduce higher frequencies is the _____.
   a) woofer
   b) crossover
   c) tweeter
   d) bass reflex

5. For proper stereo sound, the listening angle formed between the speakers and the listener should be 90 degrees.
   a) true
   b) false

6. Which broadcast connector has a guide pin?
   a) RCA
   b) phone
   c) XLR
   d) phono

7. The most practical place to locate monitor speakers in a production room is often _____.
   a) near the upper corners, close to the wall
   b) on the counter
   c) not in the room at all, but in an adjoining room
   d) in the middle of the wall, close together

8. If two speakers are out of phase, _____.
   a) the bass sounds will be generated at the rear of the cones
   b) both negative wires will be connected to negative terminals
   c) both positive wires will be connected to positive terminals
   d) the cone of one speaker will be moving out while the cone of the other speaker will be moving in

9. Which broadcast connector is always mono?
   a) phone
   b) miniphone
   c) ¼-inch phone
   d) RCA

10. Which type of monitor speaker will most likely be found in the production studio?
    a) ribbon speaker
    b) electrostatic speaker
    c) dynamic speaker
    d) condenser speaker

11. Which component of a speaker system divides the incoming audio signal into different frequencies and sends the proper frequencies to the appropriate driver?
    a) pigtail leads
    b) tweeter
    c) woofer
    d) crossover

12. Which type of headphone is designed with a porous muff that rests directly on the ear?
  a) closed headphone
  b) circumaural headphone
  c) earbud
  d) supra-aural headphone

13. Unbalanced audio cables are more susceptible to interference than balanced cables.
  a) true
  b) false

14. Having a high-power, external monitor amplifier in your production studio will allow you to record or broadcast a louder signal than using the internal monitor amp in the audio console.
  a) true
  b) false

15. Small speakers set on short stands, placed left and right of the audio console, so the listener hears mostly direct sound at ear level are known as _____ monitors.
  a) dynamic
  b) near-field
  c) acoustic suspension
  d) out-of-phase

16. When a patch panel is normaled, a patch cord is used to link broadcast equipment assigned to the top row of the panel to the equipment assigned to the bottom row.
  a) true
  b) false

17. Which broadcast connector has a sleeve, ring, and tip?
  a) RCA
  b) Cannon
  c) XLR
  d) phone

18. Which connector is most likely to be used for a patch bay?
  a) phone
  b) miniphone
  c) RCA
  d) multipin connector

19. A connector adapter is used _____.
  a) to transfer a signal in a patch bay
  b) to change a connector from one form to another
  c) to make a balanced line unbalanced
  d) to change a telephone signal to an audio signal

20. A balanced cable usually has _____.
  a) two wires
  b) three wires
  c) three ground wires
  d) two ground wires

21. The normal outputs of a CD player produce which level of audio signal?
  a) mic
  b) line
  c) speaker
  d) none of the above

22. Which production room accessory is used to protect compact discs?
   a) Discwasher
   c) degausser
   c) jewel box
   d) timer

23. When using a degausser, you should turn it on while holding the tape an arm's length away from it so that
_____.
   a) you give the degausser time to come up to full power
   b) you don't demagnetize your watch
   c) you don't erase tapes that are in the vicinity
   d) you don't put a click on the tape

24. Which production room accessory is used to connect telephone lines directly to broadcast equipment?
   a) audio routing switcher
   b) telephone coupler
   c) patch panel
   d) XLR connector

25. The best type of monitor to use when you need to use a microphone in the production studio to record a voice over music would be _____.
   a) a headset
   b) a tweeter
   c) an acoustic suspension
   d) a bass reflex

■ ANSWERS

If You Answered A:

1a. No. This speaker complement would be in a three-way system. (Reread 8.3.)

2a. No. A tweeter is a speaker designed to produce high frequencies. (Reread 8.2 and 8.3.)

3a. No. The acoustic suspension design is relatively inefficient. (Reread 8.4.)

4a. Wrong. The woofer is designed to reproduce the lower frequencies. (Reread 8.3.)

5a. No. This would put the listener directly in front of one of the speakers, and all the sound would appear to be coming out of that speaker. (Reread 8.6; check Figure 8.6.)

6a. No. (Review Figures 8.11 to 8.14; reread 8.12 to 8.14.)

7a. Correct. This gives the operator good sound and also leaves the counter clear for other equipment.

8a. No. You're confusing this with speaker enclosures. (Reread 8.4 and 8.7.)

9a. No. The phone connector can be either stereo or mono. (Review Figures 8.11 to 8.14; reread 8.12 to 8.14.)

10a. No. Ribbon speakers are generally too exotic in design and too expensive for broadcast use. (Reread 8.2.)

11a. Wrong. You may be confused because this is a part of an individual speaker that receives an input signal, but after it has been divided into the proper frequencies. (Reread 8.3.)

12a. No. This is a headphone with a ring-shaped ear cushion designed to encircle the ear and rest on the head. (Reread 8.10.)

13a. Right. Because one wire conducts the signal and also acts as ground, they are more likely to pick up unwanted noise.

14a. You haven't understood the concept of a monitor amp. It has no relation to the broadcast or recorded signal; it only controls the volume of the monitor speakers. (Reread 8.8.)

15a. Although they may be dynamic speakers, this term usually refers to the speaker driver. There is a better answer. (Reread 8.2 and 8.6.)

16a. Wrong. A normaled patch panel is actually unpatched. (Reread 8.11.)

17a. No. The phono connector only has an outer sleeve and tip. (Review Figures 8.11 to 8.14; reread 8.12 to 8.14.)

18a. Right. A male phone plug is the most likely connector to use with a patch bay.

19a. No. You would be very unlikely to use an adapter with a patch bay. (Reread 8.11 and 8.14.)

20a. No. You have it confused. (Reread 8.15.)

21a. Wrong. Mic level is a low output level, which must be preamplified to be usable, primarily produced by microphones, as the name implies. (Reread 8.16.)

22a. No. You're close because Discwasher has a CD cleaning system that helps keep dust and fingerprints off the disc, but there's a better answer. (Reread 8.19 and 8.20.)

23a. Wrong. Bulk erasers are at full power as soon as you turn them on. (Reread 8.18.)

24a. Wrong. An audio router can be involved in selecting various inputs and outputs, but it can't connect a telephone line by itself. (Reread 8.11 and 8.21.)

25a. Yes. A headset would prevent feedback and allow the operator to hear the music when the speakers are muted because the mic is on.

If You Answered B:

1b. Correct. These are the basic components of a two-way speaker system.

2b. Wrong. The crossover divides the electrical signals and sends them to the speaker drivers. (Reread 8.2 and 8.3.)

3b. Right. This answer is correct.

4b. No. The crossover is not a speaker but an electronic device for sending various frequencies to different speaker drivers. (Reread 8.3.)

5b. Correct. An angle of about 60 degrees should be formed between the listener and the speakers for the best stereo sound.

6b. No. (Review Figures 8.11 to 8.14; reread 8.12 to 8.14.)

7b. No. The sound can be good, but the speaker takes up counter space that could be used for something else. (Reread 8.6.)

8b. No. One negative connected to a positive would put them out of phase. (Reread 8.7.)

9b. No. The miniphone connector can be either stereo or mono. (Review Figures 8.11 to 8.14; reread 8.12 to 8.14.)

10b. No. Electrostatic speakers are generally too exotic in design and too expensive for broadcast use. (Reread 8.2.)

11b. Wrong. This is a part of a speaker system that reproduces high frequencies. (Reread 8.3.)

12b. No. This is a headphone with a ring-shaped ear cushion designed to encircle the ear and rest on the head. (Reread 8.10.)

13b. Wrong. (Reread 8.15.)

14b. This is the right response because monitor amps have no relation to the broadcast or recorded signal.

15b. Yes. Some production people feel the best sound is heard through near-field monitoring.

16b. Yes. When a patch cord is put into a patch panel, it is no longer normaled.

17b. Wrong. Cannon is just another name for the XLR connector. (Review Figures 8.11 to 8.14; reread 8.12 to 8.14.)

18b. No. You're warm but not correct. (Reread 8.11 and 8.13.)

19b. Correct. It transfers the signal so that another form of connector can be used.

20b. Right. There are three wires.

21b. Right. Line-level outputs are standard for most broadcast production equipment, such as CD players and audio recorders.

22b. No. This has nothing to do with compact discs. (Reread 8.17 and 8.20.)

23b. No. You take the risk of demagnetizing your watch regardless of how you turn it on. (Reread 8.18.)

24b. Correct. This is the best answer.

25b. No. This is only part of a monitor speaker. (Reread 8.3 and 8.10.)

If You Answered C:

1c. No. You're close though. (Reread 8.3.)

2c. No. A woofer is a speaker designed to reproduce low frequencies. (Reread 8.2 and 8.3.)

3c. There's no such enclosure design. (Reread 8.4.)

4c. Correct.

6c. Right. The XLR jack has a guide pin that prevents it from being connected incorrectly.

7c. No. You couldn't hear it if it were in another room. (Reread 8.6.)

8c. No. One positive connected to a negative would put them out of phase. (Reread 8.7.)

9c. No. A ¼-inch phone or phone connector can be either stereo or mono. (Review Figures 8.11 to 8.14; reread 8.12 to 8.14.)

10c. Yes. The dynamic speaker is found most often in the production studio.

11c. Wrong. This is a part of a speaker system that reproduces low frequencies. (Reread 8.3.)

12c. No. This is a type of headphone that is designed to fit into the ear. (Reread 8.10.)

15c. Although they may be acoustic suspension speakers, this term is usually associated with the speaker enclosure. There is a better answer. (Reread 8.4 and 8.6.)

17c. No. (Review Figures 8.11 to 8.14; reread 8.12 to 8.14.)

18c. No. (Reread 8.11 to 8.14.)

19c. No. Adapters are not related to balance. (Reread 8.14 and 8.15.)

20c. No. Although there are three wires, they aren't all ground wires. (Reread 8.15.)

21c. No. Speaker level is quite high and is designed to drive a monitor speaker. Most production equipment, like a CD player, would have to have its output signal amplified to reach speaker level. (Reread 8.16.)

22c. Yes. Jewel boxes are plastic protective cases for compact discs.

23c. No. Nearby tapes can be erased regardless of how you turn it on. (Reread 8.18.)

24c. Wrong. A patch panel could be involved in wiring a telephone line to an audio console, but it can't connect a telephone line by itself. (Reread 8.11 and 8.21.)

25c. No. You're confusing this with enclosures. (Reread 8.4 and 8.10.)

If You Answered D:

1d. Wrong. Only a single crossover is required in a speaker system. (Reread 8.3.)

2d. Yes. The driver transforms electrical signals into mechanical energy and thus audible sound.

3d. No. This is another name for an acoustic suspension speaker, which is relatively inefficient. (Reread 8.4.)

4d. No. Bass reflex describes a speaker system design, not an individual speaker. (Reread 8.3 and 8.4.)

6d. No. Phono is just another name for the RCA connector. (Review Figures 8.11 to 8.14; reread 8.12 to 8.14.)

7d. Wrong. This would really limit sound dispersion and any stereo imaging. (Reread 8.6.)

8d. Right. The sounds will be fighting each other when this happens.

9d. Correct. You must use two RCA connectors for stereo, one for each channel.

10d. No. There is no such speaker. (Reread 8.2.)

11d. Correct. A crossover is a network of filters that divides the audio signal into different frequencies and sends it to the proper individual speaker.

12d. Yes. Also known as open-air headphones, supra-aural headphones are designed to rest directly on the ear.

15d. No. Out-of-phase speakers are miswired, and this has nothing to do with speaker placement. (Reread 8.6 and 8.7.)

17d. Correct. The miniphone connectors also have them.

18d. No. (Reread 8.11 to 8.14.)

19d. No. There are devices to do this, but they are interfaces, not connector adapters. (Reread 8.14 and 8.21.)

20d. Wrong. (Reread 8.15.)

21d. No. There is a correct answer and this isn't it. (Reread 8.16.)

22d. No. This has nothing to do with a compact disc. (Reread 8.17 and 8.20.)

23d. Correct. Bring the tape in gradually to the degausser.

24d. Wrong. You're quite confused if you chose this answer. (Reread 8.12 and 8.21.)

25d. No. You're confusing this with speaker enclosure designs. (Reread 8.4 and 8.10)

Projects

■ PROJECT 1

Listen to the sound of the monitor speakers from different places in the production studio.

Purpose

To make you aware of how sound can change as the relationship between speaker and listener changes.

Advice, Cautions, and Background

1. If your studio is too small for you to hear any differences, just indicate this.
2. The most important thing for your drawings will be to show the relative dimensions of the studio and the position of the speakers.

How to Do the Project

1. Make three sketches of your control room, showing where the speakers are located.
2. On the first drawing, put an X where the production person usually sits. On the second drawing, put an X at another spot in the control room where you can stand and listen to the monitors. Do the same for the third drawing.
3. Play some music (you can use the music provided on the CD-ROM that accompanies this text) through the monitor speakers, and position yourself in each of the three places where you have placed Xs. Listen for any differences in the way the music sounds at the three locations.
4. Write a short report detailing how the music sounded at each position.
5. Put your drawings and your report into a packet labeled SPEAKER-LISTENER RELATIONSHIP. Give the packet to your instructor for credit for this project.

■ PROJECT 2

Inventory the broadcast accessories found in your production facility.

Purpose

To familiarize you with available accessory items.

Advice, Cautions, and Background

1. Design a form to conduct your inventory.
2. You can use items in any studio available at your facility, but note the exact locations.

How to Do the Project

1. List the brand name and model of *each item*, if possible.
2. Make sure you record the location of each item (e.g., Production Studio A or PDX 1).
3. Provide specifics about an item, if appropriate. For example, is the degausser handheld or designed for tabletop use?
4. If your production facility doesn't have a particular item mentioned in this chapter, indicate this on the form.
5. Turn in your inventory form to the instructor for credit for this project. Don't forget to put your name on it and label it BROADCAST ACCESSORIES INVENTORY FORM.

CHAPTER NINE

Signal Processing Equipment

Information

9.1 INTRODUCTION

Signal processing is nothing more than altering how audio, such as an announcer's voice or a CD, sounds. We've already seen a few forms of audio processing in the equalization capabilities of some audio consoles and the bass roll-off feature of some microphones, but most signal processing is accomplished by the use of separate audio components. Some digital equipment, especially editing software and digital audio workstations, also includes features that allow for signal processing the audio signal.

Usually signal processing involves the manipulation of the frequency response (tonal balance), stereo imaging, or dynamic range of the sound signal. Frequency response refers to the range of all frequencies (pitches) that an audio component can reproduce and we can hear, that is, around 20 Hz (deep bass) to 20 kHz (highest treble). **Imaging** refers to the perceived space between and behind monitor speakers and how we hear individual sounds within that plane. Dynamic range refers to the audible distance between the softest sounds that can be heard over noise and the loudest sounds that can be produced before distortion is heard.

Several signal-processing devices will refer to the terms "wet" and "dry." The incoming, or unprocessed, audio signal is considered a *dry* signal, and the outgoing audio signal that has been processed is considered the *wet* signal.

This chapter focuses on the capability of editing software to signal process and other electronic audio processors commonly used in radio. The amount of equipment available for signal processing in any one production facility, however, can vary widely, from essentially none to a veritable smorgasbord of electronic black boxes.

9.2 EQUALIZERS

One of the most commonly used signal processors is the equalizer. An equalizer allows for manipulation of frequency response by adjustment of the volume of selected frequencies and can be thought of as a fancy **tone control**.

You're familiar with bass and treble tone controls—most home stereo systems have them. When you turn up the treble control, you increase the volume of the higher frequencies. Unfortunately, a treble control turns up all the higher frequencies. An equalizer, on the other hand, offers greater flexibility and allows the operator to differentiate, for example, between lower high frequencies and upper high frequencies, and to make different adjustments to each.

Most equalizers found in the radio production studio are **unity-gain** devices. The sound signal that has passed through the equalizer's circuits is no stronger or weaker overall than the input sound signal was. In other words, if the processor's controls are set at zero they should have no processing effect on the incoming audio signal. Of course, if the signal is processed by increasing the level of several different frequencies, then the overall volume of the outgoing signal will be louder than the unprocessed signal.

9.3 THE GRAPHIC EQUALIZER

The two main kinds of equalizers found in radio production are the graphic equalizer and the parametric equalizer. The **graphic equalizer** is more common and derives its name from the rough graph of a sound's altered frequency response formed by the slider control settings on the equalizer's front faceplate (see Figure 9.1).

A graphic equalizer divides the frequency response range into separate bands, usually at one-third- (30 bands), one-half- (20 bands), or full-octave 10-band intervals. If the first band of a full-octave equalizer was at 31 hertz, the second would be at or near 62 hertz, the third at 125 hertz, and so on. Obviously, the more bands you have to work with, the greater control you have, but it also becomes harder to correctly manipulate the equalizer. Most broadcast-quality graphic equalizers are at least full-octave, 10-band equalizers. Each band has a slider volume control that's off in a middle or "flat" position and can move up to increase ("boost"), or down to attenuate ("cut"), the volume at that particular frequency. The volume range varies, but +12 to −12, or 12 decibels of boost or cut, is a common configuration.

FIGURE 9.1 The graphic equalizer can boost or cut the audio signal at various frequencies and provide a visual representation of the equalization being applied. (Image courtesy of Rane Corporation.)

To understand equalization techniques, look at the simple five-band equalizer shown in Figure 9.2. You may have a similar equalizer in your car radio system. Note how the slider setting would demark a frequency response graph, indicating how the original sound was being manipulated. If we were playing a piece of rock music through this equalizer, the increased setting at 60 hertz would give the drums extra punch; cutting back at 250 hertz would help minimize bass boom; the increase at 1 kilohertz would add brilliance to the voices; the decrease at 4 kilohertz would minimize the harshness of the sound; and the increase at 8 kilohertz would add presence to the highs. There is no one correct setting for an equalizer, and we could just as easily have had all different settings and yet produced an excellent sound. There are, however, settings that could make the sound very poor, and the production operator needs to beware of altering the sound too much.

As previously noted, audio editing software often includes signal processing capability. Figure 9.3 shows the screen for *Cool Edit's* graphic equalizer, which allows you to select a 10-, 20-, or 30-band unit. Clicking on the virtual slider control lets you cut or boost the volume of the specific frequency. The position of the sliders and the top portion of the screen give a visual representation of what is happening to the audio signal. Equalization procedures are exactly the same as with any other graphic equalizer. Clicking on the PREVIEW button lets you hear the equalized signal and actually change settings as it is playing back. When you have the sound you're looking for, click on the OK button and the original audio will be changed according to the EQ settings.

9.4 THE PARAMETRIC EQUALIZER

The **parametric equalizer** gives the operator even greater control over the sound because it allows not only volume control of specified frequencies, but control over the actual frequency and bandwidth selected. In other words, the parametric equalizer is used for finer control of the frequencies within a sound than the broad control offered by graphic equalizers. For example, the five-band graphic equalizer mentioned above had fixed frequency bands at 60, 250, 1000, 4000, and 8000 hertz, but a parametric equalizer allows the operator to select an exact frequency. For

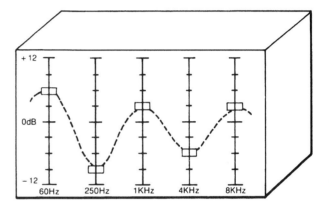

FIGURE 9.2 A simple five-band graphic equalizer.

example, instead of a set band at 1000 hertz, you might choose a band at 925 hertz or 1200 hertz.

If the graphic equalizer were increased at 1 kilohertz, not only would that frequency get a boost, but so would the adjacent frequencies (perhaps from 500 to 1500 hertz), according to a preset bandwidth determined by the manufacturer. Many parametric equalizers also allow the operator to adjust that bandwidth. For example, still using the 1-kilohertz frequency, the parametric equalizer operator could select a bandwidth of 800 to 1200 hertz or a narrower bandwidth of 950 to 1050 hertz to be equalized. Most equalizers also have a switch that allows the sound signal to pass through the equalizer unaffected or unequalized. Figure 9.4 shows one type of parametric equalizer.

9.5 EQUALIZER USES

Whether a feature of an audio editing program or a stand-alone unit, the general use of an equalizer is to alter or change the sound character of an audio signal. The term **EQ** refers to the general process of equalization when an equalizer is used to cut or boost the signal level of specific frequencies. Specifically, equalizers are often used in the production studio to cut down on various forms of audio noise, to alter recordings to suit individual taste, and to create a special effect.

FIGURE 9.3 The graphic equalizer screen from an audio editing software package. (Image courtesy of Syntrillium Software Corporation.)

FIGURE 9.4 A parametric equalizer offers greater control of various frequencies within a sound than the graphic equalizer. (Image courtesy of Orban Associates, Inc.)

EQ is often used to deal with hiss, one of the common forms of noise in production work. **Hiss** describes a high-frequency noise problem inherent in the recording process. Hiss sounds exactly as you would imagine and is heard by the human ear within the frequency range of 2 to 8 kilohertz. Using an equalizer to cut or turn down the frequency settings closest to this range can attenuate hiss to a less noticeable level. However, even with careful adjustment, it's often impossible to eliminate noise entirely. Remember, you also affect the program signal as you equalize, so EQ is usually a compromise between less noise and a still discernible signal.

EQ is sometimes used to combat hum, which is another form of noise in production work. **Hum** is a low-frequency problem associated with leakage of the 60 hertz AC electri-

cal current into the audio signal. A poor or broken ground in any part of the electrical circuit can cause hum, and it, too, sounds exactly as you would imagine. Attenuating frequencies right around 60 Hz would lessen the problem.

The equalizer may also be used for altering the sound of CDs (or actually any music) to suit an individual's taste. For some production work, you may need to accent the bass in a particular piece of background music, and boosting frequency settings around 50 Hz certainly could help do so. Equalizing anything is very subjective, and what sounds good to one listener may not to another. The key is to use any effect moderately and experiment to find just the right sound.

Sometimes equalization is undertaken to achieve a special effect. For example, cutting down most of the lower frequencies leaves a very tinny-sounding voice that might be perfect as a robot voice for a particular commercial or radio drama. You could produce an effect that approximates an old-fashioned, poor-quality telephone sound by boosting the frequency settings from about 600 to 800 Hz and cutting the frequency settings on either side of this range. Many such effects are achieved by experimenting with various settings of the equalizer.

9.6 FILTERS

Filters are less likely to be found in the radio production room, but since they are a type of equalizer, a short discussion of them may prove useful. Instead of manipulating a specific frequency, filters affect a whole range of the audio signal. For example, a **low cut filter** cuts, or eliminates, frequencies below a certain point, say 500 hertz. Instead of a normal frequency response of 20 to 20,000 hertz, once the signal goes through this filter, its response is 500 to 20,000 hertz. A **low pass filter** works in the same fashion but lets frequencies below a certain point pass or remain unaffected. In other words, a cut filter and a pass filter are opposites in their action. A **band pass filter** cuts frequencies except for a specified band. It has a low cut point (maybe 1,000 hertz) and a high cut point (maybe 3,000 hertz). When a signal is sent through this filter, only that portion of the signal between the two cut points is heard. A **band reject** (or **cut**) **filter** is just the opposite of the band pass filter in that it

allows frequencies to pass except for a specified frequency range. A **notch filter** is a special filter that completely eliminates an extremely narrow range of frequencies (such as telephone hiss) or one individual frequency (such as AC hum).

Usually filters are used to correct a specific problem. For example, a record may have a scratch that shows up around 11 kilohertz, and a notch filter is used to eliminate that frequency. Of course, filters eliminate both the problem *and* the actual program signal, so careful use is necessary to maintain a good audio signal after filtering has taken place.

Figure 9.5 shows a digital editing program that has a filtering function. This screen illustrates a low pass filter so that low frequencies are allowed to pass through the filter unaltered. The cutoff point has been set at 661.5 hertz so the high frequencies above this point are rejected or removed from the original audio. The graph gives a visual representation of what is happening to the audio.

9.7 NOISE REDUCTION

We've mentioned the problem of noise inherent in the production process. Signal-processing devices, known as noise-reduction systems, have been devised to help prevent noise. Note that these electronic devices can't get rid of noise that already exists; their job is to prevent noise from being added to a recording. Digital recording does not need to use noise-reduction devices because the noises they are

FIGURE 9.5 Digital editing software can replicate an analog filter. (Image courtesy of Syntrillium Software Corporation.)

meant to eliminate are ones inherent in the analog recording process. There are two systems commonly used with analog systems: Dolby and dbx. Both are **companders**—their general operation is to compress (reduce the dynamic range of) an audio signal during recording and then expand the signal during playback—but they are not compatible systems.

9.8 DOLBY NOISE-REDUCTION SYSTEMS

There are several **Dolby** noise-reduction systems in use in recording studios, broadcast stations, home stereo equipment, and movie theaters. The Dolby B and C systems and Dolby S and SR are most likely to be found in the production studio, often built into the electronics of various audio tape recorders.

The two-part Dolby process consists of increasing the volume of the program signal at certain frequencies (specifically at the upper end of the frequency spectrum, where the signal is most likely to be lost to noise) before the recording begins. If the particular frequencies aren't affected by noise, they aren't altered by the Dolby encoding process. During playback, levels that were increased are decreased, but noise in the recording process was not boosted, so it seems lower in relation to the program level. Depending on the system employed, 10 to 25 decibels of noise reduction can be attained using the Dolby process. As with all other signal-processing equipment, careful use is required to achieve the results the operator wants. Setting proper levels prior to recording with Dolby is important so that both encoding (recording) and decoding (playback) of the audio signal are at the same level.

Dolby SR (for spectral recording) and Dolby S are newer and more sophisticated noise-reduction systems from the Dolby Laboratories. Dolby S (derived from the SR system) is designed to be an improved version of the Dolby B and Dolby C systems.

9.9 DBX NOISE-REDUCTION SYSTEMS

There are several **dbx** noise-reduction systems: Type I, Type II, and Type III. Type II is often found in broadcasting (see Figure 9.6), and there is no compatibility between the various dbx systems. Unlike Dolby, dbx compresses the signal over the entire frequency range during recording. Again, since the signal goes through the noise-reduction unit before recording, is processed and recorded, and then is played back through the noise-reduction unit, inherent recording noise is mostly covered up.

Noise reduction of 40 decibels can be attained using the dbx system. The audio signal is compressed during recording by a two-to-one ratio (in other words, the dynamic range is cut in half), with the loud levels greatly reduced and the soft levels boosted by a carefully designed frequency response preemphasis. During playback, the signal

FIGURE 9.6 The dbx® noise-reduction system, like Dolby, is designed to lessen noise that can occur during the analog recording process. (Image courtesy of dbx®, a division of AKG Acoustics, Inc.)

is expanded by a one-to-two ratio, with deemphasis, so that the original dynamic range is restored. Noise buildup usually introduced in the recording process is dramatically reduced; however, as with all noise-reduction systems, any noise present in the original audio signal is not reduced.

Although digital audio recording will not generally introduce noise, most software programs have features for noise reduction so that audio recorded outside the system and then brought into it can be improved. For example, a sound effect or piece of music from a vinyl record may contain "pops" and "clicks" from excessive use. Some software programs include a feature that would eliminate this noise by first analyzing the audio to determine where the pops are and then repairing or reconstructing the audio at that point. There may be several parameters to set, and a bit of trial and error is usually required to get the correct settings, but salvaging just the right piece of music may be important to a production project. Other noise-reduction features may help eliminate or reduce tape hiss, 60-cycle AC hum, microphone background noise, or other noise problems heard in the audio. However, since the noise is embedded in the audio you want to keep, noise reduction is a trade-off between how much noise level you can decrease and how much loss of audio quality you can afford. Still, depending upon the sophistication of the software program you may have available, there is a great deal that can be done to improve a noisy audio signal.

9.10 REVERBERATION

A signal processor that affects the imaging of sound is the reverberation unit, probably the second most common type of processor. It manipulates the sound signal to artificially produce the sound of different acoustic environments. As we've mentioned, reverb is reflected sound that has bounced off two or more surfaces. Sound heard (or produced) in a small studio sounds different than sound produced in a large hall or auditorium, and reverb is the main characteristic that audibly produces the difference.

The modern production studio is likely to have a **digital reverb** unit that is either an electronic device (see Figure 9.7) or a feature of an audio editing program. The original signal is fed into the unit and is electronically processed to achieve

FIGURE 9.7 A digital reverb unit can simulate various acoustic environments altering the "image" of the sound. (Image courtesy of Yamaha Professional Audio Division.)

FIGURE 9.8 A digital reverb program, within audio editing software, can have various preset acoustic environments, ranging from a coat closet to a concert hall. (Image courtesy of Snytrillium Software Corporation).

the reverb effect; then the altered signal is sent out of the unit.

Besides a black box digital reverb, audio editing software may also have reverb, echo, or delay functions. Figure 9.8 shows a reverb screen from one audio editing program. In addition to building your own reverb sound by setting various parameters, note that several preset acoustic environments can be chosen, such as a medium-sized auditorium or a tiled bathroom shower. Merely selecting the appropriate preset and clicking on OK will transform the original audio so that it sounds as if it had been recorded in that environment with the corresponding reverb effect.

9.11 DIGITAL DELAY

A **digital delay** unit can be used in both the production studio and on-air control room. As its name implies, this

signal processor actually takes the audio signal, holds it, and then releases it to allow the signal to be used further. The time the signal is held or delayed can be varied from fractions of a second to several seconds. Although there are analog delay units, most systems are digital, and the incoming signal is converted from its analog form to digital for processing and back to analog after processing.

In the on-air studio, a delay unit is often used in conjunction with a telephone talk show. The program signal is sent through the delay unit to provide approximately a 7-second delay before it is sent to the transmitter. If something is said by a caller that should not be broadcast, the operator has time to "kill" the offending utterance before it is actually broadcast. (This is why callers are asked to turn their home radio down if they're talking to an announcer on-air, because the sound they hear on the radio is the delayed sound and not the words they are actually saying into the telephone. It's extremely difficult to carry on a conversation when you can hear both sounds.)

Production Tip #9—"Reverse Echo"

You don't need any special signal processing equipment to create a **reverse echo** effect used to "punctuate" a key word in commercial copy. Follow these steps to accomplish this effect: First, record the important phrase on reel-to-reel tape recorder #1 (for example, "This gigantic sale saves you . . . 50 percent!"). Be sure to pause before, and really emphasize, the key word(s) (in this case, "50 percent"). Record it several times at both 7 1/2 and 15 IPS, and leave a lot of room between each "take."

Don't rewind the tape, but dub the tape you just recorded to reel-to-reel tape recorder #2 *backward*. Either thread it for backward playback or literally remove the reels and reverse them (i.e., take-up reel becomes feed reel and vice versa). As you're dubbing, you need to add some "echo" to the key word. You do this by having recorder #2's output selectors set to "reproduce" or "tape" and having this recorder in "program" on the audio console. As you increase the gain for this recorder on the console, you are increasing the "echo" effect. You'll have to experiment to find the right amount.

Finally, reverse the tape on recorder #2 (this is the backward dub), and play it back. You should hear a nice "sneak," or "pre-echo," of the key word before you actually hear the emphasized word. Since the echo comes before the word, this effect is also known as a "forward echo." Splice this phrase into the copy at the appropriate point, add background music and other effects, and you should have a production spot that stands out from the rest. However, remember that one small effect used as part of a production can be very effective, but too many special effects in a production take away from their uniqueness.

In the production studio, delay units are used to create special effects similar to reverb. Set for an extremely short delay, the units can create an effect that sounds like a doubled voice or even a chorus of voices.

9.12 DYNAMIC RANGE

When we mention **dynamic range** in a radio production context, we're referring to the range of volumes of sound that broadcast equipment can handle. This intensity of a sound is measured in decibels (dB). One decibel represents the minimum difference in volume that we can hear, but a change of 3 decibels is often necessary before we actually perceive a difference in volume.

The dynamic range goes from 0 decibels at the **threshold of hearing** to 120+ decibels at the **threshold of pain**. A whisper is around 20 decibels, normal conversation is near 60 decibels, and shouting is about 80 decibels. Average music-listening levels are between 30 and 80 decibels, but some rock concerts have been measured above 110 decibels.

Dynamic range also relates the volume of one signal to another, such as signal to noise or input to output. We should note that dynamic range is measured on a logarithmic scale. For example, to hear one audio signal twice as loud as another, you would have to increase the volume of one by 10 decibels in relation to the other.

A 60-decibel dynamic range was once considered quite adequate for high-quality broadcast production equipment; today's digital equipment, however, offers an increased dynamic range and a 90-plus decibel range is now common.

Audio editing software often includes some type of dynamics processor that can emulate stand-alone compressors, limiters, expanders, and noise gates.

9.13 COMPRESSORS AND EXPANDERS

The compressor (and the limiter) are two of the most common signal-processing devices used to affect the dynamic range of the audio signal. Although they are most often used to process the signal between the studio and the transmitter and therefore aren't pure production room devices, they were the first processing devices used in radio, and virtually every radio station uses them. They are also occasionally used in the production room to process the signal before it's sent to an audio recorder.

The **compressor** operates as an automatic volume control and reduces the dynamic range of an audio signal. If the audio signal is too loud, the compressor automatically lowers it, and if the signal is too soft, the compressor increases it. Several adjustments on the compressor determine its actual operation. The threshold of compression is the setting of the level of signal needed to turn on the compressor. As long as the audio signal stays below this point, the compressor doesn't do anything. Input level can be adjusted on the compressor, although this level is also determined by the output of the audio signal source.

In any case, the compressor really needs to work only some of the time. If the input is too low, the threshold of compression will never be reached, and if the input is too high, the compressor will severely restrict the dynamic range. The compression ratio determines how hard the compressor works. A ratio of five-to-one means that if the level of the incoming signal increases ten times its current level, the output of that signal from the compressor will only double. Compressors also have settings for attack time (how quickly volume is reduced once it exceeds the threshold) and release time (how quickly a compressed signal is allowed to return to its original volume). The release time adjustment is very important because too fast a setting can create an audible pumping sound as the compressor releases, especially if there is a loud sound immediately followed by a soft sound or a period of silence.

An expander is essentially the opposite of a compressor and therefore is used to expand the dynamic range of an audio signal. The dynamic range of an incoming audio signal is stretched out by boosting the high-volume signals and attenuating the low-volume signals. A **noise gate** is a type of expander used to reduce noise by heavily turning down the level of an audio signal that falls below a set threshold point. For example, it could be set so that pauses in a piece of music would be attenuated so that background noise would not be recorded.

9.14 LIMITERS

A **limiter** is a form of compressor with a large compression ratio of ten-to-one or more. Once a threshold level is reached, a limiter doesn't allow the signal to increase anymore. Regardless of how high the input signal becomes, the output remains at its preset level. If they're adjustable, attack and release times on limiters should be quite short.

Both the limiter and the compressor can be rather complicated to adjust properly. Too much compression of the

FIGURE 9.9 The compressor/limiter is used to process the dynamic range of an audio signal. (Image courtesy of Symetrix, Inc.)

dynamic range makes an audio signal that can be tiresome to listen to, and pauses or quiet passages in the audio signal are subject to the pumping problem mentioned earlier. Since they're often associated with the transmitter only, compressors and limiters are usually the domain of the engineer. If you do have access to them in the production facility, it may take some experimenting to get the kind of processing that you're looking for because there are no standard settings for signal-processing devices. Figure 9.9 shows a system that combines both a compressor and limiter in a single unit.

9.15 OTHER SIGNAL PROCESSORS

A **flanger** is another processor for producing a specific special effect. This unit electronically combines an original signal with a slightly delayed signal in such a way as to cause an out-of-phase frequency response that creates a filtered swishing sound. Flanging, also called phasing, was originally accomplished by sending an audio signal to two reel-to-reel tape recorders and then physically slowing down one of the reels by holding a hand on the flange or hub of the reel. As the two signals went in and out of sync with each other, the audio would cancel and reinforce, creating a psychedelic phase-shift effect.

Figure 9.10 shows the flanger screen from *Cool Edit's* audio editing software. The Original-Delayed slider on the top left side of the screen controls the mix between the dry (original) audio and the wet (flanged) signal. Portions of both must be mixed to achieve the effect of slightly delaying and phasing the signals. Like many of the other signal-processing effects using audio software, there are other

FIGURE 9.10 Flanging—a psychedelic, swooshing sound—is a phase-shifted, time-delay effect easily created with audio editing software. (Image courtesy of Syntrillium Software Corporation.)

FIGURE 9.11 This multi-effects processor, an Eventide Harmonizer "named" Orville, puts more than one signal-processing function in a single "black box." (Image courtesy of Eventide.)

adjustments to create just the effect you're looking for, or you can just choose a preset effect by clicking on one of the names on the right side of the screen.

A **de-esser** is an electronic processor designed to control the sibilant sounds without affecting other parts of the sound signal. As the name implies, a **stereo synthesizer** is a processor that takes a mono audio signal (input) and simulates a stereo signal (output). Some processors use a form of delay to provide separation between the left and right channel outputs; others use a form of filtering to send certain frequencies to one channel and certain other frequencies to the other channel to provide a synthetic stereo effect.

9.16 MULTI-EFFECTS PROCESSORS

Many signal-processing devices are designed so that they perform more than one function—that is, to put more digital effects in a single black box. For example, Eventide, Yamaha, and Lexicon are all manufacturers who provide popular signal processing tools for the production studio (see Figure 9.11). These devices offer a variety of audio effects in one unit, including the ability to alter the pitch of an incoming audio signal, time compression and expansion, delay, natural reverb effects, flanging, time reversal, and repeat capabilities. Any production person should find it enjoyable to experiment with the variety of creative effects that can be produced with a multi-effects processor.

As we've noted throughout this chapter, another form of multi-effects processor is the digital audio workstation or audio editing software. In addition to offering improved editing capabilities, most workstations or software programs have provisions for adding special effects to the audio signal. Often you can add an effect to the audio by mouse-clicking on a preset effects button. Otherwise, you may have to set various parameters to create the signal processing effect that you desire, and that can range from being fairly easy to extremely complex. Regardless of this fact, editing software or workstation systems are still, in many cases, simpler to set up and operate than their black box counterparts.

9.17 CONCLUSIONS

This chapter is not a complete guide to signal-processing equipment. There are other units in use in radio production facilities, and there are other effects available through audio editing software programs. Nor is this chapter intended to make you a professional operator of such equipment. What is intended is that you become aware of a number of the more common processors and that you have an understanding of their basic purpose. The actual operation of most of this equipment will take some trial-and-error work in your production facility. Use signal processing in moderation, and bear in mind that a lot of great radio production has been produced using no signal-processing equipment at all.

Self-Study

■ QUESTIONS

1. The equalizer processes an audio signal by altering which of the following?
   a) volume
   b) imaging
   c) dynamic range
   d) frequency response

2. An audio signal that has been equalized would be called a "dry" signal.
   a) true
   b) false

3. Which type of equalizer can select an exact center frequency and bandwidth as well as alter the volume at that frequency and bandwidth?
   a) graphic
   b) parametric
   c) dielectric
   d) full-octave, 10-band

4. What type of filter would most likely be used to attenuate or eliminate a 60-hertz hum in a recording?
   a) low pass filter
   b) band pass filter
   c) notch filter
   d) low cut filter

5. The 60-hertz hum mentioned in question 4 could also have been eliminated by the use of either Dolby or dbx noise reduction.
   a) true
   b) false

6. A signal processor that affects the imaging of a sound is the _____.
   a) equalizer
   b) noise-reduction unit
   c) de-esser
   d) reverb unit

7. Using signal processing equipment to create a tinny voice, you would _____.
   a) cut out most of the lower frequencies
   b) cut out most of the higher frequencies
   c) eliminate the EQ
   d) increase compression

8. The noise-reduction system most likely to be found in the radio production studio is _____.
   a) Dolby A
   b) Dolby S
   c) Type I
   d) Flanger

9. In the Dolby system of noise reduction, _____.
   a) volumes of certain frequencies are increased during recording and decreased during playback
   b) the dbx is increased with a calibrated tone so that it attains the level of 30 decibels
   c) all frequencies pass through, except ones that have been preset by the notch filter
   d) once a threshold level is reached, the signal isn't allowed to increase anymore

10. A noise gate is a type of _____.
   a) limiter
   b) equalizer
   c) expander
   d) imager

11. A compressor _____.
   a) usually has a compression ratio of ten-to-one
   b) lowers a signal that's too loud and raises one that's too soft
   c) doesn't operate unless it's connected to a digital delay unit
   d) produces an out-of-phase, filtered, swishing sound

12. Any signal-processing equipment that's labeled a unity-gain device would amplify all frequencies of the signal going through that equipment an equal amount.
    a) true
    b) false

13. Which of the following is *not* a type of Dolby noise reduction?
    a) Dolby S
    b) Dolby B
    c) Dolby C
    d) Dolby D

14. Which signal-processing device is most likely to offer a variety of effects, such as pitch change, time compression, reverb, and flanging?
    a) dbx Graphic Equalizer
    b) Eventide Broadcast Delay
    c) dbx Compressor/Limiter
    d) Eventide Harmonizer

15. Which signal-processing device inputs a mono signal and outputs a simulated stereo signal?
    a) digital delay
    b) band cut filter
    c) flanger
    d) stereo synthesizer

16. Today's digital equipment offers an increased dynamic range, and a _____ decibel range is now common.
    a) 120
    b) 90
    c) 60
    d) 3

17. A digital audio workstation usually includes digital reverb and delay effects but rarely any other type of signal-processing capability.
    a) true
    b) false

18. Which graphic equalizer setting would most likely be used to add "brilliance" to an announcer's voice?
    a) boost at 60 Hz
    b) cut at 250 Hz
    c) boost at 1 kHz
    d) cut at 8 kHz

19. Which signal processor is designed to help control sibilance in an announcer's voice?
    a) compressor
    b) limiter
    c) de-esser
    d) digital reverb

20. Which of the following is the opposite of a compressor?
    a) equalizer
    b) expander
    c) flanger
    d) limiter

■ ANSWERS

If You Answered A:

1a. No. You're headed in the right direction. Equalizers do increase or attenuate volumes at specific frequencies, but they do this to alter another sound characteristic. (Reread 9.1 and 9.2.)

2a. No. A dry audio signal is an unprocessed signal. (Reread 9.1.)

3a. No. Center frequencies and bandwidths are preset on graphic equalizers. (Reread 9.3 and 9.4.)

4a. No. This type of filter allows lower frequencies to pass and would not eliminate noise at 60 hertz. (Reread 9.6.)

5a. No. Noise-reduction units, regardless of brand name, can't eliminate noise that already exists in a recording. They only prevent noise during the recording process. (Reread 9.7.)

6a. No. Equalizers affect frequency response. (Reread 9.2 and 9.10.)

7a. Correct. Cutting the bass will give a tinny sound.

8a. No. (Reread 9.8 and 9.9.)

9a. Correct. It's a two-step process.

10a. No. In a way it is the opposite. (Reread 9.13 and 9.14.)

11a. Wrong. That's a limiter. (Reread 9.13 and 9.14.)

12a. No. A unity-gain device doesn't amplify the overall level of the incoming signal at all. (Reread 9.2.)

13a. Wrong. This is one of the newest and most sophisticated Dolby noise-reduction systems. (Reread 9.8.)

14a. No. This doesn't really exist. It's a mixture of signal processing. (Reread 9.3, 9.9, and 9.15.)

15a. No. You may be thinking about a stereo synthesizer that uses a form of delay. (Reread 9.11 and 9.16.)

16a. No. You may be getting this confused with the threshold of pain. (Reread 9.12.)

17a. No. Most DAWs have multi-effect capability. (Reread 9.1 and 9.15.)

18a. No. This would punch up the bass. (Reread 9.3.)

19a. Wrong. This is a form of automatic volume control used to affect dynamic range. (Reread 9.13 and 9.16.)

20a. No. You might be confusing frequency response and dynamic range. (Reread 9.2 to 9.5 and 9.12 to 9.13.)

If You Answered B:

1b. No. Imaging can be affected by other signal processors. (Reread 9.1 and 9.2.)

2b. Correct. This is the right response.

3b. Yes. The parametric equalizer gives the operator the greatest control over the EQ process.

4b. No. This type of filter is usually used to allow a range of frequencies to pass, not to eliminate a single frequency. (Reread 9.6.)

5b. Yes. Because you can't eliminate existing noise with noise-reduction units.

6b. No. Noise-reduction units affect dynamic range. (Reread 9.7 and 9.10.)

7b. No. That is where the tinny sound would be. (Reread 9.5.)

8b. Correct. It's one of the newer common ones.

9b. No. (Reread 9.8 and 9.9.)

10b. No. A noise gate has nothing to do with frequencies. (Reread 9.2 and 9.13.)

11b. Yes. It lowers and raises signals in that manner.

12b. Yes. Unity-gain devices don't amplify the overall level of the incoming signal.

13b. Wrong. Dolby B is a common noise-reduction system found on cassette recorders. (Reread 9.8.)

14b. No. This isn't correct. (Reread 9.11 and 9.15.)

15b. No. You may be thinking about a stereo synthesizer, which uses a form of filtering. (Reread 9.6 and 9.16.)

16b. Correct. This is the right response.

17b. Yes. Most DAWs have multi-effect capability.

18b. No. This would minimize bass boominess. (Reread 9.3.)

19b. Wrong. This is a form of automatic volume control used to affect dynamic range. (Reread 9.14 and 9.16.)

20b. Correct. Since the expander increases dynamic range, it is the opposite of a compressor.

If You Answered C:

1c. No. Dynamic range can be affected by other signal processors. (Reread 9.1 and 9.2.)

3c. There's no such thing. (Reread 9.3 and 9.4.)

4c. Correct. This type of filter allows all frequencies to pass except a specified one, which we could specify at 60 hertz to eliminate the hum.

6c. Wrong. A de-esser is an electronic processor designed to control sibilant sounds. (Reread 9.10 and 9.16.)

7c. Wrong. That wouldn't really be possible. (Reread 9.5.)

8c. No. (Reread 9.8 and 9.9.)

9c. No. You are confusing this with filters. (Reread 9.6 and 9.8.)

10c. Correct. A noise gate is a type of expander.

11c. No. They have nothing to do with each other. (Reread 9.11 and 9.13.)

13c. Wrong. Dolby C is a common noise-reduction system found on cassette recorders. (Reread 9.8.)

14c. No. This isn't correct. (Reread 9.9 and 9.13 to 9.15.)

15c. No. You're thinking about another signal-processing device. (Reread 9.16.)

16c. Wrong. You may be getting this confused with the level of normal conversation. (Reread 9.12.)

18c. Yes. This would add brilliance to a voice.

19c. Right. This is the correct answer.

20c. No. Flanging concerns phase-shift and time delay, but not dynamic range. (Reread 9.12 to 9.13 and 9.15.)

If You Answered D:

1d. Correct. Equalizers allow you to adjust selected frequency volumes and thus alter the audio signal's frequency response.

3d. No. This would be a type of graphic equalizer. (Reread 9.3 and 9.4.)

4d. Although it could eliminate a 60-hertz hum, low cut filters normally are designed to eliminate *all* frequencies below a certain point. There's a better response. (Reread 9.6.)

6d. Yes. This is what reverb units do by electronically changing the apparent acoustic environment in which we hear the sound.

7d. No. A compressor acts as an automatic volume control affecting the dynamic range of an audio signal. (Reread 9.5 and 9.13.)

8d. No. This is not a noise-reduction unit. (Reread 9.7 to 9.9 and 9.15.)

9d. Wrong. This happens in a limiter, but not during noise reduction. (Reread 9.8 and 9.14.)

10d. No. A noise gate does not deal with imaging. (Reread 9.1 and 9.13.)

11d. No. You're thinking of a "flange" effect. (Reread 9.13 and 9.16.)

13d. Right. This is not a current Dolby noise-reduction system.

14d. Yes. This is a multi-effect processor.

15d. Correct. As the name implies, a stereo synthesizer makes a mono signal a "fake" stereo signal.

16d. Wrong. You're thinking about the amount of change in volume that's usually necessary before we actually hear a difference in level. (Reread 9.12.)

18d. No. This would decrease the highs, if anything. (Reread 9.3.)

19d. Wrong. This is a type of processor used to affect imaging of an audio signal. (Reread 9.10 and 9.16.)

20d. Wrong. A limiter is a type of compressor, not the opposite of it. (Reread 9.12 to 9.14.)

Projects

■ PROJECT 1

Record a radio commercial that uses a signal-processing effect.

Purpose

To develop your skill in incorporating a signal processing effect into a radio spot.

Advice, Cautions, and Background

1. This project assumes you have enough familiarity with your studio equipment to accomplish basic recording and production techniques.

2. The production incorporates a single announcer voice, a music bed, and some type of signal processing technique.

3. You will need to write a simple script that can be read in about 20 seconds. Write the copy about a department store and use the phrase, "One Day Sale!" several times in the script.
4. There are many ways to accomplish this project, so don't feel you must follow the production directions exactly.

How to Do the Project

1. Record the script (voice only) onto a recorder, such as a reel-to-reel or digital recorder. Each time the "sale" phrase is read, add some type of signal-processing effect (reverb, flanging, echo, EQ, etc.).
2. Select a music bed that is appropriate for the style of the spot. You might find one on the CD-ROM.
3. You can play back the music bed directly from a CD, or you may have to record it on another recorder from the CD-ROM.
4. Set correct playback levels for both the vocal track and the music bed. Both will start at full volume. Then cue both to the beginning sound.
5. Record your completed spot onto an audio cassette, so set your cassette recorder to record mode.
6. Begin recording. Start the music bed at full volume. Start the vocal track and simultaneously fade the music bed slightly so the vocal track is dominant.
7. As the vocal ends, bring the music bed back to full volume and then quickly fade it out as you approach 30 seconds.
8. It may take you several attempts to get the spot to come out correctly. If you need to "do it over," just recue everything and try again.
9. On the tape write your name and SIGNAL PROCESSING RADIO SPOT, and turn it in to your instructor to receive credit for this project.

■ PROJECT 2

Visit a radio station or recording studio, and learn about the signal-processing equipment used there. Write a report about what you learn.

Purpose

To give you more familiarity with signal-processing equipment.

Advice, Cautions, and Background

1. Find a place that has enough signal-processing equipment to make your trip worthwhile. Your instructor may arrange a trip for the entire class.
2. Find someone at the facility who's willing to spend some time with you explaining how the equipment works.
3. Prepare the questions that you want to ask so that you can guide the visit to some extent.
4. If possible, experiment with some of the equipment yourself. If the facility is unionized, you won't be able to do this. Don't push on this particular point because some people are very sensitive about who touches their equipment, but don't back away from any opportunity.
5. Once you have an appointment, keep it, and arrive on time.

How to Do the Project

1. Call various radio stations and recording studios until you find one that's both willing to let you visit and has sufficient signal-processing equipment.
2. Visit the facility, and talk with someone who can give you information for your report. Make a list of all the equipment you are shown, and take notes regarding it. Some of the things you may want to find out are:
   a. Is the equalizer graphic or parametric?
   b. Do they have band pass or notch filters or both?
   c. Do they use Dolby or dbx and, if so, which system?
   d. Do they have digital audio workstations with signal-processing features?
   e. Is there a digital delay unit, and, if so, how many seconds of delay does the station use?
   f. Do they have a compressor? A limiter?
   g. Do they have any multi-effects signal-processing equipment?
   h. What other signal-processing equipment do they have, and what does it do?

3. As soon as you leave the facility, organize your notes so that you remember the main points.
4. Write a report. It should be several pages long, preferably typed. Write your name and SIGNAL-PROCESSING EQUIPMENT TOUR on a title page.
5. Turn in the report to your instructor for credit for this project.

■ PROJECT 3

Record and play back material, using Dolby noise reduction.

Purpose

To make you aware of some of the characteristics of noise-reduction signal processing.

Advice, Cautions, and Background

1. You'll need a recorder with Dolby noise-reduction capability to complete this project.
2. You'll also need a prerecorded tape that has been encoded with Dolby.
3. Other configurations can be used, but this project will assume that a cassette recorder with Dolby B is being used.

How to Do the Project

1. Set up the cassette recorder to play back the prerecorded cassette tape with Dolby B. Make sure the packaging of the cassette indicates that it was recorded with Dolby.
2. Listen to the tape for several minutes. Stop the tape and rewind it to the start point.
3. Turn the Dolby B switch to the off position, and play the tape again, listening for a comparable amount of time.
4. Note any differences in the sound quality of the recording as it's played back with and then without Dolby.
5. On a blank cassette tape, record several minutes of an announcer talking. Make sure the Dolby B switch is in the on position.
6. Listen to this recording. Then make a similar recording with the Dolby B switch in the off position.
7. Listen to this recording, and note any differences in the sound quality between the recording with and without Dolby noise reduction.
8. If your recorder also has Dolby C, repeat steps 5 to 7 with the Dolby C switch on.
9. Write a short paper that describes any differences you noted. Label the paper DOLBY DIFFERENCES.
10. Turn in this paper and the tape you made to your instructor to receive credit for this project.

Multitrack Production Techniques

Information

10.1 INTRODUCTION

Even though larger facilities have had multitrack reel-to-reel recorders in their production studios for years, the majority of radio production work was done in either mono or two-track stereo. Now, as more digital equipment finds its way into all production studios, more and more of the production that's done will be multitrack. In this chapter you'll learn some of the basic techniques of multitrack production; however, these should merely suggest new ways to approach your future production work. You'll quickly learn that the biggest advantage of multitrack recording is that it opens the door to faster, easier, and more creative production work.

10.2 THE DIGITAL MULTITRACK RECORDER

From the desktop audio editor to the complex workstation, most digital systems have multitrack capability. Figure 10.1 shows the multitrack view screen from *Cool Edit Pro*. In this view, the first few tracks of the system are shown with some of the controls associated with those tracks. Like the editing portion of the program, pull-down menus provide access to all the multitrack functions, and tool bar icons also can be used to select the most used functions. The audio data in each track is graphically displayed as a waveform block as shown in Figure 10.2. The bottom of the waveform display window, along the horizontal axis, shows a time line. In the multitrack mode, audio can easily be mixed, moved, copied, or deleted, and information can be displayed on the screen in different sizes with a "zoom" control. Each track has various virtual faders and pan controls that allow for level setting and balance control during the mix of the production.

All the multitrack techniques mentioned later in this chapter can be utilized with digital systems, but you'll probably find that actually manipulating the audio is much easier digitally. For example, to move a waveform block,

right mouse click on it and continue to hold down the mouse button. You can now "drag and drop" that audio from one track to another, from one part of a track to another part, or, with other simple mouse moves, mix, copy, divide, or delete the audio.

From a simple combining of a music bed and voiceover track to a complex production using hundreds of audio blocks, digital multitrack offers ease of operation and new creative possibilities to the modern production person. Remember, when you copy or otherwise manipulate the audio in digital form, the sound doesn't degrade as it does with dubbed analog generations.

10.3 OTHER MULTITRACK RECORDERS

In addition to the DAW or audio editing software already mentioned, some production facilities have a digital multitrack recorder like the one shown in Figure 10.3, or the analog multitrack reel-to-reel like the one shown in Figure 10.4.

Any machine that can record more than one track is technically a multitrack recorder. However, in radio production, multitrack generally means recorders that have four, eight, or more tracks. The digital recorder shown in Figure 10.3 is a multitrack system that employs S-VHS tape as the recording and storage medium.

The multitrack recorder is really part of a system that contains not only the recorder, but also an audio mixer, input sources and output devices, and sometimes signal-processing equipment. Several elements may be combined; for example, a multichannel mixer with equalization capability and a multitrack recorder with noise-reduction capability may be combined in a single unit.

The audio mixer may be the production room board or a dedicated mixer that is associated only with the multitrack recorder like the one shown in Figure 10.5. In either case, it will need a good number of inputs and outputs—although a microphone is usually assigned to just one

FIGURE 10.1 Most digital audio editing software also incorporates a virtual multitrack recorder. (Image courtesy of Syntrillium Software Corporation.)

FIGURE 10.2 Audio segments are shown as waveform blocks that can be manipulated with drag-and-drop mouse clicks. (Image courtesy of Syntrillium Software Corporation.)

FIGURE 10.3 A digital multitrack recorder that uses S-VHS tape as its recording and storage medium. (Image courtesy of Fostex Corporation of America.)

channel, stereo sources (such as a CD player) are usually assigned to two channels. In general, the mixer should have at least one input/output channel for each track of the multitrack recorder. In other words, an eight-track recorder should have an audio mixer with at least eight channels associated with it. In addition, the mixer must be able to input each of the tracks of the multitrack recorder so that monitoring and mixing can take place. One arrangement

FIGURE 10.4 One of the first multitrack recorders used in the radio production studio was a four-track reel-to-reel recorder. (Image courtesy of Sturder Revox America, Inc.)

might put all the normal inputs (mics, CDs, etc.) on "program" of the mixer and all the tape inputs on "audition" or "auxiliary."

Signal processing usually includes equalization, noise reduction, and reverb effects at the least, and they can be much more elaborate. Some signal processing is usually associated with individual channels of the mixer; for example, each channel may have some EQ adjustment. In other cases, the output of a channel (such as a mic) may be sent to a signal-processing device (such as a digital reverb), and then the output of the signal-processing device is sent back to another input on the mixer, where the "processed" signal can be routed to the multitrack recorder.

The input sources are normal production inputs, such as microphones, CD players, or other audio players, and the output devices are either headphones or monitor speakers that allow for listening to the mix of all the tracks.

The multitrack recorder operates like any other audio recorder. Many multitrack recorders employed in radio production use audio tape that is $1/2$-inch or 1-inch wide; however, there are some that use standard $1/4$-inch tape, cassette tape, various videotape formats, and hard disc drives. Recorders that use 2-inch tape, such as those found in recording studios, record on 24 (or more) tracks. Reviewing the tape track configuration in Chapter 6, "Analog Audio Players/Recorders," shows that a four-track recorder would have four separate tracks being recorded on the audio tape in one direction. Each track can be recorded and played back separately so that you can record one track while listening to another, and this is a primary advantage of multitrack recording. Regardless of

the actual type of multitrack used, you'll find that you're employing a handful of multitrack techniques as you begin your production work.

10.4 OVERDUBBING TRACKS

One of the most basic techniques used in multitrack work is **overdubbing**, or the process of adding new tracks to existing tracks. Refer to Figure 10.1 as you follow the steps of a basic overdub using the multitrack function of *Cool Edit Pro*. Assume the correct device settings have been made; then to begin recording click on FILE and select NEW SESSION. A window will pop up that allows setting the recording characteristics for this session, so choose the sample rate and bit resolution you want. Now click on the small red "r" button (for enable recording) for Track 1. Then when you click on the master RECORD button on the Transport Controls, you can record, for example, a music bed from a Production Library CD onto this track; click the Transport STOP button when you're done. To accomplish the overdub, click on the "r" button for Track 1 again, which will make this track playback only. Click on the "r" button for Track 2. This time, when you click on the master RECORD button, you will record your voice on Track 2 while you hear the music bed on Track 1. Click on the STOP button when you're done recording. Remember to click on the Track 2 "r" button when you've finished recording the vocal track to disable recording on this track. With a few other mouse clicks, you can adjust the volume levels between the two tracks. The exact steps described are unique to this software, but most systems will employ a similar type of process.

A comparable procedure would be followed if you used a multitrack analog reel-to-reel recorder. This time, record the music bed on two separate tracks: Track 1 for the left channel and Track 2 for the right channel. Then you recue the recorder to the beginning of the music bed. Now, while you listen to the playback of the music bed (usually through headphones) on Tracks 1 and 2, you record a vocal on Track 3. All multitrack recorders have a sel sync feature that lets you listen to one track and record on a different track in synchronization.

Overdubbing allows you to build a production in "layers" because you don't have to record everything at the same time. If you decided later to add a sound effect to the production, you could just record it on another track, move it to the appropriate spot where you want it to occur, and set the proper volume. Playing back all the tracks at the same time would let you hear how all the elements fit together.

10.5 PUNCHING IN TRACKS

If you've recorded a vocal on one track, but a portion of the vocal contains a mistake, a multitrack recording technique

FIGURE 10.5 A small audio mixer, independent of the studio console, is often associated with the multitrack recorder. (Image courtesy of Mackie Designs, Inc.)

known as the **punch in** allows you to record over just the part that contains the mistake, and leave the rest of the track undisturbed. Once you've completed the initial recording, recue the track to the beginning. The multitrack recorder will allow you to monitor both the playback of the track and the live rerecording. It's important that you don't change volume levels or mic position of the original setup so that the rerecording is consistent with the original recording. The multitrack recorder also allows you to put the recorder into "record" mode by pressing a record button for the individual track you want to record on or putting that track into a "record ready" mode, then pressing a master record button on the multitrack. The technique is a punch in because you play back the track to the point where you want to rerecord, then punch in the record button and record over the portion of the track that you wish to correct. You punch out of record mode at an appropriate point after you've fixed the mistake. Essentially you're doing an "edit" on the fly with a punch in; in fact, it's also known as an **insert edit**. You might need to practice a few times, so you know exactly where you want to punch in and punch out. It makes sense to choose logical spots, such as the end of a

sentence or at a pause between words; otherwise the punch in may be noticeable.

To punch in using *Cool Edit Pro*, first highlight the section of audio you want to rerecord by clicking and dragging. Click EDIT on the menu, select the PUNCH IN option, and put the track into record enabled mode. Place the cursor a bit before the section where the punch in will occur. Click RECORD and you will hear the audio up to the point of the punch in where you begin your rerecording. You can record several different "takes," and the program will allow you to select the one you feel is best.

10.6 BOUNCING TRACKS

Bouncing, or **Ping-Ponging**, tracks is the process of combining two or more tracks on a multitrack recorder and rerecording and transferring them to another vacant track of the same recorder. If you were building a music bed for example, record drums on Track 1 and a bass on Track 2. Then bounce those tracks to Track 3. Now you have Track 1 and Track 2 free, and you can record stereo strings on those two tracks, and, if you want, bounce all three tracks to Track 4. Bouncing is most often used when the multitrack recorder has a limited number of tracks, such as four, and you're doing complex production work. In other words, it's a technique to increase the number of tracks that you can utilize.

However, bouncing tracks brings with it two disadvantages that the production person must be aware of. First, once several tracks are combined, they can't be uncombined. You can't change the balance of the mixed tracks, and if you equalize or otherwise process the track, it impacts all elements on the track. Second, each "bounce" causes a degradation of the sound quality of the track if the recorder is analog. It's just like dubbing from one tape to another; once you've bounced to one track, that track is a second-generation recording. If you bounce that track again, it's become a third-generation recording with resulting lower audio quality. Careful planning can help keep the number of tracks that you must bounce to a minimum.

Digital editing software also has a function to bounce tracks even though many programs allow you to add "unlimited" tracks controlled only by hard drive space. Even with a large number of tracks, there are two main reasons for bouncing several tracks to one. First, at the end of the production you will want to create a final stereo mix. For many programs, including *Cool Edit Pro*, this is simply a menu item selection to "mix down" all files. Second, you may need to bounce some tracks together to reduce the hard disk space and processing time needed to manipulate the audio. If you have a large number of tracks, making a "submix" of some of them will speed up CPU processing. Again, you can just highlight the tracks you want to combine and choose a "mix down" option for selected files.

Live bouncing is a similar technique, but at the same time that you're mixing several tracks onto a vacant track, you add a live track to the mix. Again, it's a technique to get a maximum number of sources onto a minimum number of tracks.

10.7 TRACK SHEETS

As you can tell just by reading about the techniques above, multitrack recording can become complicated. Good production practice dictates that you keep notes of what material is recorded on which track. Although there is no standard form, Figure 10.6 shows one possible **track sheet**, or format, for keeping notes regarding a multitrack production. The top of the page indicates the number of tracks the recorder has, the edge of the page indicates the various takes, and the boxes show what was put on each track during each take. As shown, during the first take, an announcer vocal was put on Track 1, a sound effect was put on Track 2, a music bed was put on Tracks 3 and 4, and Track 5 was left open. This doesn't mean that these elements were all recorded at the same time; most likely they were

put down separately, but these were the first elements assigned to those tracks. During the second take, the announcer vocal was not changed, but the sound effect on Track 2 and the music bed on Tracks 3 and 4 were all bounced to Track 5. On the third take, Tracks 1 and 5 did not change; however, a new music bed was put on Tracks 3 and 4, and the announcer vocal was rerecorded on Track 2.

You could also put any signal-processing settings, music bed cuts used, or special notes regarding the production on the track sheet.

10.8 MIXING TO STEREO/MONO COMPATIBILITY

As noted, regardless of how many tracks you work with in a multitrack production, you will ultimately mix the production down into a stereo mix with just a left and right channel. Certain tracks from the multitrack master may be panned to the right channel, some tracks may be panned to the left channel, and some tracks may be balanced to both left and right. This is where the production person needs a good monitoring system and some good judgment to create just the right mix.

Make sure that you listen to your final sound in both stereo and mono. Most likely you're working in stereo and hearing the final mix in stereo; however, you need to hear the same mix in mono because sometimes a mix sounds great in stereo, but not in mono. Often by listening in cue (assuming the cue signal is in mono) you can tell if a stereo mix is not going to be compatible with mono. It's possible that portions of the audio signal will be out of phase when the left and right channels are combined for the mono signal, causing a cancellation and diminishment of the sound at different spots. A fine-tuning of some track equalization, a slight volume change, or minor panning adjustment will usually correct the mono signal, but it's always important to make sure the stereo and mono signals are compatible.

10.9 THE MULTITRACK COMMERCIAL SPOT

There isn't a "standard" way to record a commercial using multitrack techniques, but let's look at the production of a spot that includes two announcer voices, a background music bed, and two sound effects. In most cases, the music bed would begin first at full volume for a few seconds, and then fade under the vocals and hold at a background level. The first announcer begins his or her voiceover on top of the music bed, probably trading lines with the other announcer until the end of the copy. Sound effects are added at the appropriate points, and the music bed is brought up to full volume at the end of the voiceover. The music bed ultimately ends cold or may fade out. Of course, all of this takes place in a 30- or 60-second time frame.

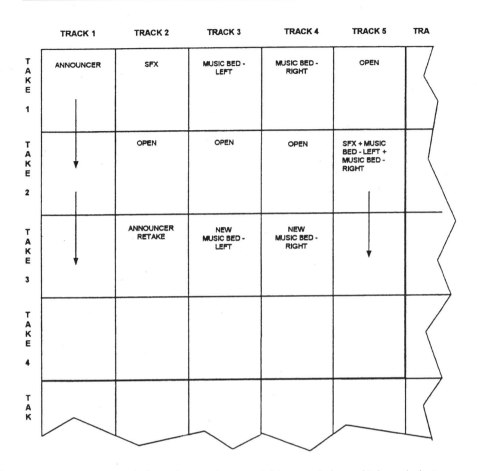

FIGURE 10.6 A track sheet shows what material is recorded on which track during a multitrack recording session.

Assuming a production studio setup with an eight-track recorder, refer to Figure 10.7 to help visualize what is happening during this "typical" production.

Each sound source (mic, CD, etc.) should be assigned a channel on the mixer and corresponding track on the recorder. Let's put announcer #1 on Track 1, announcer #2 on Track 2, a CD sound effect on Tracks 3 and 4, a CD music bed on Tracks 5 and 6, and a MiniDisc sound effect on Tracks 7 and 8. The first track you record is extremely important because it's the reference for all the other tracks. In radio production, the music bed or vocal track is often put down first. In this case, the music bed is a preproduced and timed music bed from a CD production library. We just have to dub it from the CD onto our recorder. Of course, the music bed could have come from another source—for example, a music bed directly from a record or perhaps a music bed that was edited on reel-to-reel to be exactly the length of the spot. Now set the multitrack recorder to record on Tracks 5 and 6 only (the music bed). Dub the entire music bed at full volume onto the recorder, even though you'll be fading it under the announcers. The various levels can be balanced during the final mix.

Now put the recorder Tracks 5 and 6 into a "safe" and "sync" mode. This allows you to overdub on the other

tracks at the same time that you monitor the music bed tracks. Set Tracks 1 and 2 into the record position. Since the announcers "trade" lines throughout the commercial, you should record them at the same time. Rewind the tape to the beginning of the music bed. While monitoring Tracks 5, 6, 1, and 2, record announcers #1 and #2. You should fade the music at the appropriate place, so the announcers get the proper feel reading the spot, but remember the actual "blend" of all the elements will take place later. At this point, if the vocal tracks came out OK, the announcers could leave, and a production person would finish the spot. That makes sense if the announcers are "high-priced" talent, and that's why many multitrack productions are started by putting down the vocal tracks first. Suppose announcer #2 misspoke the final line in the spot. Depending on the complexity of the spot, it would be possible to rewind the tape, set up Tracks 5, 6, and 1 to play, and have announcer #2 rerecord Track 2 to correct the mistake with a punch-in.

By additional overdubbing, the various sound effects would be added by playing back the tracks that were previously recorded and recording only those tracks that were assigned to sound effects, doing one effect at a time. Unlike basic commercial production, if you miscue a sound effect,

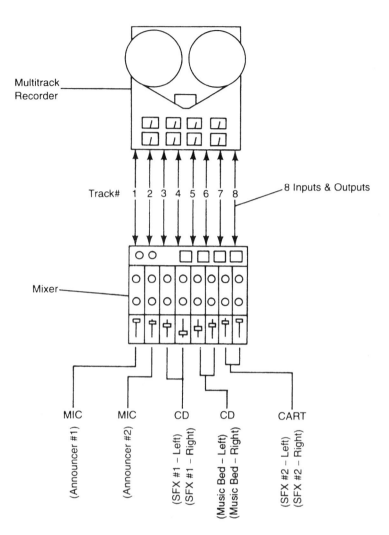

Track# 1 2 3 4 5 6 7 8   8 Inputs & Outputs

MIC   MIC   CD   CD   CART

(Announcer #1)

(Announcer #2)

(SFX #1 – Left)
(SFX #1 – Right)

(Music Bed – Left)
(Music Bed – Right)

(SFX #2 – Left)
(SFX #2 – Right)

FIGURE 10.7 Multitrack Recording routes various audio sources through a mixer and to individual tracks of the recorder, which can also play back those tracks through the mixer.

you don't have to reset every element and start all over again. You would merely rerecord the track that had the mistake on it.

Once you have all eight tracks recorded, you can begin to "mix down" the final spot. Since most commercials are played on a stereo format, they are usually mixed down to a two-track (stereo) master. You'll probably play back all eight tracks several times now (through the mixer, monitoring the multitrack recorder outputs) to adjust the levels. For this commercial, you can get the announcer and sound effect levels balanced and leave them set, but you'll have to fade the music bed up and down manually at the appropriate points as you record onto the two-track. With a more complex spot, you might have to manipulate more than one fader during the final mix—and that's where practice and experience come in to produce the perfect spot! If you're using digital multitrack software, you can adjust volume levels and pans so they will automate during playback and

you don't have to manipulate a bunch of faders during the mix.

10.10 VOICE DOUBLING, CHORUSING, AND STACKING

Multitrack techniques open the door to many special effects that can turn a basic production into a creative masterpiece. Voice doubling, chorusing, and stacking are three forms of overdubbing that can give your next production a unique sound. They are often used to add a "thickness" to the vocal by making it seem like several voices are speaking at the same time. **Voice doubling** is exactly what the name implies. Record your voice on Track 1. Then recue the multitrack recorder. Now, while monitoring Track 1, record your voice again on Track 2. Even though you read the same script, it's impossible to record both tracks exactly alike. The effect, also known as "voice dubbing," will be closer to two people reading the same script at the same time. **Chorusing** is taking voice doubling one step further. Record at least two additional tracks in sync with the original track, creating a "chorus" effect. The more additional tracks you record, the larger your "chorus" will sound. It's a way for one announcer to become a group of announcers. **Stacking** is a similar multitrack technique in which an announcer *sings* harmony to a previously recorded track.

Since it is actually a form of delay, chorus effects are often included on audio editing software (see Figure 10.8). In this case, up to twelve voices can simulate various chorus effects, and even though only one voice recorded the script, the program will slightly change timing, intonation, and vibrato of the original audio to give each voice created a distinct sound.

announcers reading a dialogue script. Obviously you must slightly change one of the voices so that it sounds like two different announcers, and you'll probably need to practice a few times to get the timing correct. Remember, you usually "mentally" read lines slightly faster than you do when you actually speak them. It can take a little time to perfect this technique, but it can be well worth the effort. The same effect can be produced using editing software without having to mentally leave pauses. Just record the lines for each announcer on the appropriate track of the multitrack, changing one voice slightly. Now cut, move, and paste the lines to create the dialogue. You can create the natural pacing of "two" announcers by slightly overlapping the end of one line with the beginning of the next line, and since you can move the audio around on the tracks, this is very easy to do.

10.11 DOVETAILING

One announcer can appear to be two different announcers trading lines using a technique referred to as **dovetailing**. On Track 1, the announcer records the *odd* lines of the script. While doing so, the even lines of the script are also mentally read. This leaves space between the odd lines on Track 1. Now, record on Track 2 the *even* lines of the script while mentally reading the odd lines to keep the timing correct. When both tracks are played back, you get the effect of two

10.12 SLAPBACK ECHO

To produce a slapback echo with a multitrack recorder, record your voice on Track 1. Now, dub Track 1 to another track, but without synchronization. Play back both tracks, and you'll get a unique echo effect. If you do the recording at a higher recorder speed, then you'll get a "closer" echo effect. Since this is another form of delay, look for this special effect to be a menu item on your editing software's special effects section (see Figure 10.9).

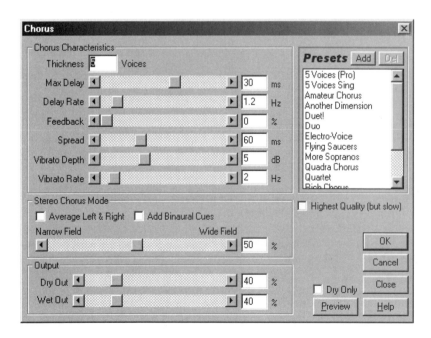

FIGURE 10.8 The chorus effect adds richness or thickness to sound by making it seem as though several voices are being played at the same time. (Image courtesy of Syntrillium Software Corporation.)

FIGURE 10.9 Echo effects can be created with a multitrack recorder or with editing software that features effects options. (Image courtesy of Syntrillium Software Corporation.)

**Production Tip #10—
"Telephone Tones"**

Even though it's not the best copy-writing practice to put phone numbers in a radio spot, local production spots often require including one. You can help emphasize the telephone number by underscoring the reading of the number with "touch tones." You obviously need a touch tone phone and the ability to record the phone. Your production studio might have a phone coupler (review section 8.21 in Chapter 8, "Monitor Speakers, Cables, Connectors, and Studio Accessories") to bring the phone audio into a channel of the audio console. With a little practice, you should be able to punch out the phone number at the exact same time as you say the numbers, recording both on an audio recorder. If you've got a multitrack recorder, just record the tones separately and place them on an empty track aligning them with the vocal track as the phone number is read. It's a nice way to add an ear-catching "effect" underneath a phone number.

10.13 CONCLUSIONS

As we've noted, much of the digital equipment that has made its way into the radio production studio has multi-track capability. The modern production person is going to have to be skilled in working in the multitrack environment to be successful. Although this chapter is only designed to give you some basic familiarity with the equipment and techniques of multitrack production, it should serve as a good starting point. Like most everything about radio production, the real learning comes when you go into the studio and try out different concepts. You'll really become skilled in multitrack production work only if you spend time in the studio to understand the creative possibilities it offers.

Self-Study

■ QUESTIONS

1. Of the following number of tracks, how many tracks is a multitrack recorder found in the radio production studio likely to have?
   a) 1
   b) 2
   c) 4
   d) 6

2. When two or more tracks of a multitrack recording are combined and rerecorded on another vacant track, this is known as _____ tracks.
   a) overdubbing
   b) bouncing
   c) punching in
   d) combo-cording

3. Which of the following is *not* part of a multitrack recorder system?
   a) audio mixer
   b) multitrack recorder
   c) DSP audio card
   d) microphone

4. Which type of tape is *not* used as a recording medium in multitrack recording systems?
   a) cassette tape
   b) videotape
   c) reel-to-reel tape
   d) all of these are multitrack recording media

5. In multitrack recording, the process of adding new tracks to existing tracks is known as _____.
   a) bouncing tracks
   b) overdubbing tracks
   c) punching in tracks
   d) Ping-Ponging tracks

6. One announcer can appear to be two different announcers reading a dialogue script using a multitrack recording technique known as _____.
   a) voice doubling
   b) chorusing
   c) dovetailing
   d) stacking

7. The main reason announcer voices are often recorded first on a multitrack recording is because vocal sources are usually assigned to Track 1 and Track 2.
   a) true
   b) false

8. Which of the following statements is *not* associated with bouncing tracks during a multitrack recording?
   a) you can combine two or more tracks on a vacant track of the same recorder
   b) several combined tracks can't be uncombined
   c) several bounces can cause degradation of sound quality
   d) you are rerecording a portion of a track

9. A track sheet is a manufacturer specification sheet that lists the number of tracks that a multitrack recorder has.
   a) true
   b) false

10. Multitrack productions are usually mixed down to a two-track stereo master. If the stereo master is slightly out-of-phase when combined into a mono signal, it can be corrected by all but which of these adjustments to one of the stereo tracks?
    a) change track equalization
    b) move track to a vacant track
    c) change track volume
    d) change track panning

11. During multitrack recording, which technique allows you to rerecord just a portion of a track to correct a mistake while leaving the rest of the track undisturbed?
    a) punching in
    b) overdubbing
    c) voice doubling
    d) bouncing

12. Bouncing tracks on a multitrack recorder is also known as _____.
    a) chorusing
    b) overdubbing
    c) Ping-Ponging
    d) dovetailing

13. On an analog four-track reel-to-reel tape recorder _____.
    a) all the tracks go the same direction
    b) two tracks go left and two go right
    c) only Tracks 1 and 3 can be used
    d) you can record eight tracks of sound

14. What is one advantage of digital multitrack over analog multitrack?
    a) digital multitracks have six tracks, but analog can have no more than four tracks
    b) the sel sync feature is in better synchronization on digital than analog
    c) you can punch in on digital, and you can't on analog
    d) you can manipulate sounds easier with digital because you can move them with the mouse

15. The "drag and drop" function of a multitrack audio editor would allow you to move audio segments from one part of a track to another, but not from one track to a completely different track.
    a) true
    b) false

■ ANSWERS

If You Answered A:

1a. No. One would not be "multi." (Reread 10.3.)

2a. Wrong. Overdubbing is the normal technique for multitrack recording. (Reread 10.4 and 10.6.)

3a. No. This is part of the multitrack setup. (Reread 10.3.)

4a. No. There are multitrack recorders that use cassette tapes. (Reread 10.3.)

5a. No. This is another multitrack recording technique. (Reread 10.4 and 10.6.)

6a. Wrong. While this is a "voice doubling" technique, it's another multitrack trick. (Reread 10.10 and 10.11.)

7a. No. It really doesn't matter what sources are assigned to what tracks. (Reread 10.9.)

8a. No. This is exactly what bouncing tracks is. (Reread 10.5 and 10.6.)

9a. No. A track sheet is a way of keeping notes during a multitrack production. It usually lists track numbers and what is recorded on each track. (Reread 10.7.)

10a. Wrong. This will often correct the mono signal. (Reread 10.8.)
11a. Yes. The punch in is also known as an insert edit because you can just rerecord a portion of a track.
12a. No. This is a different multitrack technique. (Reread 10.6 and 10.10.)
13a. Yes. All the tracks must go in the same direction, so you can listen and record at the same time.
14a. No. Both can have a varying number of tracks. (Reread 10.2 and 10.3.)
15a. Wrong. You would be able to move the audio from track to track as well as anywhere on an individual track. (Reread 10.2.)

If You Answered B:

1b. You're close because two-track recorders are usually found in the production studio, and technically they are multitrack, but this is not the best answer. (Reread 10.3 to find out why.)
2b. Correct. Bouncing tracks or Ping-Ponging tracks is the multitrack technique described here.
3b. No. This is an obvious part of the multitrack setup. (Reread 10.3.)
4b. No. There are multitrack recorders that use S-VHS videotape. (Reread 10.3.)
5b. Yes. This is a primary advantage of multitrack recording and one of the most basic techniques used in multitrack production.
6b. Wrong. Although this is a technique for adding voices, it's another multitrack technique. (Reread 10.10 and 10.11.)
7b. Yes. It doesn't really matter what sources are assigned to what tracks, but announcers are often recorded first because it's easier to lay down other tracks to the vocals, and "high-priced" talent can be finished with their part of a production once their tracks are recorded, even if the entire spot isn't completed.
8b. No. This is a minor disadvantage of bouncing tracks. (Reread 10.5 and 10.6.)
9b. Yes. This is not a correct statement.
10b. Correct. Just moving a track's location won't help.
11b. No. This technique allows you to add additional tracks to a production. (Reread 10.4 and 10.5.)
12b. No. This is a different multitrack technique. (Reread 10.4 and 10.6.)
13b. No. This would be very confusing. (Reread 10.3.)
14b. No. You are way off. (Reread 10.2 and 10.3.)
15b. Correct. This is false because you can move audio from track to track as well as anywhere on an individual track.

If You Answered C:

1c. Yes. Of the answers offered, this is the most likely configuration of a multitrack recorder in the production studio.
2c. Wrong. To punch in is a technique that allows you to record a segment of a track without affecting the material before or after that segment. (Reread 10.5 and 10.6.)
3c. Correct. A DSP audio card is part of an audio editing system, and although the system may have multitrack recording capability, it's different from a multitrack recorder system.
4c. No. Many multitrack recorders use reel-to-reel audio tape. (Reread 10.3.)
5c. No. This is another multitrack recording technique. (Reread 10.4 and 10.5.)
6c. Correct. By reading even lines of a script on one track and then odd lines on another track, one announcer can sound like he or she is talking to another with this technique.
8c. No. This is a minor disadvantage of bouncing tracks. (Reread 10.5 and 10.6.)
10c. Wrong. This will often correct the mono signal. (Reread 10.8.)
11c. No. This technique is a form of overdubbing that allows you to "voice double." (Reread 10.5 and 10.10.)
12c. Yes. This is another term for bouncing tracks.
13c. No. This would limit the usefulness of the recorder. (Reread 10.3.)
14c. No. You can punch in on analog. (Reread 10.2 and 10.5.)

If You Answered D:

1d. No. This is not a common number of tracks for a radio production multitrack recorder. (Reread 10.3.)
2d. Wrong. There is no such thing. (Reread 10.6.)
3d. No. This is a possible input source for a multitrack recorder system. (Reread 10.3.)
4d. Yes. This is the correct answer.
5d. No. This is another multitrack recording technique. (Reread 10.4 and 10.6.)
6d. Wrong. Although this is a technique for adding voices, it's another multitrack technique. (Reread 10.10 and 10.11.)
8d. Yes. This is not accomplished by bouncing tracks, but by a technique known as the punch in.
10d. Wrong. This will often correct the mono signal. (Reread 10.8.)

11d. No. This technique allows you to combine tracks and transfer them to a vacant track. (Reread 10.5 and 10.6.)
12d. No. This is a different multitrack technique. (Reread 10.6 and 10.11.)
13d. No. It's only a four-track recorder. (Reread 10.3.)
14d. Yes. A few clicks of the mouse can easily move sounds with a digital multitrack system.

Projects

■ PROJECT 1

Record a 60-second "concert commercial."

Purpose

To develop your skill in creating a spot for a concert by a recording artist, a type of commercial frequently heard on radio.

Advice, Cautions, and Background

1. This project assumes you have some type of digital audio editor in your studio; however, it can also be accomplished with analog equipment.
2. The production incorporates two announcer voices, a music bed, and several "clips" from the artist's songs.
3. You can write the actual script as you want it, but follow the basic concept given below.
4. Exact production directions aren't given in this project because there are many ways to accomplish the recording and editing.

How to Do the Project

1. Record four or five segments of songs from the artist's biggest hits. Each clip should be about ten seconds long, but some may be longer and others shorter.
2. You should pick segments of the song that are readily identifiable; usually the chorus or "hook" of the song. Try to end the clip at the end of a phrase so that it isn't just cut off in the middle of a word. Make sure the last clip doesn't fade out, as you want to finish the spot with a strong, natural ending.
3. Start recording each segment a bit before the point you actually want and record a bit beyond the actual end. Mark the true start point and end point using your audio editor and then label and save each segment.
4. Record the announcer lines with each announcer "trading lines." However, both announcers should read the last line together. If your editor has "effects" capability, add some reverb or a flanging effect to the voices.
5. Your script should use lines similar to this:
   Announcer 1: "Appearing live at the Rock Arena, (Artist Name)!"
   Announcer 2: "Join (Artist Name) on June 25th for (his/her/their) first tour of (Your City)!"
   Announcer 1: "Here's the summer concert you've been waiting for!"
   Announcer 2: "Tickets are just $50 and can be purchased at the Rock Arena Box Office or all Ticket Seller locations!"
   Announcer 1 & 2: "Don't miss this chance to see (Artist Name) in concert at the Rock Arena, June 25th!"
6. Using your audio editor, assemble the spot in a sequence that alternates between announcer tracks and song clips, beginning with Announcer 1's first line.
7. Now, add a background music bed that will pull the whole spot together. You might edit an instrumental segment from one of the artist's songs to do this, or you might find a music bed from the CD-ROM that fits the style of the other music used in the spot.
8. When you mix the music bed in you should start with the bed at full volume for a couple of seconds and then fade it under the announcer segments. When the music clips are playing, the music bed should be faded out entirely.
9. Listen to the finished commercial. If it's good enough, prepare it for the instructor by dubbing it onto a cassette tape.

10. On the tape write your name and Concert Commercial, and turn it in to your instructor to receive credit for this project.

■ PROJECT 2

Use a multitrack recorder to bounce tracks, and keep a track sheet to show what you have done.

Purpose

To enable you to learn the commonly used multitrack technique of bouncing and to allow you to learn how to keep a track sheet.

Advice, Cautions, and Background

1. This project assumes you have a multitrack recorder in your studio. If you don't have one, but you have a digital audio workstation, you can use that instead.
2. The project also assumes that you have a multitrack recorder or multitrack software in a system that has an audio board (real or virtual), a microphone, and something (such as a CD player) that can play music.
3. Make one track of music and one of voice so that you can get practice mixing these two types of sounds.
4. You may find music appropriate for this project on the CD-ROM that came with this text.

How to Do the Project

1. Record music on Track 1.
2. Record voice on Track 2. If you make a mistake, rerecord your voice on this track.
3. Mix Tracks 1 and 2 onto Track 3 so that the voice is easily distinguishable.
4. As you're doing your recording, keep a track sheet similar to the one depicted in Figure 10.6 that shows what you did.
5. Put your name on the multitrack tape and the track sheet.
6. If you've used a DAW, you'll need to dub your work onto an audio tape. If so, dub each track separately.
7. Label the tape and track sheet with your name and Bouncing Tracks.
8. Turn in the tape and track sheet to your instructor to receive credit for this project.

■ PROJECT 3

Use a multitrack recorder to undertake chorusing.

Purpose

To teach you the multitrack technique of chorusing and to further your skills with multitrack bouncing.

Advice, Cautions, and Background

1. This project assumes you have a four-track recorder or DAW software with four tracks. If what you have has more than four tracks, only use four of the tracks.
2. You can use any dialogue you want, but the first line of "Mary had a Little Lamb" works well.
3. You will use Track 1 twice when doing this project.

How to Do the Project

1. Record your selected dialogue on Track 1.
2. While playing back Track 1, record the dialogue again on Track 2.
3. Mix Tracks 1 and 2 onto Track 3.
4. While listening to Track 3, record the dialogue again on Track 1.

5. Mix Tracks 3 and 1 onto Track 4.
6. Listen to Track 4. It should sound like a chorus of four voices.
7. If you use a DAW, dub each track onto an audio tape.
8. Turn in the tape, with something on all four tracks, to your instructor to receive credit for this project. Put your name and CHORUSING PRODUCTION on the tape.

CHAPTER ELEVEN

Production Situations

Information

11.1 INTRODUCTION

Producing "spots" or commercials is one of the greatest concerns of the production person, but some additional production tips that apply to particular types of radio programming—namely, music shows, news, public affairs programs, call-in talk shows, play-by-play sports, and radio drama—are discussed in the next few pages. Entire books have been written about each of these types of programming, so you won't be given the in-depth knowledge you need to perfect any of the program forms. This chapter will, however, get you started in the right direction. Experience and advanced training can then propel you into more specialized skills. Although music shows, news, public affairs programs, call-in talk shows, play-by-play sports, and radio drama are the most common forms of radio programming, other forms do exist. For example, some stations air children's programs, and others produce documentaries. Still others are no doubt open to new forms of programming that may become popular in the future.

11.2 COMMERCIALS

Much of what has been detailed in this text applies to producing a 60-second or shorter commercial. Most radio production people are involved with producing commercial or station promotional spots. At some stations it's a full-time position, and at many stations the disc jockeys spend a portion of their workday doing commercial production work. At their simplest level, commercials are simply straight copy that the announcer reads over the air. At their most complex, they are highly produced vignettes that include several voices, sound effects, and music. In between are commercials that feature celebrity testimonials, dialogue between two announcers, and an announcer reading over a music bed, to name a few.

Commercials are usually exactly 30 seconds or exactly 60 seconds. Because they are inserted within other programming elements, they must have exact times. Otherwise part of the commercial will be cut off if they run long, or there will be **dead air** if they run short. At some stations commercials are brought on and taken off the air by com-

puters, which are very unsympathetic to anything that's too long or too short.

Anyone reading commercial copy should use a natural, sincere style. Reading commercials in a condescending manner is definitely uncalled for. Commercials pay station salaries and should be treated with respect. If you're to read commercial copy live, you should read it over ahead of time to avoid stumbling on words. If the commercial involves both reading live and playing a prerecorded segment, make sure you rehearse the transition between the two. Sometimes a prerecorded spot sounds like it's ending, but it actually contains additional information—perhaps new store hours or a bargain price. If you're to read material after the recording ends, make sure you don't read over the top of the recorded information.

Probably the most basic form of commercial you'll produce involves an announcer reading over a **music bed** or sound effects. The usual format for a commercial with music is that the music bed begins at full volume for a few seconds and then fades under and holds as the announcer begins reading the spot. The voiceover is read on top of the music bed, and then the music bed is brought up to full volume at the end of the voiceover for a few seconds until it fades out or ends cold. Although this seems simple enough, it won't come easily until you've practiced and accomplished it many times. Not only must you be concerned with timing, but you have to determine how much music to use to establish the spot, balance the levels between voice and music bed, select appropriate music, and correctly manipulate the broadcast equipment. Often you do a lot of this at the same time, although it is possible to record the voiceover and mix it with music at a later time.

Reading over sound effects is similar to reading over music in that the sound will need to fade up and down. Sound effects are usually short, however, so often they need to be looped (recorded over several times) in order to cover the 30-second length of the commercial. This is easy to accomplish with computer editing. The sound can simply be copied and laid on the time line as many times as needed.

Highly produced spots usually take a relatively long time to prepare. Minidramas, which start with music and involve two people bantering to the accompaniment of sound effects, involve a great deal of preproduction, rehearsing, mixing, and editing. They are, however, among the most challenging, creative products a radio production person handles. Often different parts of them are recorded at different times. The talent will record their parts and then leave, especially if they're highly paid talent. Then the production person will mix the talent skit with music and sound effects.

As you can see, mixing complex commercial spots (or any type of production) can be complicated. As you've learned by reading this text, production work of this type can be accomplished much more easily by using a multi-track recorder and/or digital editing.

11.3 MUSIC

Music constitutes the largest percent of radio station programming and is usually introduced and coordinated by a **disc jockey**. If you become a disc jockey, you'll be spending most of your time in the on-air studio doing all your production work live. This is actually a more challenging production situation than that in the production studio, where you have the time and luxury of rerecording until you get things just the way you want. On-air broadcasting is fast-paced, pressure packed, and, for most people, a lot of fun.

FIGURE 11.1 The radio disc jockey manipulates all the broadcast equipment and adds the element of live announcing within the style of the radio station's format. (Image courtesy of Alan R. Stephenson.)

Although the main element of the programming is music, the main duty of the disc jockey is talking. Much of this talk involves introducing music. For this, your announcing style must fit the format of the radio station. For example, fast-paced, high-energy, rapid-fire speech is not appropriate for a classical music or big band format but may be required at a contemporary hit or rock radio station.

Develop a variety of ways of getting into and out of the music. Many beginning announcers latch onto one record introduction and use it over and over ("Here's a classic from The Beatles . . ."; "Here's a classic from Bob Dylan . . ."; "Here's a classic from . . ."). If you have trouble thinking of clever material, read the liner notes on the CD or record. This will often give you an idea for something to say that's unusual or informative. Additional ad-lib material can be found in music trade publications, Internet "show prep" sites, and artist or record label Web sites. Your station may have certain policies regarding what you say and how you say it. For example, some stations require you to talk over the beginning and ending of every record. Other stations have particular slogans ("All hit radio") that they want repeated at regular intervals, or you may be required to say the station call letters every time you open the microphone.

As a disc jockey, you'll also be talking about things other than music. For example, you may need to give the time, temperature, commercials, weather, news, or traffic reports. Or you may introduce other people, such as the newscaster, who will give some of this information. Station policy will probably dictate whether you must be very formal about these introductions or have the latitude to banter with the other person. At some stations, the good-natured joking between, say, a disc jockey and helicopter traffic reporter is part of what keeps listeners tuned in.

Regardless of what's going on within the live production situation, always assume the microphone may be open. Don't say anything that you wouldn't want to go out over the air. This includes personal conversations and, of course, indecent language. Many studios have an on-air light *inside* the studio as well as the one outside the door. This inside light is to alert the announcer to the fact that the mic is live, but the best rule is to assume the mic is always on.

Obviously, as a disc jockey, you need to be proficient at operating the equipment so that you can cue up and play tapes and CDs. But this involves more than just equipment manipulation since you're normally operating equipment and talking. This means you have to plan ahead. For example, if you have to join a network, you must know exactly when and how to do it. If you aren't sure whether you've cued up a CD, redo it. You must have everything cued up and ready to go, and have a routine for what you are doing. It's also good practice to have an alternative if something goes wrong. If the CD player you want to play doesn't start, have in mind what you'll do immediately. A good announcer can overcome most miscues so that the listening audience doesn't even know that anything went wrong.

Make sure you have previewed your music, especially to know how songs begin and end. This will insure that you avoid **walking over** (beginning to "outro" a song before it's really over) a false ending. Previewing also helps you know how much instrumentation there is at the beginning of the record before the vocal starts. In this way you can talk over the instrumental but not the vocal part of the beginning. Sometimes timing information is provided on the CD, and this helps you with **voiceovers** on the intro and outro of the song. In any case, there is no excuse for a disc jockey playing a CD on the air that he or she isn't completely familiar with.

Plan how you'll get from one piece of music to the next if you play them consecutively. You might want to review the sound transitions mentioned in Chapter 3, "The Audio Console." Remember to work for a variety of ways rather than using the same method time after time. Listen to the on-air monitor frequently, if not continuously. Most audio consoles allow the announcer to hear the program line, the audition line, or the on-air signal; however, only the on-air signal allows you to hear exactly what the listener hears.

Production Tip #11—"Trade Publications"

If you're serious about having a career in radio broadcasting, you might want to subscribe to some of the following publications to keep abreast of current events in the industry. Subscription information can be found at the publications' Web sites, which are given at the end of this "tip." *Broadcasting & Cable* is considered by many to be the "bible" of the radio, television, and cable industry. In addition to the top news stories of the week, *Broadcasting & Cable* focuses on programming issues, technology developments, and features a classified section. Those interested in the music aspects of the industry will want to check out *Billboard* for both music charts in all formats and music news. *Radio & Records* (known in the industry as *R&R*) is a publication that provides both music and business information in a newspaper style format. Another publication for the latest news and information of the radio industry, with emphasis on technical aspects, is *Radio World*. If you meet certain publisher qualifications, you can get *Radio World* on a complimentary basis. These aren't the only trade magazines, by any means, but any one of them will provide valuable reference knowledge for any person interested in the radio industry.

Broadcasting & Cable—www.broadcastingcable.com
Billboard—www.billboard.com
Radio & Records—www.rronline.com
Radio World—www.rwonline.com

When your shift is over, clean up around the studio. It's also thoughtful to pull the first couple of songs or the first commercial break material for the next announcer so that he or she can get off to a smooth start. Playing music on radio is a hectic but rewarding job. Disc jockeys are, in every sense of the word, production people. Not only do they have to manipulate all the broadcast equipment, but they must add the element of announcing and present it all live and within the fast pacing of the radio station's format.

11.4 NEWS

If you're involved with radio production, you're likely to do some news work at some point in your life. In some instances the disc jockey may just **rip and read** from the news service on the hour or half hour. In a worst case scenario, the announcer would literally just rip some news copy off the wire and read it on-the-air. Of course, most radio news is now read directly off a computer screen so "rip 'n' read" just refers to the practice of reading a newscast cold or with no preparation. As we'll note in a moment, this is *not* good broadcast practice. At the other extreme are all-news stations, which usually have separate on-air people for news, weather, sports, traffic, commentaries, business news, and the like. This is a complicated format that necessitates using people who are very knowledgeable in their specialties and who have established themselves and their voices as personalities. Whatever situation you find yourself in, some knowledge about newscasting will prove useful.

Even if you're expected to simply read a short newscast each hour, you should give some time and thought to your news presentation. First, you must decide which news to present. Of course, you probably have a station news format to follow, but you should also try to select those items that are most likely to be of interest to your listeners. You may find that you need to do some rewriting of the wire service news and write some transitions to take the listener from one story to the next.

Timing is important on a news break. Make sure you read your news copy in the time prescribed. Sometimes beginning newscasters run out of news to read before the newscast time is up. To prevent this, you should pad your newscast with some extra stories that you can cut if you have to but that provide a cushion if you need extra material. You'll usually need to get commercials in at an appropriate time during a newscast, so make sure you know when this happens and are prepared for it.

Don't ever read a newscast cold. Read it over first so that you're familiar with the material. Rewrite anything that isn't natural for you, such as tongue-twisting phrases that you might trip over. Also rewrite if there are long sentences that make you lose your breath before you finish them. Avoid too many numbers or facts jammed into a single sentence. Whenever something is unclear, rewrite to make it simple and easy to understand. Remember,

FIGURE 11.2 In the modern studio, radio newscasters write, edit, and read the news directly from a computer screen. (Image courtesy of Alan R. Stephenson.)

FIGURE 11.3 Radio news persons can often find themselves recording actualities in the field for use in a later newscast. (Image courtesy of Alan R. Stephenson.)

broadcast news should be conversational and written for the ear, not the eye.

When a news story includes the actual voice of the person in the news, such as the mayor commenting on the new city budget, that segment is called an **actuality**. Most radio news operations strive to include many actualities within a newscast because these bring life to the news. It's more interesting to hear the mayor's comments than the voice of an announcer telling what the mayor said. Actualities are best reserved for opinion or reaction. The facts about the story can be given by the reporter, and then the newsmaker can say what he or she thinks about the subject. Obviously, many news actualities are gathered in the field with portable audio recorders; you can, however, also make use of the phone to gather them. Many small radio stations have one-person news departments, and in these cases the phone actuality is especially crucial. In some situations, newsroom phones are semipermanently hooked up to an audio recorder. But if not, you can use a contact mic that's specifically made to attach to the phone for this purpose. You must obtain permission to record someone for broadcast use, and your station newsroom probably has specific guidelines to follow for doing this.

Actualities generally need to be edited. For this, you should use all the editing techniques presented in Chapter 7, "Audio Editing," and then add one very important rule: Make sure that when you edit, you don't change the meaning of what someone has said. Ethical news procedures dictate that a great deal of care be taken in this area

because the elimination of a single word can significantly alter a news report. For example, "The mayor did not agree with the city council's decision . . ." could easily become just the opposite if the word "not" were edited out, leaving, "The mayor did agree with the city council's decision. . . ." When you're editing and need to eliminate part of what a person said, either because it's too long or it's irrelevant, try to match voice expressions where the statement leaves off and where a new one begins. Edits are usually best if made at the end of thoughts, because a person's voice drops into a concluding mode at that point. Be careful not to edit out all the breaths the person takes because this will destroy the natural rhythm. People do breathe, and actualities without any breathing sound unnatural. If an edit is going to be too tight because the person runs words together, add in a little background noise, or add a breath from a different place on the tape. Either of these will make for a natural-sounding pace between two edit points.

Try to maintain a constant background level throughout the actuality. To do this, you may have to mix in background noise from one part of the tape to another part. If you mix narration with an actuality, known as a voice-actuality, make sure you maintain the same level for both, and try to have background noises that are similar—or at least not jarring.

Whether you're a disc jockey reading a few newscasts or a broadcast journalist at an all-news station, you may wish to consult one of several good books available on techniques and ethics of gathering, writing, editing, and presenting news. Some of these books are listed in the Suggested Reading section at the end of this book.

11.5 PUBLIC AFFAIRS PROGRAMS

Public affairs programming usually consists of long programs that explore a news or community issue in depth. Some public affairs programs take a lighter tone and profile an individual or group. The typical public affairs show is a half-hour interview or discussion between host and guest(s). Although some stations have a specific public affairs host, many stations delegate this responsibility to a news person or an announcer.

The key to good public affairs programming is proper preparation. The host needs to research the subject and the guest before doing the program. Not only will this provide background, but it should enable the host to make a list of questions to ask. Asking the right questions really means asking good questions. For example, ask questions that require more than a simple yes or no answer. Don't ask, "Do you agree with the mayor's new policy regarding the police?" but rather, "What do you think of the mayor's new policy regarding the police?" Ask short, simple, and direct questions. The question, "Given the salaries of employees and the possible raises they will receive, what do you think the effects will be on the social security system and the GNP?" will most likely get a response of, "Huh?" Break

FIGURE 11.4 The public affairs program often involves an interview or discussion between the program host and a studio guest. (Image courtesy of Alan R. Stephenson.)

complex questions down into a number of questions such as, "How do you think increasing salaries five percent will affect the GNP?" Ask questions that don't require long answers. Don't ask, "What would you do to improve the city?" but, "What is the first thing you would do to improve the city?"

Asking good questions also means knowing how to handle the answers you get. For example, if the answer is too wordy, ask the person to summarize the response. If the answer is muddy or unclear, ask the material over again in smaller parts. If the answer is evasive, come back to it later, or ask it again from a different angle. If the response gets off track, redirect. And if the response goes on and on, interrupt politely and redirect. Listen carefully to what the guest says so that you can ask appropriate follow-up questions. Sometimes interviewers become so engrossed in thinking about the next question that they miss an important point the guest has made that could lead to something significant. Although you should write questions ahead of time so that you remember to cover all important points, don't slavishly stick to those questions. In all probability, when you ask question one, the guest will also answer questions three and seven, so you must constantly flow with the conversation. The more you can lead off what the guest says, the more natural the interview will appear. But make sure you do get the information you want.

If you're going to be recording the program at a remote location, make sure all the equipment works before you leave the station. This also holds true for recording in the studio; check everything out before your guest arrives.

You may be using a single microphone, so talk at the same level as the interviewee. As a broadcast professional, your voice may be stronger than the interviewee's, in which case lower your voice or else keep the mic farther away from yourself than from the guest. If you're talking with several guests, move the mic back and forth as each person talks. Also, follow speakers if they move their heads. Never let the guest take the microphone. He or she probably won't know how to use it properly, and you'll lose control of the conversation.

When you have a number of different guests, identify them frequently because the listener has difficulty keeping track of the various voices. Even a single guest should be reintroduced during a 30-minute program. Not only does this remind listeners who your guest is, but it introduces him or her to those listeners who joined the program in progress.

When you record at a remote location, listen to at least part of the tape before you leave to make sure you have actually recorded something. It's embarrassing to get back to the station and discover that you have nothing on the tape or disc, and it can be impossible to rearrange the interview for another time. If you're doing the interview in the studio, make sure you have a recording before the guest leaves.

Many public affairs programs are aired live or "as taped," but sometimes it's necessary to edit the tape. If you're going to be editing extensively, make a log of the material so that you know what is on the tape and where it is.

An understanding of the public affairs programming concepts and techniques, especially interviewing, will help you handle many types of production situations.

11.6 CALL-IN TALK SHOWS

Not everyone is cut out to handle hosting a call-in talk show. You must be fast on your feet and able to ad-lib in an entertaining and effective manner. For many programs, you're expected to have more than broadcast production knowledge. For example, a sports program or radio psychology show requires a host with some expertise in those areas. Sometimes the telephone talk show host has an engineer handling the equipment and a producer screening the calls so that the host can concentrate on dealing with the callers on-air, but this is not always the case, especially in smaller market radio.

A telephone talk show host has to be able to handle people tactfully (or, in some cases, abrasively, if that's the style of the program). As when interviewing for public affairs programs, the host must remain in charge of the program. Many of the other principles of public affairs interviewing also apply to call-in shows.

If you have a guest that people are asking questions of, you should give information about the guest and redirect questions if they're not understandable. The host must be able to establish good communication, without the aid of body language.

11.7 PLAY-BY-PLAY SPORTS

Many announcers also handle some sports broadcasting duties, and **play-by-play** (**PBP**) announcing skills can be a valuable asset for anyone entering the radio business. As a radio sports announcer, you must keep up the chatter, and you must describe completely what is happening. Since the listeners don't have the video image of TV, you have to be their eyes. Sports announcers often work in a team, with one announcer providing the play-by-play while another offers color commentary along with game statistics.

The PBP sportscaster operates remote equipment designed for sports broadcasting. Most of it is similar to studio equipment but extremely portable. A small audio console and headset microphone make up the bulk of sports remote equipment. The headset mic arrangement allows the sportscaster the use of both hands and keeps the counter or tabletop free for equipment and "stat sheets." The signal is sent from a remote console to the station by phone line or a remote pick-up unit or RPU (portable transmitter) that relays the signal to a special receiver at the station. You should also have some other way of communicating with the studio, such as a separate telephone line. This way you

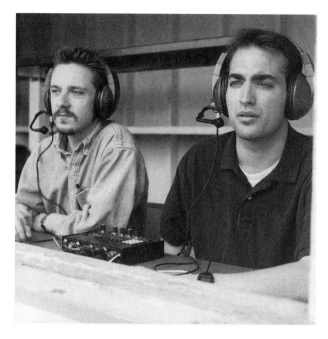

FIGURE 11.5 Sports announcers often work in a team, with one announcer providing the play-by-play while another offers color commentary along with game statistics. (Image courtesy of Alan R. Stephenson.)

can talk with the station about production matters that should not be heard by the audience. For example, commercials are usually played from the station, and you might need to coordinate when and how many will be played during a break in the action. Many remote consoles have some type of talk-back feature that allows off-air communication with the radio station.

Pregame preparation is very important for sports broadcasting. Gather all the information and facts about the teams and players, make sure all the equipment is ready to go, and get to the game in plenty of time to check out the broadcast booth, so you know everything is in order, especially the phone line connection. Sportscasting is one of the most glamorous aspects of radio production, but it is time-consuming and requires quick thinking plus a thorough knowledge of the sport.

11.8 RADIO DRAMA

Drama isn't produced very often on radio anymore, but when it is undertaken, it employs the use of many production skills, such as microphone techniques and the blending of sound effects and music into the production. Quite often, radio commercials are really a short form of the radio drama. The setting and action must be conveyed by the talent, sound effects, and music. Drama is best recorded with one microphone, but you may need to have people with louder voices position themselves a little farther away from it. It's also important to keep **perspective** during a production. In other words, people who are coming toward the supposed location of the play should sound far away at first and then nearer. The best way to do this is for the talent to walk away or toward the mic. You can mark the studio floor as to where they should start or stop talking to be on mic or off mic.

Sometimes one actor performs several parts. The actor needs to be able to create distinctly different voices in order to do this. In fact, all voices used within a drama should be distinctively different because audience members have trouble distinguishing one character from another. Talent should avoid using an affected radio voice but rather talk in their character's natural, conversational style.

Sound effects can be simulated in the studio, usually on a different microphone than the talent is using. Or they can be prerecorded or taken from a sound effects CD and edited into the production at a later time. They can be used to establish locale, tell time, create mood, indicate entries and exits, and establish transitions. Music is also an effective way to create mood and establish transitions. Most radio dramas open and close with music that's appropriate to the overall theme of the drama.

11.9 CONCLUSIONS

Whether producing a commercial, disc-jockeying a radio show, calling play-by-play sports action, or performing any of the other forms of programming, audio production is an exciting aspect of the radio business. The various types of programming allow for a great deal of variety in your day-to-day occupation and for numerous opportunities to be creative and innovative. Most people who enjoy radio production find it difficult to call it "work." You should have gained insight into the basic procedures, techniques, and concepts of modern radio production by this time. Now you need to continue working in the studio gaining the practical, hands-on experience that will help you develop into an experienced radio production person.

Self-Study

■ QUESTIONS

1. A fast-paced announcing style would be most appropriate for a disc jockey working at which type of radio station?
   a) contemporary hit radio format
   b) classical music format
   c) big band format
   d) all-news format

2. To "walk over" a false ending of a song, the radio DJ would _____.
   a) leave the mic open when it should be off
   b) recue a CD
   c) begin the outro of a song before it is really over
   d) imitate other announcers heard on the radio

3. The term "actuality" refers to _____.
   a) the voice of a person in the news
   b) a pad for a newscast
   c) wire service copy
   d) the voice of the news announcer

4. Radio news copy should contain _____.
   a) as many facts and numbers as possible
   b) simple, easy-to-understand sentences
   c) tongue-twister phrases
   d) long explanatory sentences

5. Which of the following would not be a good reason for editing a news actuality?
   a) to cut out a cough
   b) to cut out material that is irrelevant

c) to change the meaning of the story

d) to shorten the length of the story

6. A 30-second radio commercial produced with a music bed is usually _____.
   a) 35 seconds long because of the music
   b) read live by the disc jockey
   c) produced with a voiceover on top of the music
   d) recorded with two announcers and sound effects mixed in

7. Which of the following would be the best radio interview question?
   a) Do you favor capital punishment?
   b) What do you think will be the outcome of the present attempt to outlaw capital punishment?
   c) What do you think will happen regarding an amendment against capital punishment being added to the Constitution after it has been discussed by the state legislature in light of the case pending in Florida at the present time and the one recently decided in Illinois?
   d) You favor capital punishment, don't you?

8. Which of the following is good radio interviewing technique?
   a) let the interviewee hold the microphone
   b) ask all your questions in the order you have them written down
   c) ask follow-up questions based on the interviewee's response
   d) ask complex questions so you cover the topic thoroughly

9. Which of the following is *true* regarding radio sports announcers?
   a) usually project an abrasive announcing style
   b) cue up commercials while the game is in progress
   c) usually work in teams
   d) require very little preparation prior to the game

10. Radio drama is often recorded _____.
    a) at a remote location
    b) with a single microphone for the entire cast
    c) without regard for the "perspective" of sound
    d) with announcers using an "affected" radio voice

■ ANSWERS

If You Answered A:
1a. Right. Most rock music formats utilize a fast-paced announcing style.
2a. No. While the mic needs to be open, this doesn't describe what a walk-over is. (Reread 11.3.)
3a. Right. Actualities are statements from the people involved in a news event.
4a. No. Too many facts and numbers in radio news stories can be confusing because the listener can't refer back to them. (Reread 11.4.)
5a. No. Cutting out a cough or vocal stumble would be a reason to edit an actuality. (Reread 11.4.)
6a. Wrong. Commercials must be exact lengths; a 30-second spot is 30 seconds, and this includes the music bed. (Reread 11.2.)
7a. No. This type of question can be answered with a simple yes/no response. (Reread 11.5.)
8a. No. You can lose control of the interview if you let the interviewee take the microphone. (Reread 11.5.)
9a. No. While a few are abrasive, most sports announcers are not; radio talk show hosts are more likely to have this demeanor. (Reread 11.6 and 11.7.)
10a. No. Radio drama is best produced in the controlled environment of the studio. (Reread 11.8.)

If You Answered B:
1b. No. Classical music announcers are generally more subdued. (Reread 11.3.)
2b. Wrong. Cueing a CD has nothing to do with a walk-over. (Reread 11.3.)

3b. No. A pad refers to extra news stories used if the news announcer comes up short with his or her timing. (Reread 11.4.)

4b. Correct. Radio news copy should be easily understood.

5b. No. Cutting out unimportant or irrelevant material would be a reason for editing a news story. (Reread 11.4.)

6b. No. Commercials with music beds have usually been recorded before they are aired, not read live. (Reread 11.2.)

7b. Yes. This is the best choice.

8b. No. An interview can become very stilted if you ask every question in order from a list. You need to be prepared to deviate from any order of questions based on the interviewee's responses. (Reread 11.5.)

9b. Wrong. Commercials, during a sports broadcast, are usually played from the studio. (Reread 11.7.)

10b. Correct. A single mic is often sufficient for recording radio drama.

If You Answered C:

1c. No. Announcing for a big band format is probably more laid back. (Reread 11.3.)

2c. Correct. This describes what a walk-over is.

3c. Wrong. Wire service copy is not an actuality. (Reread 11.4.)

4c. No. These would be difficult for a newscaster or any announcer to read so they should be avoided. (Reread 11.4.)

5c. Never. This is a definite ethics violation. (Reread 11.4.)

6c. Correct. This describes the basic music bed commercial.

7c. No. This question is much too complex and convoluted. (Reread 11.5.)

8c. Yes. During an interview, you should listen carefully and ask appropriate follow-up questions.

9c. Right. One person does the actual play-by-play while the other adds color commentary.

10c. No. Radio drama must be careful to be sure the correct perspective is maintained during recording. (Reread 11.8.)

If You Answered D:

1d. Wrong. The disc jockey is normally associated with music formats and a fast pace isn't the best announcing style for news. (Reread 11.3 and 11.4.)

2d. No. This has nothing to do with a walk-over and it's not something you'd want to imitate. (Reread 11.3.)

3d. No. An actuality isn't the voice of the news announcer, in fact, it's just the opposite. (Reread 11.4.)

4d. Wrong. Although radio news copy must explain the elements of the news story, long, complex sentences should be avoided. (Reread 11.4.)

5d. No. Editing is essentially shortening and news stories often have to be a specific length, so this is a reason to edit. (Reread 11.4.)

6d. Wrong. This type of commercial may include a music bed, but you're getting confused with a highly produced radio vignette when all these elements are employed. (Reread 11.2.)

7d. No. This is just a rewording of the first question which can be answered with a simple yes/no response. (Reread 11.5.)

8d. No. Complex questions should be broken down into simpler, easy-to-follow questions. (Reread 11.5.)

9d. Wrong. Pregame preparation is extremely important and the key to good sports announcing. (Reread 11.7.)

10d. No. Radio drama announcers use a natural sounding, conversational voice even when the announcer is playing the role of a particular character. (Reread 11.8.)

Projects

■ PROJECT 1

Record an air-check tape.

Purpose

To instruct those interested in doing on-air broadcasting in how to make an audition or demo tape, something required when applying for a job.

Advice, Cautions, and Background

1. To apply for on-air jobs in broadcasting, you will send your resume and an air-check tape to many stations. An air-check tape is an audio tape of about 5 minutes that you record to show how you handle on-air broadcast situations.
2. Ideally, an air-check tape is an edited-down sample of your actual on-air work, but if you aren't on-air on a regular basis, a simulated air check can be put together in the production studio.
3. Try to make the tape as general as possible so that it could be sent to several different types of stations.
4. Put those things you do best at the beginning of the tape. Many potential employers don't have time to listen past the first 30 seconds and will rule you out if they don't like the beginning. Don't structure the tape so that it builds to a climax because probably no one will listen that far.
5. Feel free to use things you've done for other projects for your tape.
6. Keep the pace of the tape moving. Don't do any one thing for too long.

How to Do the Project

1. Plan what you intend to include in your tape. An air-check format might include ad-lib introductions to a few songs (either fade out the music after a few seconds, or edit to the end of the songs so that the listener doesn't have to hear the whole song), some production work (commercials, station promos, etc.), and a short newscast. If you can do play-by-play, you might want to put a short example at the end of the tape. There is no standard format, so do whatever showcases your talent best.
2. Plan the order of your tape. Make it sound like a continuous radio show as much as possible.
3. Record your tape and listen to it. Redo it if it doesn't present good broadcast skills.
4. On the tape, write your name and Air-Check Project. Turn in the completed tape to the instructor for credit for this project.

■ PROJECT 2

Record a 5-minute interview show in which you are the interviewer.

Purpose

To prepare you for this very common type of broadcasting situation.

Advice, Cautions, and Background

1. Your interview must be exactly 5 minutes. Making an exact time without having an awkward ending will probably be the hardest part of the project, but it's a lesson worth learning because broadcasting is built around time sequences.
2. Don't underprepare. Don't fall into the trap of feeling that you can wing this. In 5 minutes you must come up with the essence of something interesting, and you can't do this unless you have an organization of questions in mind. You'll also only be able to record the interview once. You can't redo this project.
3. Don't overprepare. Don't write out the interview word for word. It will sound stilted and canned if you do.
4. Five minutes is actually a long time; you'll be amazed at how much you can cover in this time.
5. As the interviewer, don't talk too much. Remember, the purpose is to get the ideas of your guest over to the audience, not your own ideas.

How to Do the Project

1. Select someone to interview. If you're taking a course, it will probably be easier to do this project with someone in class.
2. Decide what the interview will be about. You may select any subject you wish. You could talk about some facet of a person's life or his or her views on some current subject, or you could pretend the interviewee is a famous person.
3. Work up a list of questions. Make more than you think you'll actually need just in case you run short.
4. Think of a structured beginning and ending for the show since those will probably be the most awkward parts.

5. Discuss the interview organization with your guest so that you are in accord as to what is to be discussed, but don't go over the actual questions you're going to ask.

6. Tape the interview, making sure you stop at 5 minutes. Listen to it, and check that it has recorded before your guest leaves. You are finished with the project once the interview is taped. Even if it didn't come out as you had hoped, do *not* redo this project.

7. On the tape write INTERVIEW PROJECT and your name. Give the interview tape to your instructor to receive credit for this project.

■ PROJECT 3

With several other students, record a radio drama.

Purpose

To allow you to practice your dramatic abilities and to give you the experience of performing radio dramas.

Advice, Cautions, and Background

1. Make sure you have a group of congenial, dependable people. You don't want to start rehearsal and then have to switch cast members.

2. Sound effects will probably give you the most trouble. Make sure you have all that you need. Some are available on the CD-ROM.

3. Participants can get credit for this assignment without being on-air. For example, you might want to have one person in charge of sound effects, one in charge of engineering, and one as director.

4. If you want to write a play rather than use one that's already written, this is fine.

5. One person can play more than one role in radio by changing voices, but all voices used in the drama should be distinct.

How to Do the Project

1. Select the group and choose a director.
2. Have the director or the group select a play. The following are some books you may be able to find in a library that contain radio plays:
   a. Carol Adorjan, et. al., *WKID: Easy Radio Plays*, 1991
   b. Alonzo Cole and David Siegel, *The Witches Tale: Stories of Gothic Horror from the Golden Age of Radio*, 1998
   c. Metheun Books, *Best Radio Plays of 1985*, 1986
   d. David Pownall, *Radio Plays*, 1998
   e. Emil Sher, *Making Waves: Three Radio Plays*, 1998
3. Decide what each person is going to do for the production.
4. Check with the instructor about what you're planning to do and what problems you expect to experience.
5. Make sure that everyone gets a copy of the script. You can check with the instructor about ways to get the script duplicated.
6. Have set times to rehearse. Rehearse section by section both with and without microphones, and then put the whole thing together. Rehearse music and effects as well as dialogue.
7. When the production is polished enough, record it. Listen to it, and if it's good enough, give the tape to the instructor. If not, redo it.
8. On the tape write RADIO DRAMA PROJECT and the names of all the people who are involved.
9. On a sheet of paper, list the names of all involved, and write what each did for the production. Give this sheet and the completed tape to the instructor to receive credit for this project.

CHAPTER TWELVE

Internet Radio and Other Distribution Techniques

Information

12.1 INTRODUCTION

Digital technology has changed not only the production techniques of radio but the very nature of the industry itself. Radio stations have found that in order to keep up with the times, they must align themselves with the Internet. For many stations this means building **Web pages** that tie to their programming by promoting contests, concerts, and special events. Many also **netcast** their broadcast signal over the Internet, broadening their audience from a local area to the potential for the whole world.

The Internet has been important to radio at colleges and universities. College radio stations that have existed as over-the-air FM stations can now have an international audience. This has been a particular benefit to students who go away to college as their friends and relatives back home can now hear their radio programs. Alumni can use Internet radio to stay informed about their school, perhaps listening to the sports events. In addition, colleges that have not had stations in the past due to lack of funds or lack of available frequencies in their particular area can now create radio stations that are Internet only. In fact, any group or person with the proper equipment can now program a radio station that can be heard throughout the world.

This chapter will look at the techniques for creating an Internet radio station and then discuss, in briefer fashion, other radio distribution techniques, both new and tried-and-true.

12.2 WEB PAGES

In order to construct a radio station on the Internet, you must create at least one Web page. Known as the **home page** (see Figure 12.1), this page should contain an icon that potential listeners can click on to hear your station live. Once they click on this icon, they will hear whatever it is that is coming from your on-air studio. However, if you wish, you can also build files of program material from the past or even program material that you never even broadcast live. This is usually referred to as programming **on-demand**. For example, one file might contain last night's basketball game, and another file might be a talk show from a week ago. When listeners click on those files, they hear the programming from the past, not what is currently being programmed.

Your home page can contain a list of all the on-demand files, but if there are many of them you may want to lead the listener to other Web pages where they can get more information. For example, you might say "Click here for Sports Programs" on your home page and then have a list of seven or eight on-demand sports programs on a different page with brief summaries of each game. You may also want to include written information about your disc jockeys, contests, schedule, and other features. How you organize your Web pages is largely up to you and is beyond the purview of this book. There are many programs (Front-Page, Web CT, Flash, PageOut, DreamWeaver) that you can use to build eye-catching Web pages. We will concentrate on what you need to create the audio portion of your Internet radio station.

12.3 OVERVIEW OF THE AUDIO PROCESS

To undertake real-time **streaming audio** of a live broadcast, you need to get the output of your on-air console to the **sound card** (also called an **audio card**) of a computer that contains encoding software. This **encoder** system translates the analog audio from the sound card into a digital streaming format and sends it to a **server**, which is a much larger computer. The server sends the audio data stream over the Internet to the **player** software on the listener's computer, where it is decoded and played out over the analog speakers attached to the listener's computer (see Figure 12.2). The sound must be changed from analog to digital because analog audio cannot stream. It must be converted back to analog because the human ear cannot hear digital.

listen live on-line 24/7
(simulcast) (music) (worldnews)

music   arts & culture   news   program grid   about kcrw

(find it!)

DJ cam   Studio cam

(subscribe to) kcrw

(89.9) kcrw

santa monica

KCRW's Computer of the Month

NEW in the Audio Archives

G2 Sleep Part 2 on Loh Life. 4/16/01

G2 le Show on Le Show with Harry Shearer. 4/15/01

G2 Jordan Walker-Pearlman on The Treatment. 4/13/01

G2 Bernard Cooper on Bookworm. 4/12/01

G2 Bridget Jones's Diary; Joe Dirt; Amores Perros on Film Reviews. 4/13/01

G2 Olu Dara on Morning Becomes Eclectic. 4/06/01

EVENTS Announcements & New News

Support KCRW: Take a look at our cool **Premiums** and hot **Web Only Sweepstakes** then graciously **subscribe** or **renew** online. We depend on your support.

April 2001 Highlights - Find out what's coming up on **KCRW**

Visit KCRW's **Public Newsroom** for the latest news and discussion. China. Isreal. Mississippi. Cincinnati... and much more.

↓ today's (April 18) schedule

3:00 AM - 9:00 AM
Morning Edition:
National Public Radio's morning news magazine

9:00 AM - 12:00 PM
Morning Becomes Eclectic:
Eclectic and dynamic musical adventure.

12:00 PM - 1:00 PM
The World:
International news produced by the BBC and PRI

1:00 PM - 2:00 PM
To the Point:
Fast-paced, daily national news.
George W. Bush's First Earth Day

2:00 PM - 2:30 PM
Marketplace:
Business news with a global perspective

2:30 PM - 3:00 PM
Politics of Culture:
Where politics and culture collide.

3:00 PM - 3:55 PM
Fresh Air:
Revelatory interviews and unusual insights.

3:55 PM - 4:00 PM
City Observed:
A look at life in Southern Californina

4:00 PM - 6:30 PM

UCLA CAMPUS APRIL 28-29

FIGURE 12.1 This is part of the home page for radio station KCRW, operated from Santa Monica City College. Note the area for listening on-air as well as the daily schedule and the archived programs that can be listened to on-demand. (Image courtesy of Santa Monica College-based National Public Radio station KCRW; 89.9FM; KCRW.com.)

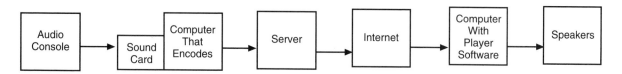

FIGURE 12.2 This diagram shows how the sound goes from the on-air console through the encoder, server, and player to the listener's speakers.

Connecting the output of the audio console to the computer sound card is fairly simple. As we discussed in Chapter 3, "The Audio Console," most consoles have several outputs, so one can be designated for the Internet. The signal can still go out over the airwaves. The input to consumer-grade sound cards is usually a **miniphone** connector, and the input on professional-grade sound cards is either **RCA** or **XLR**. There are also FM radio sound cards that can pick up an on-air FM signal and bring it into the computer.

To place files on the Internet that can be accessed on-demand, you can simply create a **soundfile** using audio editing and encoding software. There are two types of soundfiles—streaming and non-streaming. A streaming file begins to play sound on the listener's computer as soon as the listener clicks on the link to it. This kind of file provides instant access to material, but the quality of the sound may be compromised depending on the bandwidth (see below) of the Internet connection. A non-streaming file must be completely downloaded before it begins to play, but it may be played over and over since it has been downloaded to the listener's computer. The sound quality can also be of a higher quality because it is not limited by bandwidth, though the higher the quality, the larger the file and the longer the download time. Once the audio file is created, you can place it on the server and create a link to it from your Web page.

12.4 ENCODERS

The sound card in the computer that encodes is used to translate the analog signal into a digital format. The signal is sampled and then compressed so it can be sent efficiently over the Internet and be received by people who are using **modems** that operate at 28.8 or 56 kilobytes per second. This compressed signal also works with faster connections, such as DSL lines and cable modems.

One of the major considerations in this encoding process is **bandwidth**. This is the amount of frequency space that a particular signal encompasses. The more bandwidth, the more information, and the higher the quality of the signal. However, a high amount of bandwidth can slow down a system and use up all the capacity of the computer quickly.

Many audio operations strive to be CD-quality. As you learned in Chapter 5, "Digital Audio Players/Recorders," CDs are encoded using a **sampling** rate of 44.1 kHz. In other

words, they are sampled at 44,100 times per second. In addition each sample has a **bit depth** of 16 bits. One way to look at bit depth is to relate it to **signal-to-noise ratio** (see section 1.14 in Chapter 1, "The Production Studio Environment"). The higher the number of bits, the higher the signal-to-noise ratio, and hence the better the signal. You get approximately 6 **decibels (dB)** signal to noise for each bit, so 8-bit audio is about 48 dB of signal to 1 dB of noise, and 16-bit audio is a very respectable 96 dB. A 44.1, 16-bit signal uses a lot of bandwidth—roughly 1.4 megabits per stereo second (44,100 samples per second, times 16 bits per sample, times 2 for stereo, equals 1,411,200 bits). When data is sent over the Internet, it needs **overhead** (more bandwidth) so that the packets that it is sent in arrive at their destination properly. What all this means is that in order to receive pure CD-quality sound, a listener might need a connection to the Internet that operates at approximately 1.7 *mega*bytes per second. Most people have modems that operate at 56 *kilo*bytes per second or 28.8 *kilo*bytes per second. Another way to look at this is that it could take as much as 4 hours to download a 3-minute piece of CD-quality music using a 28.8 modem. Somehow the bandwidth used by an audio signal being sent over the Internet must be reduced.

There are several ways to handle this reduction. One solution is to send a monaural signal instead of a stereo one. That cuts the bandwidth needed in half. Another method is to employ **compression**. That is the method used by most of the encoding systems. It does degrade the quality of the signal somewhat, but it gets the bandwidth down to about one-tenth of what is needed for pure CD-quality sound. Most compression systems use some form of **perceptual coding** that is based on characteristics of the human ear. For example, there are certain sounds humans cannot hear (e.g., ones below 20 Hz or above 20,000 Hz). These can be eliminated. Similarly, there are also sounds human ears hear better than others. If two sounds are playing at the same time, we hear the louder one but not the softer one. By taking human hearing into account, a great deal of what is in a normal sound signal can be eliminated without much damage to the quality. Some compression systems also deal with silence. They take out the silent places within the audio and insert a code that places the silence back in when the sound is **decompressed** before it gets to the listener's audio speakers.

The encoding process requires a fairly advanced computer. Most encoding systems recommend at least a Pentium that runs at 90 megahertz with 32 megabytes of

RAM. It is best not to have anything else running on the computer that is doing the encoding because translating the signal is a fairly complex process.

12.5 SERVERS

Computers used as servers (see Figure 12.3) must be more powerful than computers used as encoders. Generally what is recommended is at least a Pentium MMX with a 266 megahertz processor and 128 megabytes of RAM.

The server audio software for audio data streaming is specially designed to handle sending out multiple audio data streams. Bandwidth again comes into play. Unlike over-the-air radio service, where one signal can reach an infinite number of listeners, for Internet service you must provide a separate audio stream from the streaming server for each listener. This can take as much as 24 kilobytes per second per listener. For this reason, Internet radio stations must limit the number of listeners who can tune in at any one time. Sometimes this number is as small as 10, but other stations choose to incorporate servers with higher bandwidth connections to the Internet that can handle about 1,000 listeners. As the popularity of Internet radio grows,

this individual serving will become more of a problem, but by then technological advances, which are coming very quickly, will probably solve the problem.

Many colleges and universities now have servers that connect to the Internet. The most common procedure for a college Internet radio station is to use part of the space on the university server. It is possible (although expensive) for a station to have its own server, or it can contract to use part of a server from an Internet Service Provider (ISP) or some other source. ISPs usually charge based on the amount of bandwidth a station occupies, so this is another reason to pay careful attention to bandwidth needs.

12.6 PLAYERS

The player software resides on the listener's computer. It receives the audio data stream from the server and decodes and decompresses it into analog sound that can be heard from the computer speakers. The streaming audio does not stay on the listener's hard drive; it streams in and then out again.

What actually happens is that the initial compressed audio data is placed into a buffer area, analogous to a small storage tank. Once a certain amount of data has partially filled the "tank," the soundfile begins to play. Streamed audio is poured into the top of the tank while the playback audio is being drained from the bottom of the tank. The filling of the tank is slightly faster than the draining of the tank, so there is always enough in reserve to continue playing back the audio if the input stream is momentarily interrupted.

The player software is available to listeners for free or at a low price. They simply download it from the Web site of the company providing it.

12.7 SOFTWARE OPTIONS

Usually the same company that provides the encoder and server software to a station is the same company that provides the listener with software. This can present a problem, especially for the listener who needs one brand of software to listen to one station and another to listen to a different station. Although both brands of software can be downloaded free or for a minimal cost, the two forms of software may compete to be the dominant (default) software on the consumer's computer. This can create nasty incompatibility problems, but the major software suppliers are working to alleviate this problem. Your Internet radio station Web page should definitely have a link to the Web page of the software company you are using so that your listeners can download the proper player software easily.

The major software players at present are Real from RealNetworks (*www.real.com*), Windows Media from Microsoft (*msdn.microsoft.com*), and QuickTime from Apple (*www.apple.com/quicktime*). Others providing software are StreamWorks (*www.xingtech.com*),

FIGURE 12.3 A server. (Image has been reproduced with the permission of Cisco Systems, Inc. Copyright © 2000 Cisco Systems, Inc. All rights reserved.)

Production Tip #12—"Kerbango"

One of the disadvantages of Internet radio is that the listener needs to be at his or her computer in order to hear the station. A number of companies have come up with what they think is a solution to this problem. One of the first was Kerbango, a stand-alone Internet radio. Dubbed the Internet Boombox, it looks like an old-time radio with large buttons and knobs (see Figure 12.4). To operate this radio you must connect to a phone line or home or office network (ethernet). You press the "on" button and you are connected to the Internet and to Kerbango's list of Internet stations displayed by format—country, jazz, talk, and so on. Using the "tuning knob,"

you select a category and then, with the "select" control you choose a specific station. If you move to a different location you can keep listening to your Kerbango as long as you connect to a phone line or ethernet port. You can also use Kerbango to play back MP3 files, and you can connect it to your stereo system. Recently, 3Com closed its Internet-appliance division, putting the Kerbango on hold. However, it's possible another company will buy and offer this Internet radio in the future, and certainly other companies will offer a similar type of radio for the Web.

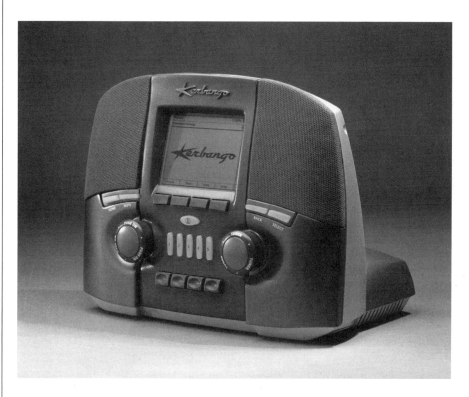

FIGURE 12.4 The Kerbango, an Internet radio appliance. (Image courtesy of Kerbango, a division of 3Com Corporation.)

Winamp (*www.winamp.com*), Destiny Media Player (*www.destinymediaplayer.com*), and Audio Active (*www.audioactive.com*).

At present RealNetworks is number one, with its products being used by the most stations and listeners (see Figure 12.5). It was the first one in the field, essentially inventing streaming audio. The tool used for encoding and netcasting is called RealProducer, the server is called RealServer, and the player is called RealPlayer. Its basic server can support up to 25 simultaneous listeners, but you can get more advanced services. Because RealNetworks has

been around for awhile, there are quite a few ISPs that provide RealServer hosting that stations can tap into (for a fee) if they don't have their own server.

Microsoft's Windows Media product is currently number two in terms of stations and listeners, having come into the business later than RealNetworks. Early versions of the product were called NetShow. Microsoft's encoder uses a proprietary system called **Advanced Streaming Format** (**ASF**) that must then be used with a server that has Windows NT loaded on it. This format can support 1,000 simultaneous listeners with 28.8 modems. Windows

Fill your room with sound.
Own the Bose® Wave® radio/CD.
CLICK HERE

BOSE

)01

RealPlayer - RealJukebox - Games | GoldPass | Help | International | RealNetworks.com

Player 8 Plus - Our Best Player

RealPlayer Plus gives you:

- cess to Major League Baseball games, all ason long
- Amazing audio and brilliant full-screen video
- Advanced picture controls and a graphic EQ
- Your choice of 2500+ radio stations

Download RealPlayer 8 Plus Now

Just US$29.70

Music
Download Music
Radio/TV Stations
Live
Entertainment
News, Sports and more!

TOP MUSIC DOWNLOADS

The all-new 2002 Mercury Mountaineer

1. Tim Buckley
2. Depeche Mode
3. Stevie Nicks
4. Snoop Dogg
5. New Order
6. Madonna
7. Monica
8. Alice Cooper
9. Wolfgang Amadeus Mozart
10. Dolly Parton

SEARCH ○ real.com
◉ NBCi.com (the web)

[Search]

GET READY FOR THE NBA PLAYOFFS

Get Live Sports with RealPlayer GoldPass:

Listen to the NBA Playoffs Here!
Now that the NBA regular season is over, get ready for the playoffs with NBA.com TV! Interviews, analysis, news- everything you need to keep your hoops knowledge solid.
Live Now!

Live Audio of MLB Games
Ricky Henderson re-launches his assault on the record books as the Padres face off against Deny Neagle and the Colorado Rockies. Listen to this game live, or pick another from today's schedule!
Colorado @ San Diego
Thursday @ 5:00 pm ET

MOVIES   **more movies**

Tomb Raider
Watch the new full-length trailer -- Angelina Jolie stars as video game heroine Lara Croft!
download RealPlayer 8

MUSIC VIDEOS   **more music**

Tribute To Joey Ramone
On April 15th, one of rock's true pioneers passed away. Sit back and remember with Real.com.
download RealPlayer 8

games
Free Downloads and Web Games!

 Action   **Strategy & Sims**

Racing   **Casino/card**

Puzzle & Board   **Web Games**

Featured Free Game:
Jetboat
Superchamps 2
A great game made better. Amazing jetboat racing!

Check it out:
Weekly Top Ten Free Downloads
Brand New Games!

RealNetworks.com

THREE basic steps
1. Creating
2. Broadcasting
3. Play ▶ PLAY

Interested in learning more about streaming media?

Streaming Media Starter Kit
Everything you need!

Content Creation Software
- RealSystem Producer Plus
- RealSlideshow Plus
- RealPresenter Plus

RealSystem iQ
▶ Intelligent Media Delivery

FIGURE 12.5 RealNetworks' Web page allows you to download easily and also links you to a large number of other services the company provides. (Web page courtesy of RealNetworks. Copyright © 1995–2000 RealNetworks, Inc. All rights reserved. RealNetworks, Real Audio, Real Video, Real System, RealPlayer, RealJukebox, RealDownload, Real Entertainment Center, and other names or logos are trademarks or registered trademarks of RealNetworks, Inc.)

Media Player can be downloaded onto a variety of Microsoft operation systems—Windows 95, Windows 98, and so on. Microsoft provides extensive documentation (see Figure 12.6) to help stations and listeners install the software, all of which can be downloaded from Microsoft's Web site.

Apple's product, QuickTime, has been around for a long time as part of the Macintosh family. Its first use was to serve as a means of providing picture and sound for jerky mini-movies that were not real-time streaming. Over the years Apple has improved the technology and added audio streaming, but it is still thought of mainly for its non-streaming applications (see Figure 12.7). Versions older than QuickTime 3 do not support streaming. As a result it is a distant third to Real and Microsoft in terms of providing streaming for Internet radio stations. Originally only available for Macintosh computers, QuickTime has branched out with a Windows version. Because of its non-streaming history, it is very easy to save files with the QuickTime player and then play them back at a later time.

12.8 ON-DEMAND FILES

As mentioned previously, one of the advantages of Internet radio is that you can place programs on the server that listeners can access at any time. This means listeners can hear your programming at times that are convenient to them.

When you record material that you want to place in an on-demand mode, you should take special care to have a high-quality recording because these files, too, go through encoding, compression, and other processes. The more useful audio information the system has to analyze, the better. You should try to record with minimal background noise and high-quality equipment.

In order to prepare on-demand material, you create soundfiles and then place these on your server so that your listeners can access them through their players. Most soundfiles end with .WAV, .AVI, .RA or .MP3.

MP3 has received particular attention because of its use in downloading music files from the Internet. It is an audio file format that is supported by a large number of shareware applications that convert music from CDs. Basically, it is a compression system for audio. Its full name is MPEG –2, Layer 3. MPEG stands for Moving Picture Experts Group, the group that developed compression systems for video data. This MPEG system encompasses a subsystem for audio compression that is referred to as Layer 3; it is based on the "perceptual coding" discussed in section 12.4.

The three major streaming providers (RealNetworks, Microsoft, and Apple) are now supporting this format in addition to their own proprietary systems. Some of the more minor players use MP3 as their streaming technology and do not have their own proprietary systems.

12.9 COPYRIGHT

Copyright in relation to the Internet has become a major concern. Because it is so easy to copy digital material, the copyright laws (written in the 1970s) either do not cover the concept or are ineffective in stemming the tide of illegal copying. Your Internet radio station must remain aware of the latest in copyright legislation and enforcement or it can find itself in major legal trouble.

There are three agencies that license music to radio stations—ASCAP, BMI, and SESAC. These organizations (see Figure 12.8) have been in business for many years and have negotiated license agreements that enable regular radio stations to play music without having to negotiate for each song. The agencies collect a set fee from each station and then have stations submit logs of what they play. They then distribute the money collected to composers and music publishers based on an approximation of how often each selection was played. There are three agencies because each of them handles different music, but a station that subscribes to all three can feel that it is playing music without violating copyright laws. These organizations have recently determined minimum fees for Internet broadcasting—$264 for ASCAP, $500 for BMI, and $50 for SESAC. If you are starting an Internet radio station, you should make sure you contact these agencies (*www.ascap.com, www.bmi.com, www.sesac.com*).

Another Website to consult regarding copyright is that of the Recording Industry Association of America (RIAA). Its address is *www.riaa.org* and it constantly updates information about copyright procedures (see Figure 12.9). This site will help you determine what licenses you need and how to obtain them.

12.10 INTERNET RADIO STATION LISTING SITES

Once you have established an Internet radio station, you want people to know about it. With all the material on the Internet, it would be hard for any but the most avid of fans to find your station. To help solve this problem, there are Internet sites that list radio stations (see Figure 12.10). They list by format type, geographic area, and various other parameters and simply link to all the radio stations they list. Some charge for listing and some don't. You would be well advised to contact as many of these as possible to see if they will list your station.

For starters, most of the companies that provide the encoder/server/player software also list radio stations and do so for free if you are using their software. Some of the other sites that you may want to check out are:

www.internetradiolist.com
www.webradio.com
www.gebbieinc.com
www.broadcast.com

Encoding the Program

After the audio is processed, it is sent to the sound card of the encoding computer: a P2-266 megahertz (MHz) Compaq computer with 64 megabytes (MB) of RAM. When the system was initially set up, the audio level was carefully adjusted, and the computer and modem were placed in a cabinet where the system runs mostly unattended.

Sending the Stream to the ISP

A 56-Kilobits per second (Kbps) data line between the encoding computer and Activate.net **MS** safely conveys the 20-kbps stream to the Window Media server. In the future, KPLU plans to upgrade to a frame relay system, which would allow them to send multiple streams to the ISP. With more than one stream, KPLU would be able to support multiple formats and bandwidths, possibly another program stream--a special local news stream, for example. There would also be bandwidth available to upload on-demand content. Kerry Swanson, KPLU Director of Operations, envisions a time when live jazz programming will be created specifically for the Internet.

Other Options

By using automation for webcasting, radio stations have a cost-effective means of covering network content that cannot be simulcast as well as an inexpensive platform for generating Internet-specific content. With the majority of the audience composed of over-the-air listeners, it is difficult to imagine a time when revenue will actually be generated from streaming on the Internet. However, every indication is that growth of streaming media is imminent. More and more radio stations are going online, more and more listeners are tuning in, Internet bandwidth is increasing, and the technologies comprising streaming media are expanding rapidly.

Aside from simulcasting, automation is the easiest, least resource-intensive way for a broadcaster to get into webcasting. The event sequencer used by KPLU provides basic automation functionality. However, there are a number of inexpensive automation programs available on the market today that provide full automation. One of them is from Broadcast Software International **MS** (BSI).

WaveStation main user interface, showing the event list

BSI's WaveStation integrates radio automation functionality with Windows Media Encoder. WaveStation automates the playback of WAV files and encodes a live Windows Media stream on a single computer. WaveStation allows a radio station to not only automate the covering of copyrighted network content, but to create original automated programming for the Internet. As a station expands its Internet usage, WaveStation will expand with it, switching seamlessly between simulcast, automation, and live-assist programming (live disk jockey assisted by automation). WaveStation also allows the radio station to send script commands live through automation. This allows a station to send URL flips, for example, to accompany programming. A jazz station could send artist information and pictures synchronized to the music.

The Internet will probably not replace over-the-air broadcasting in the near future. But as Internet broadcasting grows, and listeners begin to rely on it more and more, the radio business will no doubt go through another change. Radio has gone through many changes since the first commercial station signed on in 1920. Today's radio station competes in an often-saturated regional market. Tomorrow's Internet radio station will compete with other stations on a global scale. And because the cost of Internet broadcasting is so low, tomorrow's station will be sharing the virtual airwaves with thousands of other million-dollar facilities as well as inexpensive automated stations that can be set up in a bedroom. Technology has prevented most people from becoming broadcasters for many years; now the Internet is empowering them. To make it, the Internet broadcaster of the future will need to operate inexpensively and offer unique, compelling programming. Microsoft® Windows Media™ Technologies and automation provide the means for exploring this new world.

Additional Information

- KPLU Radio Web site **MS**
- Broadcast Software International **MS**
- CRL Systems **MS**
- Aphex Systems **MS**

Related Articles

- Windows Media Encoder Overview
- Setting up Your Windows Media Services Real-Time Encoder for Radio
- Setting Up Your Windows Media Services for Radio
- Putting Your Radio Signal on Your Web Site
- Windows Media Radio Station Guide

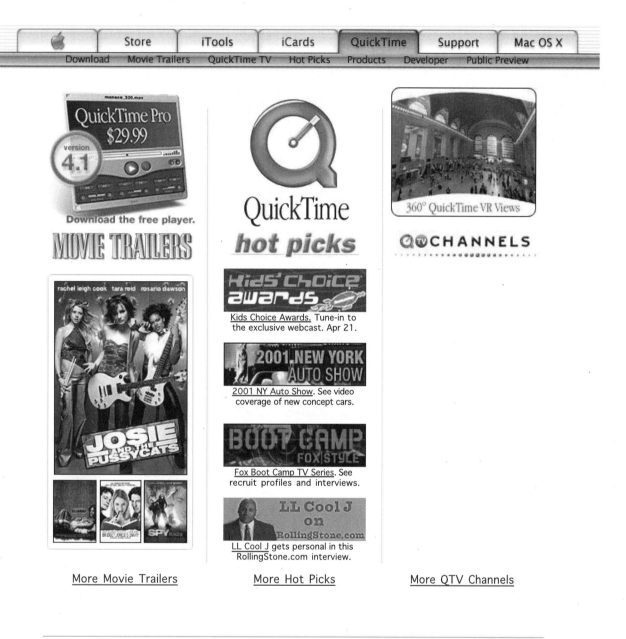

FIGURE 12.7 QuickTime's Web page emphasizes its video features as well as its audio. (Web page courtesy of Apple.)

FIGURE 12.6 This page is an outline of some of the material Microsoft provides to help customers get their Internet radio stations up and running. (Image courtesy of Microsoft.)

ASCAP LICENSING:
(What ASCAP Licenses,
 What ASCAP Does Not License)
 Frequently Asked Questions
 Common Licensing Terms
 Licensing Resources
 Contact ASCAP Licensing

BROADCAST LICENSING
Frequently Asked Questions

GENERAL LICENSING
(Nightclubs, Concerts, Hotels, Businesses, etc.)
 Frequently Asked Questions
 List of ASCAP General Licenses
 General Licensing Report Forms

INTERNET LICENSING
Frequently Asked Questions
 Internet License Agreement
 ASCAP's RateCalc™

RADIO LICENSING
Frequently Asked Questions
 Radio Licensing Annual Reports
 Radio License Forms
 ASCAP PARIS Software

TELEVISION

A S C A P
Since 1914 the Leader in Music Licensing

ASCAP licenses the right to perform songs and musical works created and owned by songwriters, composers, lyricists and music publishers who are ASCAP members and members of foreign performing rights organizations who are represented by ASCAP in the United States.

It is impossible for individual composers and publishers to monitor the hundreds of thousands of businesses that use music. It would be equally difficult, time consuming and expensive for business owners to locate and negotiate with all the owners of the music that might be used. There is a simple, fast and reasonably priced alternative. Through ASCAP, in one simple transaction, businesses can obtain the right to perform the millions of songs created or owned by more than 110,000 of America's and hundreds of thousands of the world's best songwriters, composers, lyricists and publishers. Founded in 1914, and still owned by and managed for its writer and publisher members, ASCAP grants businesses the permission they need to perform music publicly. The money collected is distributed, after deducting operating costs (currently less than 16%), directly to ASCAP members and to affiliated foreign performing rights organizations for their members.

Continue...

FIGURE 12.8 ASCAP's Web site. (Copyright © 2000 ASCAP. Reproduced with Permission of the American Society of Composers, Authors and Publishers from *www.ascap.com*.)

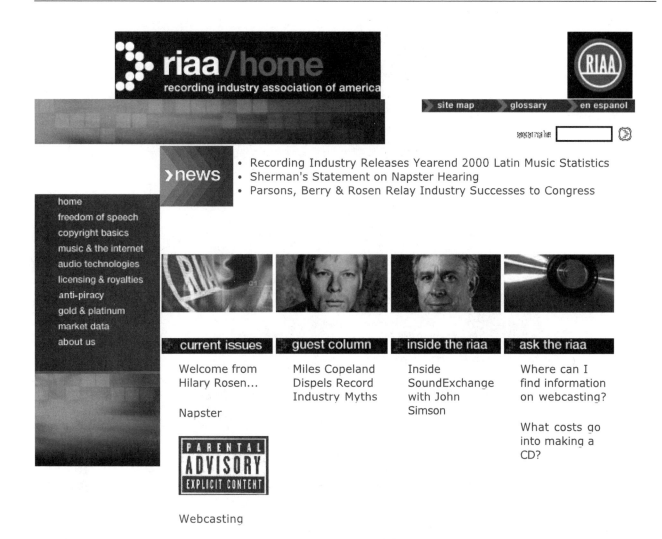

FIGURE 12.9 The Recording Industry Association of America updates its copyright information regularly. (Image courtesy of RIAA.)

Establishing and operating an Internet radio station can be a rewarding activity and a very good learning experience for anyone interested in a career in either traditional radio or new technologies.

12.11 OTHER DISTRIBUTION MEANS

New distribution techniques, such as the Internet, are not unusual in radio programming. As each new form takes hold, the old ones undergo change, but the need for programming remains. Regardless of how the material is distributed, it must be produced in such a way that meets the entertainment and information needs of the public.

AM over-the-air entertainment broadcasting was started in the 1920s and was the dominant form of radio distribution for many years. FM was developed during the 1930s but did not come to fruition until the 1960s and later overtook AM as the favored listening form. When cable TV went through a growth spurt in the 1980s, it added audio-only services to its menu, but these have never achieved great success. A new form of broadcasting that distributes directly from satellites to radio receivers is poised to create competition for traditional over-the-air AM and FM. Students and practitioners of radio need to understand these various distribution techniques in order to profit from what they have to offer and in order to produce programming that will meet the goals of the services.

12.12 SATELLITE RADIO

Satellite radio, often called **digital audio radio service (DARS)**, will beam radio programming directly from a

Search

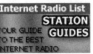

General
General Radio
International
Countries
Languages
Music
Adult Contemporary
Alternative
Alternative Rock
Brazil Radio
Classic Rock
Classical Music
Classics
College Radio
Country
Dance/Techno
General
Gospel / Spiritual
Jazz
Latin
Lite
Mixed Radio
Oldies
Rap/Urban
Rock
Top 40
News
News
Sports
Sports
Talk
Talk Radio
Whats New
New Stations
Archive
Featured Stations
Resources
Build an Internet Radio
Station

Real Player
WinAmp
Windows Media Player

HOME
Business
Daily Pick
Desktop
Featured Archive
Fonts
Games 2.0
MP3
Must-Haves
Screen Savers
Upload
Utilities
Wallpaper

INTERNET RADIO FAQ - All the information you need to start enjoying radio broadcasts on the internet!

PREVIOUSLY FEATURED STATIONS

 Need a healthy refreshing doze of Trance music? Then follow our link to the Massinova Project, an Internet based radio station with a Pre-Recorded 24/7 broadcast of today's hottest Trance music. The station's playlist has enough songs to let you listen to music whole day without getting bored by constant repetition. Massinova Project also allows users to request any song from their extensive playlist.

Tired of the constant onslaught of modern saccharine-sweet bopper music? Then take a break from it with KillerOldies.Com - an Internet based radio station broadcasting popular music of years long gone. KillerOldies.Com is fully optimized to deliver the best music experience to you with not only a great playlist selection, but also by using music player that comes on many PCs by default and differentiating its broadcast into two streams that allows folks with faster Internet connections to enjoy higher quality music, while still serving a modem-friendly music stream for all modem users out there.

 High quality Jazz music stations can be hard to come by on the Internet. However, thanks to the excellent music broadcast from the SmoothJazz.com, that is no longer a problem. SmoothJazz.com is an Internet Jazz portal where you can listen to a number of pre-recorded Jazz music shows in MP3 or Real Audio format, buy tickets to concerts, purchase Jazz related merchandise, locate a Jazz club near you and many other Jazz related features taht no fan of Jazz music can live without. You can also choose to give a listen in 32kb or CD quality 128kb, granted your Internet connection is can handle it.

October 2000

Get it

FIGURE 12.10 Here is part of the home page of Internet Radio List. Note that it features stations and shows a special list of new stations. It also covers stations from other countries. You can search by station name, country, language, and key word. (Copyright © 2000 Internet.com Corporation. All Rights Reserved. Reprinted with permission from *www.Internet.com*.)

satellite to a home or car receiver. The signals will be distributed nationally with no need for local stations that broadcast to a local area. Because DARS is a digital service, its signals will be of higher quality than current FM broadcasting.

The FCC has granted two companies, Sirius Satellite Radio and XM Satellite Radio, the right to broadcast DARS. Both services are planning to charge consumers about $10 a month. For this they will receive approximately 100 channels, most of them narrowly focused to particular interests such as classical music, new popular releases, or auto racing. Some of the offerings will be commercial free, and others will carry about 8 minutes of commercials an hour—far less than present commercial radio. The service will occupy different frequencies than current radio broadcasting, so anyone wanting to hear them will need a new radio receiver. The radios will be inexpensive, and both companies have working arrangements with auto manufacturers to have the radios offered as standard or optional equipment in new cars.

There are no definite plans to make any of the audio channels training grounds for students, but this type of service is something students should prepare for if they wish a career in radio. The multitude of channels and their narrow focus will provide an opportunity for creativity in both programming and production.

12.13 CABLE RADIO

Many cable TV systems provide digital CD-quality audio services that are piped into the home along with the cable TV service. Obviously these **cable radio** signals cannot be heard in the car but are limited to in-home listening. In some instances the cable systems charge extra for these services, and in other instances the services are part of the basic package. There are both commercial-free programs and ones that contain advertisements. Sometimes the audio is used as background for text channels listing local events or program schedules. Some of the companies providing these audio services also make them available to broadcast networks and/or commercial establishments such as doctors' offices. In some instances a company will provide only one channel of audio services while other companies provide multiple channels. The offerings are varied, such as news programs from around the world, classical music, religious programming, and foreign language programming. Many of these services have Web pages, and some you might want to check out are:

The Beethoven Satellite Network—*www.wfmt.com*
The Cable Radio Network—*www.cableradionetwork.com*
Moody Broadcasting Network—*www.mbn.org*
World Radio Networks—*www.wrn.org*
Yesterday USA—*www.yesterdayusa.com*

Many colleges operate public access cable channels and place student-produced audio on the channel, often under character-generated announcements about the school. Often this is the same programming that is going out over the Internet radio station or the on-air station, thus giving the student work a broader audience.

12.14 OVER-THE-AIR BROADCASTING

The most traditional way that radio programming is delivered is over the airwaves by local stations. The sound goes from the station's studio to the **transmitter**. Here it is **modulated**, which means the signal is superimposed onto a **carrier wave** that represents a particular station's frequency. Some stations operate in the **AM** band where the frequencies are 535 to 1,705 kilohertz, and others are in the **FM** band of 88 to 108 megahertz. These frequencies are much higher than sound frequencies (20 to 20,000 Hertz) and can travel much further than sound. Once the sounds have been modulated, they are sent out of the station antenna into the air. The carrier wave can be picked up by a radio receiver that demodulates the signal and turns it back into sound that the ear can hear.

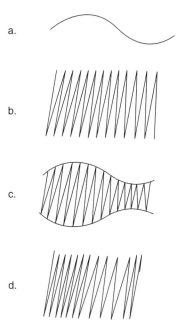

FIGURE 12.11 (A) An electrical wave that represents original sound. (B) The carrier wave of a radio station that is of a much higher frequency. (C) How the carrier wave is changed for amplitude modulation. Note that the height of the carrier wave is varied to take into account the characteristic of the sound wave. (D) How the carrier wave is altered for frequency modulation. Note that the frequency or distance between the waves is varied to relate to the original sound wave—the frequency is decreased where the sound wave is lowest.

Technically, the difference between AM and FM involves how the on-air signal is modulated. AM stands for **amplitude modulation** and involves a method that varies the amplitude, or height, of the carrier wave in order to represent the sound. FM stands for **frequency modulation** and is a process that changes the frequency of the carrier wave in order to represent the sound. Figure 12.11 shows a representation of the two types of modulation.

FM signals are better quality, in part because of the modulation techniques. For example, AM is more subject to static because static is most likely to occur at the bottom and top of the carrier wave. For FM, that part of the wave can just be cut off to eliminate static, but for AM the top and bottom must remain because they are the key to how the modulation occurs. There are many other reasons why FM is better quality. One is that FM signals occupy more bandwidth than AM because bandwidth was not given a great deal of consideration when AM was developed in the 1920s.

Fortunately for colleges, most student-operated radio stations are in the FM band. This has nothing to do with modulation or bandwidth; it has more to do with politics. Many early AM stations were operated by educational institutions, but as radio's popularity grew and frequencies were in short demand, the universities lost out to commercial interests. When FM was established, the educators convinced the FCC to reserve some of the frequencies (88.1 to 91.9) for noncommercial use so that commercial stations could not operate in that band. Today many of these frequencies are licensed to colleges and universities that use them for public radio programming and/or as student stations. As previously mentioned, sometimes the programming going out to the community from the FM antenna also goes over the Internet or over a cable TV system.

12.15 CONCLUSIONS

At present there is a wealth of outlets for student audio work. In addition to stations operated by colleges and universities, there are Internet sites, cable services, and broadcast stations that accept individual programs produced by students. Anyone wishing to get experience and exposure while a student can certainly find a distribution outlet for quality audio work.

Self-Study

■ QUESTIONS

1. The Internet has been important to college radio because _____.
   a) stations can have an international audience
   b) alums can keep in touch by listening to the college radio station over the Internet
   c) colleges that could not have a station because of lack of available frequencies can now have one
   d) all of the above

2. On-demand programming is _____.
   a) programming that is streamed live over the Internet
   b) files of programmed material that can be accessed over the Internet
   c) the icon that listeners click on to receive live streaming
   d) a home page as opposed to a Web page

3. Which of the following aspects of Internet radio is on the listener's computer?
   a) encoder
   b) server
   c) player
   d) overhead

4. Which type of soundfile begins to play on a listener's computer as soon as he or she clicks on it?
   a) streaming
   b) non-streaming
   c) FM
   d) Flash

5. Someone with a modem operating at 56 kilobytes per second can easily receive uncompressed, analog audio signals from the Internet.
   a) true
   b) false

6. The greater the bandwidth of a signal _____.
   a) the faster the system will operate
   b) the lower the signal-to-noise ratio will be
   c) the greater the frequency of the sound will be
   d) the higher the quality of the sound will be

7. Approximately how much does the signal-to-noise ratio improve with each additional bit when you are dealing with bit depth?
   a) 44.1 kilohertz
   b) 48 dB
   c) 6 dB
   d) 1,411,200 bits

8. Perceptual coding _____.
   a) takes into account what sounds the human ear can hear
   b) involves sending a mono signal instead of a stereo one
   c) is a compression system that increases the amount of bandwidth a signal uses
   d) places more silence in a signal so it can be easily decompressed

9. Computers used as servers need to be more powerful than computers used as encoders.
   a) true
   b) false

10. One difference between Internet radio and over-the-air radio is that _____.
   a) Internet radio stations do not need to pay license fees to play music
   b) Internet radio covers a smaller geographic area than over-the-air radio, enabling only people who are close to its server to receive its signal
   c) each listener is served individually for Internet radio but an over-the-air signal can be picked up by anyone who has a radio within the service area
   d) Internet radio was developed earlier than over-the-air radio

11. Streamed audio stays on a listener's computer in a large buffer area that acts like a storage tank.
   a) true
   b) false

12. Which audio streaming software is currently used by the most stations?
   a) QuickTime
   b) Windows Media
   c) RealNetworks
   d) StreamWorks

13. Microsoft's proprietary encoder system is called _____.
   a) Windows NT
   b) MP3
   c) QuickTime
   d) ASF

14. The audio compression system based on the compression system developed by the Moving Picture Experts Group is _____.
   a) WAV
   b) MP3
   c) QuickTime
   d) AVI

15. Which of the following is a music licensing agency?
   a) ISP
   b) RIAA
   c) ASCAP
   d) MPEG

16. Internet Radio List is _____.
   a) server software
   b) software to copy music
   c) an organization that gives out blanket licenses
   d) a service that lists Internet radio stations

17. Which of the following was developed the earliest?
   a) AM radio
   b) FM radio
   c) cable radio
   d) satellite radio

18. Which form of radio can go directly from a satellite to a radio receiver?
   a) cable radio
   b) Internet radio
   c) FM radio
   d) DARS

19. Which company is establishing a satellite radio service?
   a) Apple
   b) Yesterday USA
   c) Sirius
   d) Kerbango

20. One difference between AM and FM is that _____.
   a) AM stations have greater bandwidth than FM stations
   b) AM stations modulate by varying the height of the carrier wave, but FM stations modulate by varying the frequency of the carrier wave
   c) FM stations are more subject to static than AM stations
   d) more college radio stations are on the AM band than are on the FM band

■ ANSWERS

If You Answered A:
1a. This is correct, but there is a better answer. (Reread 12.1.)
2a. No. By definition, on-demand is not streamed live. (Reread 12.2.)
3a. No. An encoder would be used by the station. (Reread 12.3, 12.4, and 12.6.)
4a. Right. A streaming soundfile begins to play as soon as it is clicked.
5a. Wrong. (Reread 12.4 and select the other answer.)
6a. No. It is the opposite. (Reread 12.4 and try again.)
7a. No. This relates to sampling, not bit depth. (Reread 12.4.)
8a. You are right. Perceptual coding takes into account what a human can hear.
9a. You are correct.
10a. Wrong. They must both pay. (Reread 12.5 and 12.9.)
11a. No, not on the listener's computer. (Reread 12.6.)
12a. No. This is number 3. (Reread 12.7.)
13a. No. This is a Microsoft product that the encoder runs on, but it is not the encoder system. (Reread 12.7.)
14a. No. This can indicate a soundfile, but not a compressed one. (Reread 12.8.)
15a. No. This isn't even close. (Reread 12.5 and 12.9.)

16a. No. It is less technical than that. (Reread 12.10.)
17a. Yes, in the 1920s.
18a. No. The cable TV system is in between. (Reread 12.12 and 12.13.)
19a. Wrong. This is computer-oriented. (Reread 12.7 and 12.12.)
20a. Wrong. It is the other way around. (Reread 12.14.)

If You Answered B:

1b. This is correct, but there is a better answer. (Reread 12.1.)
2b. Correct. A listener can click on a file on a Web page.
3b. No. A server would be used by the station. (Reread 12.3, 12.5, and 12.6.)
4b. No. Non-streaming must be downloaded. (Reread 12.3.)
5b. Right. Data must be compressed or the information would take forever to download.
6b. Wrong. This has more to do with bit depth. (Reread 12.4.)
7b. No. This number was used in reference to 8-bit sound. (Reread 12.4.)
8b. No. That is a form of bandwidth reduction, but it is not related to perceptual coding. (Reread 12.4.)
9b. No. It is the opposite. (Reread 12.4 and 12.5 and select the other answer.)
10b. Wrong. It would be the opposite. (Reread 12.5 and 12.14.)
11b. This is the right answer. It does not stay on the listener's computer.
12b. No. This is number 2. (Reread 12.7.)
13b. No. MP3 is not proprietary. (Reread 12.7.)
14b. Yes. This stands for MPEG 2, Layer 3.
15b. No. This organization has been involved with copyright disputes, but it doesn't license music. (Reread 12.9.)
16b. Wrong. It doesn't deal with computer software. (Reread 12.10.)
17b. No. There is a better answer. (Reread 12.11.)
18b. Definitely not. (Reread 12.12.)
19b. Wrong. This is involved with a different distribution system. (Reread 12.12 and 12.13.)
20b. Correct. You understand the modulation well.

If You Answered C:

1c. This is correct, but there is a better answer. (Reread 12.1.)
2c. No. The program is not an icon, and they would not click to stream. (Reread 12.2.)
3c. Yes. The listener's computer has the player.
4c. No. FM is not a soundfile. (Reread 12.3 and 12.14.)
6c. Wrong. Bandwidth and frequency are not related here. (Reread 12.4.)
7c. Yes. This answer, 6 dB, is the correct choice.
8c. No. This is wrong for a lot of reasons, one of which is that compression does not call for an increase in bandwidth. (Reread 12.4.)
10c. Right. Internet radio requires a separate stream for each listener.
12c. Yes. RealNetworks is number 1.
13c. No. This is an Apple product. (Reread 12.7.)
14c. No. This is Apple based. (Reread 12.7 and 12.8.)
15c. Correct. ASCAP is one of the music licensing agencies.
16c. No. It is not involved in licensing. (Reread 12.10.)
17c. Wrong. This didn't come along until much later than some of the other choices. (Reread 12.11.)
18c. No. This does not involve satellite. (Reread 12.12 and 12.14.)
19c. Yes. And so is XM Satellite Radio.
20c. No. It is the other way around. (Reread 12.14.)

If You Answered D:

1d. Yes, this is the correct answer. All of the answers apply.
2d. No. On-demand programming could be placed on a home page or Web page, but it is not either of them. (Reread 12.2.)
3d. Wrong. Overhead is not a relevant term here. (Reread 12.3, 12.4, and 12.6.)
4d. Very wrong. Flash is a computer program involving animation that is used to design Web pages. (Reread 12.1 and 12.3.)
6d. Correct. More bandwidth equals higher quality.
7d. No. This huge number was used in relation to a minute of stereo sound. (Reread 12.4.)

8d. No. This answer doesn't really make sense and it does not relate to perceptual coding. (Reread 12.4.)

10d. Definitely not. (Reread 12.5 and 12.11.)

12d. No, this is not most used. (Reread 12.7.)

13d. Correct. It stands for Advanced Streaming Format.

14d. No. This can indicate a soundfile, but not the right one. (Reread 12.8.)

15d. Wrong. This is an organization dealing with compression. (Reread 12.8 and 12.9.)

16d. This is the correct answer.

17d. No. This is very new. (Reread 12.11.)

18d. Correct. This stands for Digital Audio Radio Service.

19d. No. You are way off. (Reread the Production Tip in this chapter.)

20d. Wrong. That's not where college radio is. (Reread 12.14.)

Projects

■ PROJECT 1

Look at the Web sites of six different radio stations and write a report on their differences and similarities.

Purpose

To give you a feel for how stations are currently utilizing the Internet.

Advice, Cautions, and Background

1. Try to select different types of stations—for example, ones that are Internet only, ones that are both broadcast and Internet, AM stations, and FM stations.
2. Try to use a fairly powerful computer that has a player or can easily download one.
3. Consider both the audio and visual elements as you do your analysis.

How to Do the Project

1. Find six different stations that have Web pages on the Internet. Feel free to use the Internet sites that list radio stations, as mentioned in section 12.10.
2. Go to one of the Web sites and click on a soundfile or on the live streaming. If necessary, download the player software.
3. Make notes about the appearance of the site and about the type of audio material that is available. Look at the various pages and see the types of materials that are included. You might want to consider such facets as: how much material is on the home page; whether or not the site contains live streaming and on-demand files and, if so, what types of on-demand files are included; the color scheme of the pages; the organizational principles around which the pages are presented; the extent to which on-air personalities are featured; and so on.
4. Do the same for five more sites.
5. Write a report that compares and contrasts the radio station presentations. See if you can find trends or recurring features. For example, do music stations tend to use the Internet in different ways than talk stations? Are there things that Internet-only stations include that broadcast stations do not? Do most of the station sites include daily schedules?
6. Put your name on your report and label it WEB SITE ANALYSIS. Give the report to your instructor for credit for this project.

■ PROJECT 2

Tour a broadcast radio station transmitting facility.

Purpose

To enable you to see a broadcast transmitter firsthand and better understand the broadcast process.

Advice, Cautions, and Background

1. Although you may have toured a radio station already, you may not have seen the transmitter facility because many broadcast studios are physically separated from the transmitter site.
2. Try to arrange to talk with an engineer as that is the person who can give you the most information.
3. Make sure that before you go you have some ideas about what you want to find out.
4. Your instructor may have set up a tour for the entire class, or the engineer at your college FM station may offer a tour of your own station. Either case is fine for completing the project.

How to Do the Project

1. Select a station. (If the instructor has arranged a station tour for the whole class, skip to step 4.)
2. Call someone at the station, tell them you would like to see their transmitter site and talk with someone about it so you can write a report for a radio production class, and ask if you may come.
3. If so, set a date; if not, call a different station.
4. Think of things you want to find out for your report. For example:
    a. How does the line out of the audio console get to the transmitter?
    b. Is there any signal processing equipment at the transmitter site?
    c. Does the station use amplitude modulation or frequency modulation, and exactly where is this modulation equipment located?
    e. What is the physical layout of the transmitter site?
    f. How does the signal get from the transmitter to the antenna?
5. Go to the station transmitter site. Tour to the extent the station personnel will let you and ask as many questions as you can.
6. Write a report about what you found out.
7. Put your name and TRANSMITTER SITE REPORT on your report and hand it in to your instructor to get credit for this assignment.

Glossary

A-B miking   A method of stereo miking where one mic feeds the right channel and another mic feeds the left channel.

Absorption   The process of sound going into the walls, ceilings, and floors of a studio.

Absorption coefficient   The proportion of sound a material can absorb in relation to the sound it will reflect back. A coefficient of 1.00 means that all sound is absorbed in the material.

Acoustic suspension   A speaker enclosure design that consists of a tightly sealed box that prevents rear sounds from disrupting main speaker sounds.

Actuality   A voice report from a person in the news rather than from the reporter.

Adaptive Transform Acoustic Coding   A data compression system used for MiniDiscs.

Adhesion   A condition that occurs when one layer of audio tape sticks to another.

Amplify   To make louder.

Amplitude   The strength or height of a sound wave or radio wave.

AMS   See *automatic music sensor*.

Analog   A recording, circuit, or piece of equipment that produces an output that varies as a continuous function of the input, resulting in degradation of the signal as material is copied from one source to another.

ATRAC   See *Adaptive Transform Acoustic Coding*.

Attack   The time it takes an initial sound to build up to full volume.

Audio card   A connection between a computer-based audio workstation and other audio equipment.

Audio chain   The route through various pieces of equipment that sound takes in order to be broadcast or recorded.

Audio console   The piece of equipment that mixes, amplifies, and routes sound.

Audio routing switcher   A type of patch panel that allows audio inputs to be switched to various outputs electronically.

Audio signal   A sound signal that has been processed into an electromagnetic form.

Audio tape recorder   A device that rearranges particles on magnetic tape in order to store sound.

Audition   An output channel of an audio console.

Automatic music sensor   A button on a digital audio tape recorder that allows the operator to skip forward or backward to the start of a new song.

Auxiliary   An output channel of an audio console.

Backing layer   The back side of audio tape—the side that does not have magnetic coating.

Balance control   A knob on stereo input channels used to determine how much sound goes to the right channel and how much sound goes to the left channel.

Balanced cable   A cable with three wires—plus, minus, and ground.

Band cut filter   See *band reject filter*.

Band pass filter   A filter that cuts all frequencies outside a specified range.

Band reject filter   A filter that allows all frequencies to pass except a specified frequency range.

Bass reflex   A speaker enclosure design that has a vented port to allow rear sounds to reinforce main speaker sounds.

Bass roll-off switch   A switch that turns down bass frequencies to counter the proximity effect.

Bias   A high-frequency signal that improves frequency response of a recording and cuts down distortion.

Bidirectional   Picking up sound from two directions; usually refers to a microphone pickup pattern.

Binary   A number system that uses two digits, 1 and 0.

Blast filter   See *windscreen*.

Boom arm   A microphone stand for use in the radio studio, consisting of metal rods designed somewhat like a human arm; one end goes into a base that can be mounted on a counter near the audio console, and the other end supports the mic.

Boom stand   A stand that can be placed away from an announcer; usually it consists of one vertical pipe with a horizontal pipe at the top of it.

Bouncing tracks   A multitrack recording technique that combines two or more tracks and transfers them to a vacant track.

Bulk eraser   See *degausser*.

Cable   Wire that carries audio signals.

Cannon connector   See *XLR connector*.

Capacitor mic   Another name for a condenser mic.

Capstan   A metal shaft that controls the speed of a tape recorder.

Cardioid   Picking up sound in a heart-shaped pattern; usually refers to a mic pickup pattern.

Cartridge   A device that converts the vibrations from the turntable stylus into variations in voltage; also, the endless-loop tape container used in a tape recorder.

Cartridge recorder   A tape recorder that uses tape that is in an endless loop.

Cassette   A plastic case containing 1/8-inch audio tape.

Cassette recorder   A tape recorder that records and plays back 1/8-inch tape housed in a plastic case.

CD   See *compact disc*.

CD player   The piece of equipment that uses a laser to play back compact discs.

CD-R   See *CD recorder*.

CD recorder   A type of CD machine that can record as well as playback compact discs.

CD-RW   A CD format that can be recorded on over and over.

Channel   The route an audio signal follows; also, grouping of controls on an audio console associated with one input.

China marker   A pen-type device used to mark edit points on audio tape.

Chorusing   A multitrack overdubbing technique in which an announcer reads the same script on several different tracks to give a "chorus" effect.

Circumaural   See *closed headphones*.

Closed headphones   A ring-shaped muff that rests on the head, not the ear, through which a person can hear sound.

Coding   In digital technology, assigning a 16-bit binary "word" to the values measured during quantizing.

Coincident miking   Using multiple microphones with pickup patterns that overlap; usually refers to stereo miking techniques.

Cold ending   Music or song that ends with a natural, full-volume ending.

Combo   The working procedure by which the radio announcer is also the equipment operator.

Compact disc   A round, shiny disc onto which sound is recorded digitally so that it can be read by a laser.

Companders   Signal processing equipment that compresses dynamic range during recording and expands it during playback.

Compression   A sound wave characteristic that occurs when the air molecules are pushed close together; also, a system for encoding digital data bits so fewer can be placed on a disc or tape yet still represent the original data.

Compressor   A volume control usually associated with the transmitter that boosts signals that are too soft and lowers signals that are too loud.

Condenser mic   A mic that uses a capacitor, usually powered by a battery, to respond to sound.

Connector adapters   Freestanding connector parts that allow one connector form to be changed to another.

Connectors   Metal devices to attach one piece of audio equipment to another.

Control board   See *audio console*.

Cross-fade   To bring up one sound and take down another in such a way that both are heard for a short period of time.

Crossover   An electronic device that sends low frequencies to the speaker woofer and high frequencies to the tweeter.

Cross-pair miking   See *X-Y miking*.

Crosstalk   The picking up on a tape track of the signal from another track.

Cue   To preview an input (such as a CD or audiotape) before it goes over the air; also, to set up an audio source at the point where it is to start.

Cue burn   Damage to the outer grooves of a record caused by backtracking the record.

Cue defeat   Switch on a cart recorder that can be set so that a cue tone is not put on the audio tape during recording; used for editing purposes.

Cue talent   A signal given to talent that means, "You're on"; it is given by pointing the index finger.

Cue tone   A tone that cannot be heard that is put on a cartridge tape to stop it automatically.

Cue wheel   Part of a CD player that allows the operator to find the exact starting point of the music.

Cupping   The turning up of the edges of audio tape.

Curling   The twisting of audio tape from front to back.

Cut   A hand signal given to talent at the end of a production; it is given by "slicing your throat" with your index finger.

DASH   See *digital audio stationary head.*

DAT   See *digital audio tape.*

DAW   See *digital audio workstation.*

dB   The abbreviation for decibel.

dbx   A noise-reduction system that compresses both loud and soft parts of a signal during recording and then expands them during playback.

Dead air   A long pause on a broadcast when no sound is heard.

Dead roll   To play music with the volume turned down at first to shorten the piece's duration.

Dead studio   A studio with very little echo or reverberation, caused by a great deal of absorption of the sound.

Decay   The time it takes a sound to go from full volume to sustain level.

Decibel   A measurement to indicate the loudness of sound.

De-esser   A processor that gets rid of sibilant sounds without affecting other parts of the signal.

Degausser   A magnetic unit that erases tapes.

Demagnetizer   A device to remove magnetic buildup on a tape-recorder head.

Desk stand   A mic stand for a person in a seated position.

Diffusion   Breaking up sound reflections by using irregular room surfaces.

Digital   A recording, circuit, or piece of equipment in which the output varies in discrete on-off steps in such a way that it can be reproduced without degradation of the signal.

Digital audio editor   Equipment that uses standard or proprietary computers to edit sound.

Digital audio stationary head   A digital recording system that records horizontally on reel-to-reel recorders.

Digital audio tape   High-quality cassette tape that can be dubbed many times without degradation because of the sampling process of its recording method.

Digital audio workstation   A computer-based system that can create, store, edit, mix, and send out sound in a variety of ways, all within one basic unit.

Digital cartridge recorder   A piece of equipment that operates similarly to an analog cart machine but stores sound on a computer disc.

Digital delay   A unit that holds a signal temporarily and then allows it to leave the unit.

Digital distribution network   A network that links ad agencies, production houses, or record companies with radio stations to deliver CD-quality audio via PC-based servers and phone lines.

Digital reverb   A unit that produces reverberation electronically.

Digital signal processor   A type of electronic audio card used for computer editing.

Digital Versatile Disc   A new video format that has the capacity to hold a feature-length movie on a compact disc-styled medium. It can also be used for music and computer data.

Direct-drive turntable   A system in which a turntable platter sits on top of the motor.

Direct sound   Sound that goes straight from a source to a microphone.

Disc jockey   A person who introduces and plays music for a radio station. The term arose because the person plays recorded discs and rides gain on the audio board.

Distortion   A blurring of sound caused by overamplification or other inaccurate reproduction of sound.

Dolby   A noise-reduction system that raises the volume of the program signal most likely to be affected by noise during production, then lowers it again during playback so that the noise seems lower in relation to the program level.

Dovetailing   A multitrack overdubbing technique in which a single announcer appears to have a dialogue with himself or herself by recording different parts of a script on different tracks.

Drop-out   A flaking off of oxide coating from audio tape so that the total signal is not recorded.

DSP   See *digital signal processor.*

DSP audio card   A necessary element in order to use standard computers to edit audio.

Dubbing   Electronically copying material from one tape to another.

Duration   The time during which a sound builds up, remains at full volume, and dies out.

DVD   See *Digital Versatile Disc.*

Dynamic mic   A mic that consists of a diaphragm, a magnet, and coils. It is extremely rugged and has good frequency response, so it is used often in radio.

Dynamic range   The volume changes from loud to soft within a series of sounds; also, the amount of volume change a piece of equipment can handle effectively.

Dynamic speaker   A speaker with a cone attached to a voice coil. Electrical current in the voice coil creates a magnetic force that moves the cone.

Earbud A headphone that fits in the ear.

Echo Sound that bounces off one surface.

Editing Splicing or dubbing material to rearrange or eliminate portions of it.

Electret microphone A type of condenser mic with a permanently charged capacitor.

Electromagnetic speaker Another name for a dynamic speaker.

Electrostatic headphones Headphones that require external amplification.

Electrostatic speaker A rarely used type of monitor speaker.

EQ The general process of equalization.

Equalization The adjustment of the amplification given to various frequencies like high frequencies or low frequencies.

Equalized Audio sound that has had the amplification of its various frequencies adjusted.

Equalizer The unit that adjusts the amount of amplification given to particular frequencies like high or low frequencies.

Equalizer/filter switch A switch on a turntable to eliminate scratchy noises in the record.

Equal loudness principle The hearing of midrange frequencies better than high or low frequencies.

Eraser/splice finder A degausser that looks like a cart machine; audio carts that are inserted into it are erased and stopped just past where the tape was joined together.

Event The start point to end point for an edit; usually associated with digital audio editors.

Fade To gradually increase or decrease the volume of music to or from silence.

Fade in To bring sound up from silence to full volume.

Fade out To take sound from full volume to silence.

Fader Part of an audio console that moves up and down to control volume.

Feedback A howling noise created when the output of a sound (usually from a speaker) is returned to the input (usually a mic).

Feed reel See *supply reel*.

Filter A unit that cuts out a particular frequency range of the audio signal.

Flanger A device that electronically combines an original signal with a slightly delayed one.

Flat See *flat frequency response*.

Flat frequency response The quality of a frequency curve wherein all frequencies are produced equally well.

Floor stand A mic stand for a person in a standing position.

Flutter Fast variations in sound speed.

FM microphone A mic that does not need a cable because it consists of a small transmitter and receiver.

Four-track recorder A machine that records four signals on a tape, all going in the same direction.

Frame The housing for a computer chassis, power supply, and motherboard.

Frequency The number of cycles a sound wave or radio wave completes in one second.

Frequency response The range of highs and lows that a piece of equipment reproduces.

Full-track A recording method that uses the whole tape for one monophonic signal.

Fundamental A basic tone and frequency that each sound has.

Gain control A knob or fader that makes sound louder or softer.

Gain trim Controls on an audio board that are used to fine-tune the volume of each input.

Give mic level A signal given to talent to tell them to talk into the mic so the audio engineer can set controls properly. It is given by "chattering" one hand, with the palm down and the thumb under the second and third fingers.

Graphic equalizer An equalizer that divides frequency responses into bands that can then be raised or lowered in volume.

Grease pencil A crayon-like substance used to mark edit points on tape.

Guard bands Small portions of blank tape between each recorded track and at the edges of the tape.

Half-track mono The recording of two separate mono signals on a tape, one going to the left and one going to the right.

Half-track stereo See *two-track stereo*.

Hand signals Method of communication that radio production people use when a live mic prohibits talk or when they are in separate rooms.

Hard disk drive A storage medium built into a computer.

Hard wiring Connecting equipment in a fairly permanent manner, usually by soldering.

Harmonics   Exact frequency multiples of a fundamental tone.

Head   An electromagnet that rearranges iron particles on tape; also, the beginning of an audio tape.

Headphones   Tiny speakers encased in something that can be placed in, or close to, the ear.

Headshell   The front part of a turntable tone arm where the cartridge and stylus are installed.

Heads out   Having tape on a reel, with the beginning of the audio tape facing out.

Hertz (Hz)   A measurement of frequency based on cycles of sound waves per second.

Hiss   A high-frequency noise problem inherent in the recording process.

Hum   A low-frequency noise problem caused by leaking of the 60-cycle AC power current into the audio signal.

Hyper-cardioid   Picking up sound well from the front, but not the sides; usually refers to a mic pickup pattern.

Idler arm   A tension part of a reel-to-reel tape recorder that will stop the recorder if the tape breaks.

Imaging   The apparent space between speakers and how sounds are heard within the plane of the speakers.

Impedance   The total opposition a circuit offers to the flow of alternating current.

Indirect sound   See *reflected sound*.

Input selectors   Switches that are used to choose mic or line positions on an audio board.

Insert edit   See *punch in*.

In the mud   Operating volume consistently below 20 percent on the VU meter.

ISDN   Integrated Services Digital Network; a type of digital phone line.

Jacks   Female connectors.

Jewel box   A plastic case for a CD.

KiloHertz (kHz)   1,000 cycles per second.

Laser   An acronym for "light amplification by simulated emission of radiation"; a narrow, intense beam in a compact disc that reads encoded audio data.

Laser diode   A semiconductor with positive and negative electrons that converts an electrical input into an optical output.

Lavalier microphone   A small mic that can be attached unobtrusively to an announcer's clothing.

Leader tape   Plastic tape that does not contain iron particles to record. It is used primarily before and after the recording tape so that the tape can be threaded.

LEDE   See *live end/dead end*.

Limiter   A compressor with a large compression ratio that won't allow a signal to increase beyond a specified point.

Line level   An input that has already been preamplified.

Live bouncing   A multitrack recording technique that combines two or more tracks plus a live recording and transfers them to a vacant track.

Live end/dead end   A studio where one end of the studio absorbs sound and the other end reflects sound.

Live studio   A studio with a hard brilliant sound caused by a great deal of reverberation.

Low cut filter   A filter that eliminates all frequencies below a certain point.

Low pass filter   A filter that allows all frequencies below a certain point to go through unaffected.

M-S miking   See *mid-side miking*.

Magnetic layer   The part of the tape that contains the iron oxide coating.

Magneto-optical design   A recordable CD that records on a magnetic alloy and uses laser light to playback.

Master fader   The control that determines the volume of the signal being sent from the audio console.

MD   See *MiniDisc*.

Mic level   An input that has not been preamplified.

Microphone   A transducer that changes sound energy into electrical energy.

MIDI   See *musical instrument digital interface*.

Mid-side miking   A method of stereo miking where three mics are arranged in an upside-down T pattern.

Mini   See *miniphone connector*.

MiniDisc   A 2.5-inch computer-type disc that can hold 74 minutes of digital music.

Miniphone connector   A small connector with a sleeve and a tip.

Monaural   One channel of sound coming from one direction.

Monitor amplifier   A piece of equipment that raises the volume level of sound going to a speaker.

Monitor speaker   A piece of equipment from which sound can be heard.

Moving-coil mic   Another name for a dynamic mic.

MP3   A compression system for audio that is a subsystem of the video MPEG compression format.

Multidirectional microphone   A mic that has switchable internal elements that allow it to employ more than one pickup pattern.

Multiplay   A type of CD player that can hold up to 200 CDs and access material on them according to a prescribed pattern.

Multiple-microphone interference   Uneven frequency response caused when microphones that are too close together are fed into the same mixer.

Multitrack recorder   A machine that can record four, eight, or more tracks, all going the same direction.

Musical instrument digital interface   A communication system that allows musical instruments and other electronic gear to interact with each other.

Mute switch   Control on an audio console that prevents the audio signal from going through a channel; similar to an on/off button.

Near-field monitoring   Placement of monitor speakers on a counter on each side of an audio console so they are extremely close to the announcer.

Noise   Unwanted sound in electronic equipment.

Noise reduction   Methods of eliminating unwanted sound from a signal.

Nondirectional   Another word for omnidirectional.

Notch filter   A filter that eliminates a narrow range of frequencies or one individual frequency.

Octave   A sound that doubles in frequency; for example, sounds at 220 hertz and 440 hertz are an octave apart.

Omnidirectional   Picking up sound from all directions; usually refers to a microphone pickup pattern.

On-air lights   A signal that comes on to indicate that a live mic is on in the studio.

On-air studio   The studio from where programming is broadcast.

Open-air headphones   Devices to hear sound that fit onto the ear.

ORTF miking   A method of stereo miking where two mics are crossed in a precise manner determined by a French broadcasting organization.

Out of phase   A phenomenon that occurs when the sound wave from one mic or speaker is up and the sound wave from a second mic or speaker is down; the combined result is diminished or canceled sound.

Output selectors   Buttons that determine where a sound goes as it leaves the audio console.

Overdubbing   Adding new tracks to something that is already recorded; usually a multitrack recording technique.

Overtones   Pitches that are not exact frequency multiples of a fundamental tone.

Pan knob   The part of an audio board that controls how much sound goes to the right channel of a stereo system and how much goes to the left channel.

Pan pot   See *pan knob.*

Parametric equalizer   An equalizer that can control the center frequency and the bandwidth that will have its volume raised or lowered.

Patch bay   See *patch panel.*

Patching   Connecting equipment together through the use of jacks and plugs.

Patch panel   A board that contains jacks that can be used to make connections with plugs.

PBP   See *play-by-play.*

Peaking in the red   Modulating a signal so that it reads above 100 percent on the VU meter.

Pegging the meter   Operating sound so loudly that the needle of the VU meter hits the metal peg beyond the red area.

Penetration   Sound that goes through a surface and is transmitted into the space on the other side of the surface.

Performance studio   A studio used primarily by actors or musicians that has microphones but no other production equipment.

Perspective   The spatial relationship of sound; for example, sounds that are supposed to be distant should sound distant.

Phantom power   Power that comes from a recorder or an audio board through a mic cable to a condenser mic.

Phase   The up and down position of one sound or radio wave in relation to another.

Phone connector   A connector with a sleeve and a tip.

Phono connector   See *RCA connector.*

Photodiode   The part of a CD player that provides the data signal that will be converted to an audio signal.

Pickup pattern   The area around a mic where it "hears" best.

Pinch roller   A rubber wheel that holds tape against the capstan.

Pin connector   See *RCA connector*.

Ping-Ponging tracks   See *bouncing tracks*.

Pinning the needle   See *pegging the meter*.

Pitch   Highness or lowness of a sound determined by how fast its sound wave goes up or down.

Planar-magnetic   A rarely used type of monitor speaker.

Plastic base   The middle part of audio tape, usually made of polyester.

Platter   The part of the turntable on which the record rests.

Play-by-play   A term designating sports broadcasting from the scene.

Play level pot   A fader or potentiometer that controls the volume of a sound signal that is being played back.

Playlist   An order into which edit events are assembled; usually associated with audio tape editors.

Plugs   Male connectors.

Polar pattern   A two-dimensional drawing of a mic's pickup pattern.

Pop filters   See *windscreen*.

Pot   See *potentiometer*.

Potentiometer   A round knob that controls volume.

Preamplification   The initial stage at which volume is boosted.

Pressure mic   Another name for a dynamic mic.

Pressure pads   Small, soft elements that keep cartridge tape pressed against the tape heads.

Pressure zone microphone   A flat microphone that, when set on a table or other flat surface, uses that surface to collect the sound waves and therefore can pickup audio levels from a fairly widespread area.

Print-through   The bleeding through of the magnetic signal of one layer of tape to an adjacent layer of tape.

Prism system   The part of a CD player that directs the laser to the disc surface.

Production studio   The place where material for radio is produced before it is aired.

Program   An output channel of an audio console.

Proximity effect   A boosting of bass frequencies as a sound source gets closer to a mic.

Punch in   Editing by recording over one section of a track but leaving what was before and after the edited section intact; a technique associated with multitrack recording.

PZM microphone   See *pressure zone microphone*.

Quantizing   In digital technology, determining how many levels or values each sample will be broken down into; the standard for most digital recording is 256 quantizing levels.

Quarter-inch phone   See *phone connector*.

Quarter-track stereo   The recording of two stereo signals on one tape in which two signals go to the left and two go to the right.

R-DAT   See *rotary head digital audio tape*.

Radio microphone   Another name for an FM microphone.

Rarefaction   A sound wave characteristic that occurs when the air molecules are pulled apart.

RCA connector   A connector with an outer sleeve and a center shaft.

Record-level pot   A control that adjusts the volume of an incoming sound signal.

Reel-to-reel recorder   A tape recorder that uses open reels of tape placed on a feed reel and a take-up reel.

Reflected sound   Sound that bounces back to the original source.

Region   In digital audio editing, a common designation for a section of audio that is to be edited or saved for later use.

Regulated phase microphone   A mic that consists of a wire coil impressed into the surface of a circular diaphragm that is suspended within a magnetic structure.

Reinforced sound   Sound that causes objects to vibrate at the same frequency as the original sound.

Release   The time it takes a sound to die out from sustain level to silence.

Remote start switches   Buttons that enable a piece of equipment to be operated from a distance.

Reverb   See *reverberation*.

Reverberation   Sound that bounces off two or more surfaces.

Reverb ring   The time it takes for a sound to go from full volume to silence.

Reverb route   The path a sound takes from a source to a reflective surface and back again.

Reverb time   See *reverb ring*.

Reverse echo   A production technique used to punctuate a key word.

RF microphone　Another name for an FM microphone.

Ribbon drive speaker　A rarely used type of monitor speaker.

Ribbon mic　A mic that consists of a metallic ribbon, a magnet, and a coil. Because it is bulky, heavy, and fragile, it is rarely used in radio anymore.

Riding the gain　Adjusting volume during production.

Rip and read　To read news copy from the wire service machine with very little editing.

Rotary head digital audio tape　Another name for digital audio tape.

RPM　Revolutions per minute.

Sampling　In digital technology, the process of taking readings from the original sound source to convert to binary data.

Sampling rate　The number of times per second that a reading of the sound source is taken in order to convert it to binary data.

Scattered wind　When tape does not spool up evenly on a reel.

Sealed baffle　See *acoustic suspension*.

Segue　To cut from one sound at full volume to another sound at full volume.

Sel sync　Selective synchronization, a tape recorder feature that makes a record head act as a play head.

Sensitivity　A mic's efficiency in terms of volume.

Shock mount　A mic stand that isolates the mic from mechanical vibrations.

Shotgun microphone　A highly directional mic that consists of a mic capsule at one end of a tube or barrel that is aimed toward the sound source.

Signal processing　Manipulating elements of sound, such as frequency response and dynamic range, so that the resulting sound is different from the original sound.

Signal-to-noise ratio　The relationship of desired sound to inherent unwanted electronic sound. The higher the ratio, the purer the sound.

Slider　See *fader*.

Slip cueing　Preparing a record to play by having the turntable motor on and holding the edge of the record until it should be played.

SMPTE time code　An electronic language developed for video that identifies each picture frame.

S/N　See *signal-to-noise ratio*.

Solo switch　A button that allows one particular audio board sound to be heard on the monitor.

Sound file　A segment of audio recorded on a hard disc; usually associated with digital audio editors.

Soundproofing　Methods of keeping wanted sound in the studio and unwanted sound out of it.

Sound signal　A noise that has not been processed into an electromagnetic form.

Source/tape switch　A switch that allows someone to monitor either the input or the output of a tape recorder.

Spaced pair miking　See *A-B miking*.

Speaker　A transducer that converts electrical energy into sound energy.

Speaker level　An input that has been amplified several times in order to drive a speaker.

Speed selector switch　On a turntable, the control that determines whether the record plays at $33^1/_3$ RPM or 45 RPM.

Splicing block　The device that holds audio tape during editing.

Splicing tape　Special tape used for holding together audio tape in the editing process.

Split-pair miking　See *A-B miking*.

Stacking　A multitrack overdubbing technique in which an announcer sings harmony to a previously recorded track.

Standby　A signal given to talent prior to going on-air by holding one hand above the head with the palm forward.

Standing wave　A combination of a sound wave going one direction and an identical sound wave going in the opposite direction.

Stereo　Sound recording and reproduction that uses two channels coming from right and left to imitate live sound as closely as possible.

Stereo microphone　A mic that incorporates small multiple-sound-generating elements within a single mic housing that can record sound in such a way that when it is played back, it sounds like it is coming from two areas.

Stereosonic miking　A method of stereo miking where two bidirectional mics are placed one on top of the other.

Stereo synthesizer　A device that inputs a monophonic audio signal and simulates a stereo output signal.

Stylus　A small, compliant strip of metal that vibrates in record grooves.

Super-cardioid　Picking up sound well from the front but not the sides; usually refers to a mic pickup pattern.

Supply reel　The reel on the left-hand side of a reel-to-reel or cassette tape recorder that holds the tape before it is recorded or played.

Supra-aural   See *open-air headphones.*
Sustain   The amount of time a sound holds its volume.
Sustain ending   Music or songs that end with the last notes held for a period of time, then gradually faded out.

Tail   The end of an audio tape.
Tails out   Having tape of a reel with the end of the audio tape facing out.
Take-up reel   The reel on the right-hand side of a reel-to-reel or cassette tape recorder that holds the tape after it is recorded or played.
Talk-back switch   A simple intercom on an audio console that allows the operator to talk with someone in another studio.
Tape guide   A stationary pin that leads tape through the transport system of a reel-to-reel recorder.
Tape loop   A piece of audio tape spliced together so that it plays around and around in a continuous circle.
Tape transport   The part of a tape recorder that moves the tape from the supply reel to the take-up reel.
Telephone coupler   See *telephone interface.*
Telephone interface   A piece of equipment that connects telephone lines to broadcast equipment.
Tensilize   To prestretch an audio tape.
Tension arm   A moveable guide for tape on a reel-to-reel recorder.
Three-pin connecter   See *XLR connector.*
Three-way system   A monitor speaker that divides sound not just to a woofer and tweeter, but also to another driver such as a midrange.
Threshold of hearing   The softest sound the human ear can hear, noted as 0 decibels.
Threshold of pain   The loudness level at which the ear begins to hurt, usually about 120 decibels.
Timbre   The distinctive quality of tone that each voice or musical instrument has.
Timer   A mechanism with a series of numbers that can be used to indicate how long something is recorded.
Tone   See *timbre.*
Tone arm   The device that holds the turntable cartridge and stylus.
Tone control   A control that increases the volume of the high frequencies or the low frequencies.
Tone generator   An element in an audio board or other piece or equipment that produces a tone that can be set to 100 percent to calibrate equipment.
Track sheet   A format for keeping notes of what material is recorded on what tracks of a multitrack recording.
Transducer   A device that converts one form of energy into another.
Tray   The area where the CD sits so that it can spin and be read by the laser.
Trim   See *gain trim.*
Turntable   A device for spinning a record and converting its vibrations into electrical energy.
Tweeter   The part of a speaker that produces high frequencies.
Two-track stereo   The recording of two tracks on one tape, both going the same direction to produce stereo sound.
Two-way speaker system   A speaker that has a woofer, a tweeter, and a crossover.
Type I   A cassette tape that uses ferric oxide as its magnetic material.
Type II   A cassette tape that uses chromium dioxide or a chrome equivalent as its magnetic material.
Type III   A cassette tape that had a dual layer ferri-chrome magnetic material; it is no longer available.
Type IV   A cassette tape that uses pure metal magnetic material.

Ultra-cardioid   Picking up sound well from the front, but not the back or sides; usually refers to a mic pickup pattern.
Unbalanced cable   Cable with two wires, of which one is positive and the other is combined negative and ground.
Unidirectional   Picking up sound from one direction; usually refers to a mic pickup pattern.
Unity-gain   A device whose circuits do not make the output signal louder or softer than the input signal.
User interface   A device, such as a keyboard or mouse, that allows a person to interact with a computer.

Variable resistor   A device that controls the amount of signal that gets through the audio console, and thereby controls the volume.
Vented box   See *bass reflex.*
Vocal stripping   Removing the lyrics from a song by manipulating the recorded channels.
Voice doubling   A multitrack overdubbing technique in which an announcer reads the same script on two different tracks to give a double voice effect.
Voiceover   Speech over something else, such as music.

Volume   Loudness.

Volume control   See *gain control*.

VU meter   A unit that gives a visual indication of the level of volume.

Walking over   Talking over the vocal portion of a song, such as when an announcer is introducing a record. Normally, an announcer only talks over the instrumental portion.

Waveform   The shape of an electromagnetic wave.

Wavelength   The distance between two crests of a radio or sound wave.

Well   See *tray*.

Windscreen   A ball-shaped accessory placed over the microphone to reduce plosive sounds.

Wireless headphone   A device to hear sound that transmits an RF, or infrared, audio signal from the source to the headphone.

Wireless microphone   Another name for an FM microphone.

Woofer   The part of the speaker that produces low frequencies.

Wow   Slow variations in sound speed.

XLR connector   A connector with three prongs.

X-Y miking   A method of stereo miking where two mics are placed like crossed swords.

Suggested Reading

Adams, John J. *Complete Guide to Audio*. Indianapolis: Howard W. Sams, 1998.

Albarran, Alan B. and Pitts, Gregory G. *The Radio Broadcast Industry*. Needham Heights, MA: Allyn and Bacon, 2000.

Alten, Stanley R. *Audio in Media*. 5th ed. Belmont, CA: Wadsworth Publishing Company, 1999.

Brooke, Pamela. *Communicating through Story Characters: Radio Social Dramas*. Lanham, MD: University Press of America, 1995.

Catsis, John R. *Sports Broadcasting*. Chicago: Nelson-Hall Publishers, 1996.

Day, Louis A. *Ethics in Media Communication: Cases and Controversies*. Belmont, CA: Wadsworth Publishing Company, 1991.

Dominick, Joseph R., Sherman, Barry L., and Messere, Fritz. *Broadcasting, Cable, the Internet, and Beyond*. 4th ed. Boston: McGraw-Hill, 2000.

Ford, Ty. *Advanced Audio Production Techniques*. Boston: Focal Press, 1993.

Godfrey, Donald G. and Leigh Frederic A. (eds.). *Historical Dictionary of American Radio*. Westport, CT: Greenwood Press, 1998.

Guralnick, Elissa G. *Sight Unseen*. Athens, OH: Ohio University Press, 1995.

Hagerman, William L. *Broadcast Announcing*. Englewood Cliffs, NJ: Prentice Hall, 1993.

Hyde, Stuart W. *Television and Radio Announcing*. 8th ed. Boston: Houghton Mifflin Company, 1998.

Keith, Michael C. *The Radio Station*. 5th ed. Boston: Focal Press, 2000.

———. *Talking Radio*. Armonk, NY: M.E. Sharpe, 2000.

McLeish, Robert. *Radio Production: A Manual for Broadcasters*. Boston: Focal Press, 2000.

O'Donnell, Lewis B., Benoit, Phillip, and Hausman, Carl. *Modern Radio Production*. 5th ed. Belmont, CA: Wadsworth Publishing Company, 2000.

Patterson, Philip, and Wilkins, Lee. *Media Ethics: Issues and Cases*. Dubuque, IA: Wm. C. Brown Publishers, 1991.

Pohlmann, Ken C. *Principles of Digital Audio*. New York: McGraw-Hill, 2000.

Reese, David E., Beadle, Mary E., and Stephenson, Alan R. *Broadcast Announcing Worktext*. Boston: Focal Press, 2000.

Sauls, Samuel J. *The Culture of American College Radio*. Ames, IA: Iowa State University Press, 2000.

Siegel, Bruce H. *Creative Radio Production*. Boston: Focal Press, 1992.

Watkinson, John. *The Art of Digital Audio*. Boston: Focal Press, 1994.

Willis, Edgar E., and D'Arienzo, Camille. *Writing Scripts for Television, Radio, and Film*. Fort Worth: Harcourt, Brace, Jovanovich Publishers, 1993.

Production Tip #13—"Cool Edit Pong"

There have been several items in the news lately about "easter eggs" placed by programmers in DVDs and computer software programs. An easter egg is a hidden sub-program or section of the disc that will be activated only when a special code is entered, usually a specific set of keystrokes. Knowledge about easter eggs is passed by word-of-mouth or even on Web sites. So here's an easter egg that you'll find in *Cool Edit Pro*, but it will only work if there are no files or multitrack sessions loaded into the program. From the main Cool Edit screen, click on the "Help" option. Now click on the "About Cool Edit Pro . . ." option. This will bring up some information about the program that includes the Syntrillium Software Corporation logo. Move your mouse pointer to the graphic of the flower blossom. Click on the center of the blossom and drag it to the left moving the blossom into the focal point of the cone. When you release the blossom, the ancient computer game "Pong" will automatically begin within the *Cool Edit Pro* program. Your mouse controls your "paddle" and you compete against the computer. When you're tired of it, just hit your computer Esc key to go back to the normal version of *Cool Edit Pro*.

Index

Special Offer!

$100 off
Cool Edit Pro

The complete multitrack recording studio for Windows™

64 tracks and more than 40 cool effects!
Supports 24-bit/96 KHz
Supports DirectX™ Plug-Ins
Crash recovery protects your data
Optional MP3 encoder/decoder available

Contents of Accompanying CD-ROM

Chapter 1   The Production Studio Environment

Various Audio Frequencies—Pitches: (1.7)
  60 Hertz Tone
  440 Hertz Tone
  1,000 Hertz Tone
Fundamental Tone, Harmonics and Overtones: (1.7)
  Fundamental Tone
  Fundamental Tone Plus Harmonics and Overtones
Tone Envelopes—Attack, Decay, Sustain, Release: (1.7)
  Examples
Echo and Reverb Effects: (1.8)
  Echo
  Reverb
Studio Environment—Dead & Live: (1.8)
  Dead Studio
  Live Studio
Signal to Noise Ratio—High & Low: (1.14)
  High Signal to Noise Ratio
  Low Signal to Noise Ratio

Chapter 2   Digital Audio Production

Dubbed Audio Degradation—Analog vs. Digital: (2.2)
  Original Recording
  Analog Recording Dubbed 10 times
  Digital Recording Dubbed 10 times
Digital Sample Rates: (2.2)
  Low Sample Rate—11,000 times per second
  High Sample Rate—44,000 times per second
MIDI—Musical Instrument Digital Interface: (2.7)
  How It Works
Tight Editing: (2.8)
  Removing A Short Glitch or Stutter
Shortening a Recording: (2.8)
  Original 17 Second Recording
  Shortened 15 Second Recording (Short silences between words removed)

Chapter 3   The Audio Console

Line and Mic Inputs: (3.5)
  Mic to mic and line inputs
  Line to line input
  Line to mic input
Audio Input Levels: (3.9)
  Riding in the Mud
  Peaking
  Pegging
  Digital Pops
Frequency Spectrum Ranges: (3.13)
  Too Little Bass
  Too Much Bass

220

Hiss and Hum: (9.5)
    Hiss
    Hiss Minimized with High Frequency Roll-off
    Hum
    Hum Minimized with 60 Hz Equalization
Filters: (9.6)
    Original Sound
    Low Cut Filter
    Low Pass Filter
    Band Pass Filter
    Band Reject (or cut) Filter
Dolby: (9.8)
    Dolby Off
    Dolby On
Reverb: (9.10)
    Reverb
Digital Delay: (9.11)
    Delay
Dynamic Range: (9.12)
    20 Decibels—whispering
    60 Decibels—talking
    80 Decibels—yelling
Compressor: (9.13)
    Uncompressed
    Compressed
Flanger: (9.15)
    Original Sound
    Flanged Sound
De-esser: (9.15)
    Original Sound
    De-Essed Sound

Chapter 10   Multitrack Production Techniques

Overdubbing: (10.4)
    Record Drums on Tracks 1 & 2
    Record Instruments on Tracks 3 & 4
    Play All Tracks Simultaneously
Punching In Tracks: (10.5)
    Original Recording
    Punch In Edit
Bouncing Tracks: (10.6)
    Record Drums on Track 1
    Record Bass on Track 2
    Bounce Tracks 1 & 2 to Track 3
    Record Strings on Tracks 1 & 2
    Record More on Track 4 and Play
Voice Doubling and Chorusing: (10.10)
    Single Voice
    Voice Doubling
    Voice Chorusing
Dovetailing: (10.11)
    Dovetailing Initial Recording
    Dovetailing Final Recording
Slapback Echo: (10.12)
    Original Recording
    Slapback Echo